Masters' Guide to Psychic Development

Dream Work, Telepathy, Auras, Astral Projection & Channeling

channeled by Mataare

compiled and edited by Carolyn Hawkins

Mountain Cat Productions ♦ Santa Barbara, CA

Masters' Guide to Psychic Development
Dream Work, Telepathy, Auras, Astral Projection & Channeling

channeled by Mataare
compiled and edited by Carolyn Hawkins

Published by:
Mountain Cat Productions
Santa Barbara, CA
805.895.4375
www.MountainCatProductions.com
www.Mataare.com
www.WhiteHawkReadings.com

ISBN, print ed. 09755546-8-9 (9780975554685)
First Printing 2013

Library of Congress Control Number: 2013905800

Table of Contents

A special thank you to Mataare for entrusting me to work alone in the task of creating the nine books in this series. It was a sacred responsibility and a powerful spiritual journey to transcribe, edit and compile the materials, putting to paper my interpretation of the concepts presented by the Guides in Spirit channeled through Mataare over the years.

About Mataare

Since 1981, Mataare, working as a clairvoyant, tarot reader, numerologist and trance channel, has traveled extensively throughout North America sharing his extraordinary gifts in seminars, classes and private readings.

Mataare, formerly named Paul Norris McClain, has been a professional trance channel since 1981. He specializes in channeling his client's own personal Spirit Guides as well as some of the most beloved and well-remembered Master teachers. Each Guide has his or her own powerful, distinguishable character filled with information and love for the client. Clients are able to make significant personal connections with all of their Guides in Spirit and are able to experience them as the available, supportive friends they are.

On September 20, 1992, Mataare experienced a powerfully transforming meditation resulting in a major shift in his awareness. He believes the personality of Paul McClain shifted into his greater soul self, whose name is Xiota-Lahmpsa Mataare. He now experiences life as Mataare, which he uses as his name. Mataare believes strongly that anyone can learn to develop psychically and spiritually, and offers courses that put others in touch with their own greater abilities and higher awareness.

About Carolyn Hawkins

For over 30 years Carolyn (known to many as Whitehawk) has provided simple, practical answers about life, love and spirituality through private readings for individuals from all walks of life. Carolyn is privileged to be serving a private ongoing intensive apprenticeship with the Native American Chief, Sun Bear. Under Chief Sun Bear's tutelage Carolyn has finely honed her natural psychic gifts, allowing a deeply intimate contact with Spirit. It is through purity of intent, empathy and insistence upon clarity that Carolyn is able to facilitate the seeker to receive personal and practical answers from their own spirit guides.

Introduction

Merlin

If you are to be active with us, you must have a desire to serve and it has to be a very important desire to you. It is something that at times you will need to be very committed to, more committed than to other things. This does not really come about in this fashion by a decision that you happen to like the idea of that, but it is something that comes out of your heart. It is a very strong feeling. It is a calling.

Not all who have a calling will answer it in the same way, nor do they need to answer it in the same way. However, to all of you who do answer it in this way, or for that matter in any other way, it will become important for you to have access to the inner or higher planes as you desire, as you wish. It must not be something you cut off from or feel cut off from because it must be something you freely feel able to go back and forth to at will.

Technique is one thing and skill is another. Skill comes with practice. For instance, many learn to play musical instruments, and there are many who are in some way born with a talent or an affinity to be able to conquer an instrument. Then there are those who have no initial ability, but have dedication. That commitment, that dedication becomes that which leads them to their greatness. There are those who have some desire and go just far enough to be able to satiate that desire, and beyond that, they have no desire to go any further.

It is for you to come to terms with whether or not what we intend to help you with is something you wish to do. It does not make you any more special than anyone else. Let us get that straight right now because it is important that you do not somehow feel spiritually more special than others are. If you do, you will find yourself with the need to always make yourself the teacher or put yourself above other people in such a way as you keep them disempowered, keep them less than you. The purpose is to help another rise above their condition, and that is service.

It is very important that you realize that this represents your dedication, your devotion, your gift back to the Creator. The Creator's gift to you is that which you experience by making yourself available for doing that. You will see what that means. It is a very special experience in that it is the greatest experience available to humankind. All have that potentially available to them if they choose it. Whether or not you use it in the form of service, we shall show you some things and help you be able to make a connection with other planes and realms of consciousness.

The goal we have is a lifelong goal to assist you in transcending the elements, the particles of thought, belief and experience that interfere with your happiness so that you can live in freedom, light and empowerment. I hope that you shall be sufficiently aimed such that you never have to be apart from your center ever again. In order that we do this, there is a commitment needed, a commitment that only you can decide to make. It is a commitment not to Spirit, but a commitment to you. It is a commitment to the power of love. It is a commitment to open the source of beauty within you and merge with it.

Commitment is different from a promise. A commitment is a choice you make, as you need to make it. A promise may or may not be a kept commitment. A commitment is the willingness to understand what your objective is and regularly ask is this in harmony with my objective. You continually make choices in favor of and actions in alignment with that objective. A commitment means the willingness to look at your actions and to make ever wiser and wiser choices. A commitment means looking at the results you are getting and the willingness to make new choices to achieve those results if those results were not achieved. A commitment is a willingness to be flexible and a dedication to the creation of that goal.

We cannot provide for you a commitment that you will need. We can only provide for you the course, the direction. The commitment has to come from you. We shall only provide you with many directions and many answers, but we are not here for giving you answer. We are here to aim you in the direction that you say you wish to fulfill that you might experience your most radiant nature, but the commitment shall have to come from you.

Everyone's levels of commitment shall be different. Some will be more committed or less committed, but we are not in a race with each other. Some may achieve better results in one area where others may achieve better results in other areas. Some may be successful in breaking through in one or another area. Others may be unsuccessful in one or another area. However, the commitment is not for measuring against each other who is more commitment or who is better at this or that. It is a commitment you have made to yourself to merge with the excellence of your being, whatever that means to you. You will decipher exactly what it means to you and you will come to understand that better. You will also come to be able to create that end much more successfully. These are our intentions.

What we shall offer you are not secrets. It is knowledge that has been in the world for ages upon ages and translated at different times in different ways. It is information we have sussed out from the universe and processed in such ways as it might be intelligible to you. It is information we gathered from Mataare's experiences and from your experiences that you have gotten in life and you have come to certain understandings about what your needs are and how best to fulfill those needs. We shall draw upon the ethers and upon the teachers and teachings of the past as well as teachers of the present and the future not yet arrived here. More importantly, we shall draw upon your own wisdom brought forward through this synergistic union, which we shall unfold together.

This is an overall statement of the curriculum that lies ahead. It will be a beautiful and pleasant journey. It will require increasing discipline on your part. The discipline that it will require is not one that shall be rote practice of any kind, but rather devoted unfolding, dependant upon whether you find yourself able to be as committed as we suggest.

Know that we are committed to drawing from you all that can rise up in you in terms of inspiration. We are committed to getting you committed. If you do not feel you are able to be successful in breaking through to some joyful and successful state of harmony and beauty within, then know that we have our ways. We shall find ways to draw out of you that which you perhaps do not even know is within you.

We are presenting to you a pathway that has many, many facets and is not for everyone. Although much that we say shall be from universal truth, you may come to discover that which is unfolding here is not for you. Know that if your place or your pathway should be different, then so be it. Know that other doorways shall open to you.

Know this as well. The truth of your ascendant nature, the truth of your breakthrough further into awakening and enlightenment does not depend upon you understanding clearly anything and everything we say. You can receive that which you are able to receive from us, and that which you are not able to receive from us, so be it. Integrate whatever you receive in whatsoever ways help you prosper and unfold in a beautiful way in your life. That which you cannot receive, that which is not for you, do not feel you must take it on.

We do not wish to change you into that which we are. Our intention is to link you to that to which we are linked, the Creator, the source of all, so that which uniquely is you can be most fully and potently expressed. You shall not all become homogenous automatons, one exactly the same as the next, carrying and holding exactly the same principles from person to person, but rather that which is divinely and uniquely yourself can be expressed in its most perfect form of expression.

Be prepared to leave behind certain things that shall stand in the way of your progress, particularly compulsions and addictions of any kind, whether those compulsions and addictions may be compulsions and addictions from the most obvious kinds of things, drugs, alcohol, food, or the most subtle kinds of compulsions and addictions, relationship addiction, anger and hostility addiction. It can be any kind of attachment to things that ground you in an energy or that you are not sovereign in, but rather gets a hold of you. Be prepared to find little fulfillment in spiritual, emotional, physical and intellectual senses, for all of these areas must be cultivated in order for you to come to know who and what you truly are and to express the full magnificence of your potential.

Guides

Cassandra: from the Goddess lineage

Devorah: Queen of the Gypsies

Enoch: Lord of Light

Kathumi Singh: Master of Wisdom

Merlin: the title of the man named Ambrosius Merlinius, THE Merlin.

Miriam: Mother of Yeshua (the man later called Jesus)

Morgana: High Priestess of Avalon during times of King Arthur

Paramahansa Yogananda: teacher of ancient wisdom, founder of Self Realization Fellowship

Olga and Helga: Romanian sisters and seers

Philos: Keeper of the Akashic Records, never been incarnate in human form.

Sanjuro: Sensei

Sun Bear: group soul of Native American Shamans. The man named Sun Bear, who died several years ago, has merged with the group soul.

Psychic Development

Sun Bear

Apprentices are those who are willing to allow us to train them to bring forward what is the God in you. It is not just for the development of your psychic abilities, not just to learn how to do some fancy psychic and spiritual tricks. It is for those of you who want to break through to the other side, those of you who are ready to see that this world is an illusion and who are not afraid of what is real. This is for those who are willing to spend some work outside of the circle that most people stand inside of, for those who are willing to walk a very long journey that is a little bit intense. It is for those who are willing to put aside all identities except your higher self and learn the meaning of unconditional and unlimited love, and in the process learn how to develop psychically.

It is all going to be a beautiful unfolding, but if you are going to keep up with us, it is not always going to be easy. It is going to have some big challenges, not hard, but big challenges. Nothing has to be hard. The only thing that will be hard is if you fight your own higher self, then it is going to be very hard, very tough. In that case, you are going to need commitment and discipline. If you want to open to your highest self, it will take a little discipline, but maybe that will be more than you anticipate.

It is going to take increasing energy. When you let go to your highest self, it does not stay limited to a few hours from week to week. It starts to take over your life. At first, you will be very much in charge, but then you give up being in charge and let go to something that is greater than what you have identified with as self. At any time, you can stop, but you cannot have a foot in both worlds. Your feet must be in one world or another, in your spirit or not. If you are not in your spirit at a certain junction and try to be a little bit in your spirit and a little bit in the world, your mind will fracture. At some point, you will have to choose if you have not already, to be here, in the world and being your best that way, which is fine, or in your spirit. There is no in between.

I have seen many who have gone for lifetime after lifetime after lifetime coming back repeatedly into the world here. They are not willing to be about the business for which they came into the world. They come into the world for the business they come into the world for and then find many distractions. Sometimes they do not know what the distractions are. Sometimes they find distractions in the name of spirituality. They think the purpose of life is to go off in the mountains and meditate or move into a cloister or an ashram and cut off all involvement from the world. Perhaps they do not realize their spirit along with their body in the world with their light.

What good is your light going to do in the mountains where no one can see it, where it can lead no one, where you cannot grow by seeing your light interact with the world? Anybody can be spiritual in a cloister, in an ashram secluded away from everything. It is fine for a while until the growth stops.

We can only show you things, but you will have to do the work. We can show you one technique after the next, and we will, but you will have to find your own desire to walk this walk.

If you are willing to walk some of this walk with us, you will walk far, very, very far. When I speak of willing, I do not mean that you agree and say yes, I will. We will see what you are willing to do by how much you are willing to work and to practice the things we show you.

Dream Journal

We ask you to get hold of a journal. You will need it. It is crucial to begin to record some dreams. You will need to do this at least twice a week.

From time to time, try to read your dreams and see if you can capture the theme, the essence of the dream in one or two sentences. See if you can state this dream was about this. This dream was about transformation. This dream was about letting go. This dream had two things. Do not try to do it at the time you are writing the dream down. Later, when you are rereading your dreams, put little notations about what the theme seems to be, even if that means you add in a little piece of extra paper affixed to the page because the page already may be filled. Eventually we want you to begin to see what the themes of your dreams are, because once you see the themes consistently, you are going to categorize the dreams by their themes.

Getting control of what is going on in your dreams is essential for the transmutation of the spirit into the higher realms. Beginning is being willing to capture them and get some themes. That is enough of the serious stuff for now.

Auras

We are going to play a little bit. Playing is good. We are going to play at seeing the aura. There are many ways to see the aura. I will talk a little bit about what auras are.

When you look at me, the body I now occupy, what you are looking at is an aura. Ha, ha, ha. You think you are looking at a body. It is not. It is just an aura. Everything is the same thing. You just classify it in different ways.

According to many Native teachings, the illusions of the different worlds are taught, but you are able to know only some of the Native teachings. You know some of the teachings you were taught in your schools, some of the basics of mathematics and physics and things of this kind. Some of you may know a little more than others know. Some of you may understand some things of light and energy. Perhaps everybody knows that nothing is really still. Everything is in motion. You know that everything you are looking at just has the appearance of solidity, but is not solid really. What goes around the center of the atom is what makes it appear to be solid. What is that called? They go very fast, six miles in one second. Do you know how fast it has to be going to go that distance of six miles in one second? Fast. That is why it looks solid. It is an illusion. It is just a particle of energy in motion.

You have an organism that is the manifestation of your consciousness called 'I'. Your consciousness, your human spirit as well as the Spirit and the intelligence of many other creatures has caused an 'I' to form in order to have a perception of reality, but it is a tiny segment of reality. It is one part of reality magnified so that those creatures given to live in that dimension, those spirits given to live in that dimension can learn something by having a certain portion of reality magnified.

Why is that? Why are you not aware of that tiny little subatomic world? Why are you not aware of that microcosmic world? You are getting more aware, but there are no lessons for you there yet.

We have sometimes told you that the little stars in the sky are just like the central points of many other points of energy, like little atoms, some of them with planets around them. Much like the way the electrons travel around the nucleus of the atom, your planets travel around the sun in a similar manner. Your entire universe is literally nothing but a speck on the physical body of a larger physical being. That physical being is in a universe not unlike your own, which also has points of lights. That universe has some different qualities. That being's universe is but a speck on the physical substance in yet a larger universe, and it goes on and on without end.

The same is true the other way, in subatomic levels below that, below that, below that. There are many, many forms of life infinitely smaller. Do you think quantum is the smallest particle? It is not. It gets smaller and smaller, but the nature of the smaller universes is a little different.

Do you know what that means? That means no end. It never stops. There is no smallest. Can you imagine? Try to imagine that. Think about that, going on forever, no smallest.

You are just organized intelligences that have chosen to organize your consciousness in such a way like the rest of the creatures here on the earth. You have manifested, over time, an organism designed to experience this part of physical reality because this is where your lessons are.

The organs you have manifested physically are not as sensitive as the organs within your consciousness. Your eyes, ears, ability to taste, touch, smell, that is not so complete in your physical universe because there are many beasts that can see, taste and smell more than you. They are aware of much more than you are. Can you imagine what the world is like for a bear that can smell miles away? What must be going on in the mind, in the consciousness of a being whose sensual reality includes so much more?

Some of the most intelligent creatures in the world, your whales, dolphins and porpoises, are all from the same family. Why they are the most intelligent is because there practically is no limit to the extent their consciousness has reached. They are so intelligent that you cannot even understand the language of the dolphin.

Language is very powerful because you can only conceptualize or understand what you can language. What you cannot put into the symbols of a language, you will not be able to understand. You can only grasp what you can language. Creatures whose consciousness extends farther than yours are smarter than you are. They are smarter along different lines and do different things with their consciousness than human beings, but that is their path.

You will be going a little into the reality of that, like the reality of the animals. What will the people around you say? Will they think you are crazy? What if you were able to attune to an aura half way around the world? Hum. What if you are aware of things to which nobody else can even relate? How will that feel? How will you handle that? Will you say, ah, I am crazy? Will you say they who cannot relate are crazy? How will you handle that?

When you walk this walk, this journey, you have to walk it like a master. This is why we say, if you do not go all the way in one world or the other, your mind will fracture. You cannot relate to both worlds at once. You must relate to one or the other and work from that realm up. You must know where to place your consciousness so that you attune not to everything, but to the appropriate thing.

What is going to go on in your minds when you are aware of so much more? How will that affect your work life? How will that affect your relationships? How will that affect your community? How will that affect your path in life, your goals? How will that affect your friends, your children? How will that affect you? On what kind of things will you focus? What will be important to you? How will that affect your dreams, your financial goals, all of those things? You are walking a sacred journey.

Aura is the key. Everything you know, you know because on some level you have become aware of the movement of energy. It does not matter whether you call it physical realm or nonphysical realm, because there is only one realm. You have just labeled things differently. A table is not more or less physical than I am when I am not in a body. It is just your organism has amplified this tiny part of reality and made it seem dominant so you call it real. However, when you die, it is so insignificant you cannot even imagine that you ever believed it was real.

Your aura, every organism, every particle of existence vibrates with energy. It produces an emanation. That is an aura, and you are able to perceive that aura. You are able to perceive that aura on five so-called physical levels and multi-dimensions of so-called nonphysical levels. The five physical levels on which you perceive auras are the impact of touch, the impact of sound between certain ranges, decibel levels and frequencies, certain frequencies of light you are able to perceive, certain levels of taste you are able to perceive and certain levels of taste you are able to perceive. It is all because of vibration. It is all because of the patterns of movement of energy that cause you to be sensitive in different ways.

The molecular and atomic structure of sugar is different than, for example, a piece of lettuce. Your tongue can sense the difference in vibration. You are able to see some patterns of light, but not able to see other patterns of light. Your eyes cannot capture ultraviolet or infrareds. You cannot see it. Everything is animated energies all the time. All the time you are interpreting and measuring all of the energies, so-called physical and nonphysical.

I want to get you out of the habit, for those of you who are in the habit, of thinking auras are something that you see. Auras are something of which you become aware. You do not see a thing. You become aware of it. An aura is something that you sense, feel, touch, measure, interpret and translate into something meaningful.

I may look at a person's aura and see blue and yellow. Another person may look and see red and green. However, what does blue and yellow mean to me? What does red and green mean to that other person? It likely means similar kinds of things.

In order to prove this point about auras, we developed an exercise. We are going to do it now as a prelude to seeing auras, their colors, but more importantly letting the impact of the aura hit you.

When you see an aura, it does not mean it is going to be a color. In addition, if it is a color, there are not specific colors, only specific ways people interpret them. Sometimes there may be agreement in the interpretation of a specific color. For example, if green is the color of healing, then when most people see an aura where there is healing going on, they will see green because that is the agreement they have. That does not mean that aura is green. It just means that is what they see. The important thing is what it means to you. For somebody else growth might be red. If they see red in an aura, that means growth to them.

Let us do a little exercise. The exercise is to look at someone and say what kind of vegetable he or she would be or what kind of automobile he or she would be. Then extrapolate from that what the symbol of the vegetable or automobile means to you. For example, if someone had a lot of orange in his or her aura, you might have thought carrot, which is orange. If your thought was, someone might be a Jaguar automobile, what association do you have with the Jaguar automobile, such as fast, powerful, sleek, etc.

Part of what we are doing is drawing forward your descriptions, your feelings, your intuition, helping you understand how your intuition works, letting it form a language for you. Later it will form symbols for you so that your messages and pictures can come in more clearly.

At this point, you can begin to see an aura by asking if they were to be a color, what color they would be. Then look and begin to see those colors around them. In addition to that, you might see other colors. Then you ask what do those colors mean to me?

Merlin

Every form of life is capable of telepathic communication, for every form of life exudes a kind of radiant vibration that all other forms of life learn how to interpret in some form or another. Every kind of radiance, everything in existence moves and therefore creates a vibrant force that all other forms of consciousness can respond to if they are sensitive to it.

Attuning to the ways you are already sensitive to each other's vibration and continually translating your experience of the radiances into images in your own mind, images that you do not even realize all of the time that you are continually translating and deriving information from, this is a form of telepathic communication. It is through telepathy that all forms of life, all forms of consciousness can be in touch with each other to a greater or lesser extent.

We wish to further intensify and expand upon the ways we read into this auric communication, which we label telepathy. We will do all of these things many times and in ever deepening levels. Each time we shall call it by a different label, for each different label represents another level of depth of that communication.

Meditation, for example, when we go very deeply into meditation, meditation technique and technology is another form of telepathic communion. Meditation is an expanded level of awareness where you commune with the messages of the universe, of the All That Is and all of its parts and particles that you are able to receive at that time and translate into a message at the largest level of universal message you can appreciate. That large message is the grand scale of that for which you are here.

In daily life, you must live in a kind of microcosm. Living life in a physical body is like living life through a microscope. It is like focusing the full radiance and expanse of your infinite consciousness through the physical organism in order to focus on the limited realm of reality available to the human being through the physical human organism. By having that focus, you can learn things. Much as a scientist might look through a microscope to look more closely at life to study it and to learn from it, you are the scientist of the macrocosmic consciousness. Your body is the microscope and this world is where you are focusing through this microscope to learn what you need to learn to appreciate greater understandings of your cosmic force.

In some instances, you are a scientist who never removes their eyes from the microscope and eventually thinks that that is all there is. The reality you perceive through the microscope, although significant, although important, is far from all there is. One can never learn what needs learning through focusing only through that microscope. Indeed, it is a most baffling situation if you do only that.

Opening the door to your telepathic self is a way to remove your eyes from the microscope and begin to use other senses that are aware of other realms, realities, truths and understandings vital to your lives. We are going to focus a little on this aspect, on yet another dimension of this, auras and telepathy.

One way we would like to speak to you of auras has to do with being aware of the physical aura that exists around people. The physical aura, so to speak, is the aura that is closer to the physical body or appears to be closer to the physical body. In addition, there is an expanded aura, you might say.

If you were to look at my body, the one I temporarily inhabit, you will see very close to the physical body a kind of radiance that you are not always certain you are in fact seeing unless you are skilled at doing this. You will see a kind of glow. You might not see the glow with equal radiance from every part of the body. You might see a greater radiance around my borrowed head or around certain parts of the body that seem to be projecting a kind of activity, a kind of energetic movement.

Not only will you see that around my body, but you will also sense that and see that around the bodies of others. If you look around, you will notice a kind of sparkling in the air around the bodies of others, perhaps around the face or above the shoulders. If you look for it, it will appear to be around the stomach, hands and around the body as though there were something going on there. Some persons may see sparkles, and very often, they will see rainbows projecting.

The reason you might question if you are seeing this is that you are not seeing the radiance with your eyes. What you are seeing with is your consciousness, which is 360 degrees. The reason you think you are seeing with your eyes is that you are accustomed to seeing with your eyes. Wherever you focus your attention, you will naturally focus your eyes there or reversed, wherever you focus your eyes, you will also focus your attention. When you see something with what in fact is your awareness, you think you are seeing with your eyes. When you try to make your eyes see it, it seems to disappear because you stop looking with your consciousness and start looking instead with your eyes. You are letting your eyes get in the way of your vision. What will happen is your psychic perception will seem to go in and out, turn off and on.

Who has thought they have seen a spirit brush by and then turn to look and see nothing? It is for the same exact reason. The Spirit occurred in your field of vision psychically. You became aware that your eyes must have seen it. You turned to look and there goes your psychic vision, and you start looking with your physical eye focus. That is why you think it disappears.

It is better to say that I have become aware of the aura rather than I see the aura, because that is in fact what has happened. It is your consciousness.

Next time you are in a room with other people, close your eyes and become aware of everybody in the room. Can you image the lights or the energy radiating from where everybody is? If there were nothing between you, do you think you might be able to find your way to where another person was in the room?

Please close your eyes. Become aware of what is behind you with your eyes closed. See what is behind you. See what is down on the floor. See what is behind you to the right. Become aware of what is around you to the left. Become aware of what is behind you and above you. Now open your eyes.

Whether or not you know what is actually in those places, you became aware of something. You became aware wherever you direct your attention. You become aware of some energy, some movement and some motion. I am calling it motion, but it is not necessarily moving as we might typically describe it. You became aware of some activity up and behind, some to the left and to the right and behind you and down. You are sensing what is with your presence.

Some of you are better at sensing that than others are. We are going to hone all of that. If we had every day with you for 365 days, you would not need your eyes, but we do not have that time with you. Those of you who are truly dedicated will be able to do this on your own. We shall give you the method, but it will be up to you to do the work that we give to you so that you get very good at knowing what is going on in this plane and in other planes.

The reason we did this little exercise was to get you in touch with your psychic vision, your psychic eyes, which simply means to direct your focus where you want to focus it. You can see that you have a kind of inner eye called attention, focus, and you can place it were you want to place it. When you place it where you want it, you become aware of what is there to whatever extent you are skilled at becoming aware, to whatever extent is important to you.

I would like you to become aware of a radiance that seems to be closer to the physical body and a different kind of radiance a little more distanced from the body. One may seem to be like an outline very close to the body and one might seem to be a little less visible and further extended where you might not be able to see it as clearly, but you might be able to sense it. It may or may not be a still shape. It may or may not be the shape of the physical body. In fact, sometimes you may think you are seeing it and sometimes it may disappear or sometimes you might see or feel the extended aura interacting with other energies around it.

Look with your psychic eye. That means become aware, relax your physical eyeballs since you will not need them, and let your physical gaze become relaxed. You will almost see it with your temples. Even though your eyes are open, the focus of which you are becoming aware may seem to be in your temples. With your temples focused, for those are the centers of your brain near what is aware of such things, you will become aware of a near aura and a more distant aura. Whatever it is, uncertain or certain, acknowledge it. The way to get certainty is to accept what you are experiencing until otherwise disproved or further enlightened.

Use your consciousness where you cannot see with what appears to be your eyes. Use the idea. Become aware. When looking at someone's aura, you might ask, for example, what about his or her hands or what about his or her feet. Choose to become aware. What of his or her eyes? Choose to become aware.

If one does not see it, there might be a reason why one chooses not to see. It might be a very valid reason. It might be a reason that is not as valid, but there are always reasons. For example, one reason not to see is that there is an investment. Maybe I will not see as much as others or in the same way as others. Maybe there is opening psychically that also opens other doors that you have previously shut, doors that you do not want to have opened because of one kind of fear or another. It could be a memory of something from the past from this life or another or a feeling or an impression of some kind. Whatever it is, you can move beyond it and we will help you acknowledge what you have seen. Whatever kind of thing you will see, you will acknowledge.

After seeing something, the next step is to ask what it all means. The little shoulder that you see or the blue light or the energy down someone's arm or the glow in the back of someone's head or the radiance about someone's knees, what does all of this mean? The question you must ask is what it means to you. You translate the images. You ask, what does this mean? What comes to mind when I think of this image? You ask what it means to you.

What does a yellow glow around someone's shoulder mean to me? What does yellow mean to me? How do I feel about the color yellow? Is it a happy color to me or is it a sad color to me? Is it a dim yellow? Is it a bright yellow? Is it a dark yellow? Is it an inspiration yellow? What kind of yellow is it? What does yellow mean to me? What does it mean that I focused on the light around a particular part of someone's body? If this relates to the physical body, what advice would I want to give to the person based upon what I see? That is the next step, what does it mean to me and what advice, if any, might I give based upon that?

The truth is all you are ever seeing is your own consciousness reflected. However, because you have chosen to let someone enter into your reality, then he or she has become a part of your dream, a part of your organism and a part of your event. You are opening up to something beyond you and beyond him or her to guide you as to what to say, what to advise that person.

When you read an aura, when you exist in reality letting the little microscope close and open up to the macrocosm, you change your relationship to what you term reality. The truth is that we are all one. That is the truth. One of the reasons we are all one is because we all interconnect with each other. There is no separate reality.

You can direct your consciousness wherever you choose. You choose to direct it in a specific direction, and you become aware. When you choose to withdraw it, you will become aware of what you choose to focus upon next.

What you are doing is entering into more of the mutual reality to get yourself higher and to get anyone who has participated in your reality higher. Whether that means you are the guide or they are the guide, you are both together in that project. That is the purpose for entering into another reality beyond your own.

When you see another's reality, the way to get higher is whatever comes to mind when you ask how can I lift this condition? What next step can we take? What advice can be given? What can be shared? When asking that, you are going to take your next step forward into another plane.

When you enter into this state of being aware, you must trust in your intention to move forward. You will make mistakes in terms of what you will advise. Any advice that you give, that person must take that under their own advisement and see if it makes sense for them. If it does not make sense for them, that is well and good. You are presenting as an instrument to do your best as a sensitive to advance the condition the best way you are able. Every individual has a responsibility to regard what makes sense to him or her and to disregard what does not make sense.

The more available you are as an instrument, the more refined your skills become as an instrument. The more you are aware of how you deciphered things, the more you can trust and refine the part of your psyche that does that. Before we go ahead, I want you to understand how that occurs to you, having it be conscious rather than an unconscious process.

One can see one's destiny in the aura. What one can see in the aura is the highest available destiny, the lowest available destiny and anything in-between. When you read an aura, you must see the highest and aim that person toward the highest available destiny. You may wish to warn them of what is available for them if they do not go toward the highest. The darkness and the light always exists together to be seen. The highest path is available and what is not the highest path is available if they do not choose the highest path.

Someone who is exactly in between can still choose either one. Sometimes you can sense whether the person has made choices about the available paths or not. In that sense, you may wish to emphasize the importance of their focus. Some have already decided and they will do it no matter what. Some you may have to push a little bit.

That is what you get from the aura, a picture of destinies and the paths where they are headed. The highest path must always compel you also. Some will get so much into the dark side because in some, it may be very present, and they may become overwhelmed by the presence of their dark side and think, oh, that person is definitely headed for it. They forget to advise, wait a minute. This is where you are going. This is how to get there, and you had better get on it. You had better move toward it. That is available. If you do not, the choices you have already made have power and you have to make the choices. That is all available in the destiny. The rest is up to them to make sense of it and to put into action what seems to go together and what does not.

When you are reading for another, they may be in denial. Oh no, I am perfectly happy. Can you not see? Everything in my life always works and everything is fine. My relationship is fine. My money is fine. Just this area is bothering me. You will say, fine, fine, fine. This is what you can do about this one area, but you had better look at this other area here. You cannot be fooled by the words. You must see what you see in the aura, the soul's destiny and how to get to it.

You cannot be fooled another way either. I have been doing everything that my Guides have told me through this one and that one, and nothing works. That is another lie. Do not be fooled. Do not be upset. There is the destiny in the aura. Keep going.

That brings us to another little point. Who has planned that even when you do everything right and things go wrong, what will you do? How will you handle that? Who are you? Do you know who you are? Do you realize that you are more than what happens to you, that you are more than the product? Everyone who says yes shall be tested.

Truth is not truth until it is tested. When you believe you are something, you have come to see yourself as something, and you do everything right and it still does not go the way you want, do you then say, I must have been wrong and start giving up on that effort, or do you say, ah, I have prepared for this? When everything goes wrong, this is what I do. I get in touch with what is good about that situation. I get in touch with what I feel is good about life, what I feel grateful for, what is working and what energies I still have to create the things I wish. Do you say I must be the one for which nothing works? Do you then claim that identity? You must know ahead of time where you are going and you must become identified with that destiny.

Auras have not only to do with health, but also all of destiny. You see a picture of that person's destiny and you get that person in touch with their destiny. Do not be fooled by anything your eyes tell you or your ears hear. On the other hand, do not try to convince them of what you see. It is not your job to convince. Only relay with a very peaceful demeanor. Yes, yes, yes, I understand all that, but this is what I see. Destiny shows in the aura.

Connecting with Guides
Miriam

We all who come here find it easy to come. Perhaps you think of us as ones who live in a separate dimension, away from you. In fact, we live here amongst you. Our dimension, if you wish to call it that, intertwines with your own. The perceptive amongst you are aware of us to a greater or lesser extent.

Perhaps you do not always sense that we are around you, but from time to time have you not felt your life, at certain junctures, to be guided or blessed? Have you not at other times felt annoyed, angry, upset when you feel something, someone ought to have been watching out for you, and yet perhaps you did not feel that something or someone was. Why was there disappointment? Was there some expectation, some sense of something that you could not name, but felt in a subtle place in your being?

We are here that that which is subtle can come to shine more brightly, but you will need to choose to be aware of it. You will need to choose to allow it to be acknowledged. It shall be no different than it is for you to acknowledge yourself, for deep within your being there is a great wisdom, a great knowing.

When I speak of that which is within your being, I do not mean within your body. I mean deep within your being, and your being is consciousness. Deep within your consciousness, there is a beautiful voice. Sometimes this voice speaks to you as one. Sometimes it speaks to you as several. Sometimes it speaks to you as yourself. However, there a voice that speaks within your being.

The voice stands apart from any other voice that is unwise, unloving or disempowering, and is present when you are attentive and when you need. If you will not be attentive, you may not hear it. If you do not think it is there, you might not look for it. If you believe you are alone, apart and separate from everything, that belief may stand like a shield, like a cloud between you and that voice. However, if you wish this voice to amplify itself that you might distinctly know of it and continually access that which is your Guide, then that is available to you.

Listen carefully as those who come speak, for if you do, something shall reach you deeply within your being. You need not understand one single solitary word, but you will know everything you need to know, for that level upon which we best communicate, you and we, is a level far beyond that of words.

Merlin

I have come to speak to you a little bit about how it is actually that you are connected to a very vast realm of spiritual influence. I will not presume that you do not have any kind of experience at all. I will presume that some of you have connected frequently, or at least from time to time, to some form of consciousness that you were not so certain was you. On the other hand, maybe you might have thought it was you, but it was as if you were in a higher state of awareness, a heightened state of consciousness where you saw things differently, clearly or more penetratingly.

For example, have you ever woken in the morning having had a dream that was very clear to you, very alive, very vital and very vivid? You were so certain that as vivid as it was that you would remember it. Then later, as time goes on, you began to forget it. It simply began to disappear. That level of consciousness seems to fade away. Who has had an experience like that?

Have you ever woken at some time of night and thought that perhaps the problems you had been thinking of suddenly seemed to have a solution? By that solution, you were then able to see your way clearly through that day or week or month with regard to that problem. Perhaps you wrote it down and perhaps you remembered it. However, have you ever had that consciousness of clarity come and then fade away as quickly as the dream has faded away or suddenly at a later time of the day the idea, this very same idea, did not seem as good, as important, as significant or something seemed wrong? Only when you are in some sort of heightened awareness does a certain level of consciousness seem practical or meaningful.

Have you ever wondered where you spend your time in terms of consciousness? Where is it that you live? Where is it that you grow? These are the different levels and planes of consciousness, of awareness. Your body does not go there, but your awareness flips into different states, different levels of awareness of height and depth every now and then.

Forces that attract you to become aware of these different levels for guidance pull you there. We quite often pull you there, but do not need to make ourselves known to you. Our purpose is not to prove our existence to you at all. Our purpose is to see to it that you are connected to your sense of empowerment and knowingness. If you show us you are interested in connecting with our level of awareness, by making certain commitments to get in that level of awareness more frequently and to live there and to be drawn there, then we shall eventually make ourselves very well known to you. However, we must see you demonstrating that you are interested beyond trying to prove the existence of a Guide, Spirit, God or anything else, but interested simply because you have a need for clarity, understanding, self-empowerment and awareness.

If we make ourselves too known to you too frequently, we find that you have a way of turning to us constantly to ask us the most useless of questions. At first it is very good sorts of questions that you ask us, like show me the way that is the purpose of my life. What is the next step for me to fulfill my existence? How might I better live my existence in such a way as I can contribute more? These are useful kinds of questions, and we come and we give you ideas. They first will be very expansive ideas, but they will become more and more particular if you are sincere.

By sincere what I mean is that you will tend to carry out the answers that you get if they feel right to you, and that you will not simply hear the answer and forget about it. You do not simply respond to everything you get because not everything you get will come from the highest guidance. Sometimes you are in states other than your higher consciousness and you get in touch with consciousness that is not near higher consciousness and that does not advise you very well. You must decide what feels to you to follow. Therefore, we ask you first to think about what you receive, and then if it seems wise, carry through with it.

You would be surprised how often you consult us, receive guidance that you acknowledge is right, and then you wait or you decide, oh, but it is not possible. For instance, some energy within you, some restlessness comes over you and suddenly you feel as though, for some inexplicable reason, there is a draw to some other part of the land, some other part of the world, and it keeps coming up Egypt or it keeps coming up Sedona. It keeps coming up, the mountains. You say, oh well, I do not have the money. Oh, I do not have the time. My children. My husband. My wife. My job. Then it comes again, the mountains, Egypt, Sedona, west. Then you start to think, I think I want to go west. I feel an attraction to Egypt, you say, and you do not pursue it.

The voice again comes. If you are attentive, it will come more often. You will start thinking thoughts like, perhaps I should begin to take a little money out and set aside for it or perhaps I should set a date several months from now, arrange an airline ticket, and see what happens. Perhaps I should commit myself in some way.

Perhaps a work keeps calling to you. Perhaps it is a creative expression, dance, dance, dance. I do not have a dancer's body. Dance. I am too old. Dance. I am not good enough. Dance. I am only happiest when I am dancing. Dance. I wonder where the dance classes are.

Sometimes we tend to become a little bit insistent, but we are not trying to force you to do anything. We are trying to get you to acknowledge what you desire, what you are here for, what you want to do. Sometimes it requires increased levels of intensity to enable you to hear us. However, we are never trying to force you. If you want to tell us no, you choose not that, then we are here at the ready. What do you choose? Let us facilitate you that you might find your radiant spirit, you might find your higher self, you might find joy and pleasure in this existence and that you might have a meaning to your existence. Name it and we shall begin to help you. Why do we do this? It makes no sense to us to do anything else except love unconditionally. That is one of the keys to getting in touch with us.

I want to talk to you a little about what it is you are, and what it is we are, for that is very important. There are many ways to describe it and no one way shall ever describe it completely. Everything I am about to tell you as well as everything I have already said is practically a lie since it is incomplete. If it is incomplete, it cannot be the truth. How can it be the truth at all? At best, perhaps it causes you to awaken to something you already know, the truth that exists in you already, but not in any words that we shall say. Only that which awakens within your being the 'I understand' feeling is a truth that wakes up inside of you.

That aside, I shall now explain some things to you on the metaphysical level for those of you who have thirsty minds and think that you want to know things only to find out that it really is not that way at some point later, but it will serve to help anyway. First, there is only a singular intelligence, one consciousness, and each of you is a part of it. The minds that you think are in your head are not in your head. Search as you might, you will not find a mind in that head. The mind exists beyond the body. The brain is really like a transformer of a kind for your consciousness to go in and out of states of physical awareness.

For example, when you sleep and there is no sensory input or minimal sensory input, you are not seeing anything, hearing anything, aware of anything to the touch or smelling anything. You have very little sensual stimulus, and if there is sensory stimulus, you tend to ignore it. In fact, if you are paying attention to any sensory stimulus, you cannot go to sleep. If you pay attention to the comfort or discomfort of the bed, if you hear sounds, smell strong smells, there is too much heat or it is too cool, in other words, too many sensory stimuli, all that will happen is you will be stuck in body consciousness.

It is only when you lose consciousness of the body that you can fall asleep. Your consciousness then leaves the body and enters into a dimension. What dimension is that? Likely, the same dimension you shall find yourself in were your body to quit altogether. If someone were to come and take your life in your sleep, then whatever you were dreaming about, whatever is your level of consciousness, whatever would be your state of mind would become your reality. If you are more expert in negotiating these planes of reality, you can create the reality that you want. You can go to that journey, that level of consciousness whereby there is beauty. If you are not successful in negotiating different levels of existence in this life, you will likely create the same kind of existence that you now have in this life after the body.

Those who commit suicide are frequently miserable after they have killed themselves because their misery is not attached to what they are going through in the world. It is attached to the way they think, which they take with them. They do not kill the way they think. They do not kill the levels of consciousness into which they are going. In fact, what they more often do is disconnect from what they are familiar with, having lived here a certain number of years, even though they may not love being here, and they have put themselves in a realm with which they are less familiar and less empowered. They often have horrible experiences, for they cut themselves off from that with which they are familiar. Eventually they are assisted so that they can grow in those planes.

By the way, the only way it makes sense to commit suicide, as we see it, is if your body has become so degenerated that it is impossible to live in anymore, that the body is the source of the trouble. Then escaping the body makes good sense.

That was a little bit of a divergence, was it not? What I started to say was you must leave the consciousness of the physical environment in order to access the higher dimensions. What is in that higher dimension? Is it filled with Guides? Let us explain it like this. Each of you here is composed of many particles of thought. You are a sum total of what you believe, what you think and so forth. Those particles of thought are actually particles of energy that band together to form an entity. The entity becomes housed in a body and you call the body you.

When you die, those particles of thought, those particles of consciousness that have become fulfilled or do not need to return here, do not wish to return here, go on to a different state of being. Perhaps they join with a larger body of consciousness similarly aimed. The rest of those particles of consciousness that may need to fulfill themselves in some further way then return to this earth.

The particles may further fracture. In other words, if you are one hundred particles bound together and fifty of them find fulfillment and fifty of them wish to return, then those fifty may not necessarily feel that by returning in a collective similar to the one they were in before that they will have any better chance of fulfilling their life. Therefore, they may further subdivide into smaller groupings that will each form other entities, and then come into the world. They may not come into this world just as those entities. Let us say there are five entities now, each of ten particles. They may join with other particles similarly aimed so that there are free and ambient particles and remnants of other consciousness that comes in and reforms. These ten entities may be connected to other bodies of consciousness so that now they are no longer entities that are groupings of ten, but each entity may be groupings of let us say fifty or a hundred. Therefore, each successive incarnation is never the exact entity that before existed here.

That is why those of you who have past life memories only remember parts of pieces of those past lives because only parts and pieces remain with you. That is why so many of you have connections with so many people because after incarnation after incarnation who knows how many people there are with which you have connected. You may have one who you feel a relationship with like a friend. This one may be another particle that you never got along with before when you were one together. Now that you are in two different bodies, you do not get along any better.

All of the particles that have banded together to form entities, to form who you are, are connected to the larger mind, from which you have drawn those particles. That larger consciousness that you have drawn those particles from is your Spiritual Guide.

Sometimes your Spirit Guide may be so expansive that you may not relate to that Spirit Guide. You may not relate to it for any number of reasons. You might not relate to it because you separated from it. If you could relate to it all that well, you would have gone with it. Perhaps you may not be able to relate to that level of consciousness that was fulfilled, achieved, accomplished, or touched upon by that which is now your Guide. Because you may not consciously relate to it, you may not know that there is any kind of connection or you might not relate to it because you may not think along the paradigm that I am describing. You may have another way of looking at the universe.

You do not need to look at the universe in the way that I am describing it in order to be connected to the Guide because something happens. Before you are born, after you have collected all of your particles, what you do is you consult with all of that Spirit you have drawn yourself from that is connected to a higher consciousness and before you come into this life, you are told what it is that you need to do in order to reach your fulfillment. This, in a sense, is discussed, worked out to the satisfaction of you and your teachers, and you are born absolutely clear, beyond a shadow of a doubt.

You may not know that, but it is one reason none of you could listen to your parents when you were very young. There was some instinct you were born with that you were trying with all your might to remember, to follow, to hold, but perhaps progressively you systematically unlearned, perhaps through abandonment experiences, loss experiences, death, sickness, abuse and so many kinds of things. Perhaps you were not loved enough or acknowledged enough. Perhaps you only were acknowledged when you were able to prove your worth, when you proved yourself intelligent enough or when you proved yourself able to do what you were asked. Perhaps you were validated only when you did what you were told.

Furthermore, in school many of you were invalidated. You were told that everything you knew and valued meant nothing. The only thing that meant anything was what you were told. Your opinions were not important. You were not asked what you thought about life. You were not asked what you had learned so far. You were not made to feel that who you were was important. You were told, sit down, shut up, listen, study, remember and put everything else out of your mind.

This first stage is the time you are within yourself drawing out from the universe your memories of what you are here to do, often staring out into space, daydreaming, imagining, drawing back some of that knowledge. After that, you are disenfranchised, which is another stage that can happen from when you are very young. The second stage is reconnecting. The third stage we shall call refining. The fourth stage we shall call ascension.

The second stage, reconnecting, is a very confusing stage. It is like a great search of everything you can find that assists you to understand that there is something more to life than what you have been told. This is the message from your Guides. The message draws you to this or that book, this or that recording, this or that teacher, running about here and there. It is most confusing. You are told a little bit of this and a little bit of that. You learn a little bit of personal growth, a little meditation, a little of this, a little of that, until you make enough of this reconnecting to decide it is time for refining. Refining is all the work that is necessary for you to have a clear connection between you and the universe.

Then ascension occurs when you have ascended in your consciousness beyond all struggles. I do not want to talk too much about these things because each can be a discourse of itself. What I am here to speak about is the reconnecting. The refinement is up to you. It is up to your desire. This shall be just one of a few ways of reconnecting. Many of you already have your own way of connecting to the universe.

There is a God force, as we can describe it, which when you are in connection with this in a most complete way, then you are simply the recipient of whatever comes into your awareness. Some of you find that experience when you are meditating. We are going to discuss a technique or two of how to connect with Spirit Guides.

The very first thing that is important to understand when you connect with a Spirit Guide is you must forget all of your conceptions about what Spirit Guides are because it shall not fit any of them. Whether it is a Guide or God, we shall never come in the way that you expect, but always in a way that you can recognize. The reason is that we are trying to get you to go beyond your beliefs, beyond your conceptions, beyond your understandings to be open to what is. We shall take whatever form necessary, whatever form we can in order to get your attention.

Would you like to meet your own Spirit Guides right now? Then let me explain what we are about to do. You are going to relax the physical body and the physical consciousness. I shall guide you through that. You are going to let yourself become very sensitive and very aware. You are going to ask for some kind of sign or symbol that you can recognize that your Guide will use in order to contact you.

Perhaps that sign or symbol will be a physical sign. Perhaps you will feel touched physically. Perhaps in your mind's eye you will see a vision. Perhaps in your inner ear you will hear a name whispered. Perhaps a thought will come to you, a picture or a name. Perhaps a certain sensation shall come over you. Whatever it shall be, you will not look for a Guide, but simply be open to a contact.

You will see some recognizable things, traits, signs and feelings and in some instance, you might be very surprised. The thing is this. In the first place, you are never really seeing anybody or anything. All you are seeing is your projection of some aspect of yourself. That is because we agree to some extent on certain basics about language.

What I am trying to say is this. As I am speaking, everybody is getting a different impression of what I am saying. One might ask what the reality of what I am saying is. What is it that people are hearing? Is there a definitive there? There is, but I do not know that it is received by anyone. It might be. When I take even one word, say a color, people have different associations of what that means to them. If I make a description, people have different understandings. Every single word I say is connected in your minds to many other words. Because it is connected to many different words, different pictures are forming, different understandings are forming.

The best you can see are your projection of your own understanding and not necessarily what it is that I am saying. The same is true when you look at what I am. You do not necessarily see that which I am. You see some projection of your own consciousness of what you have come to know as me.

My point is this. All you really see, identify and associate with, you may think it is another person, but you are really seeing yourself. It does not matter what that person is, how that person does or does not change, you are really seeing yourself at different stages of your own existence. That is all you ever really see.

Ultimately, anything you see on this side of the universe in the physical or the nonphysical, it is the same. You are only seeing one thing, self. The best other entities can do for you is reflect something back to you, which is some dimension of yourself, and yourself is everything that is. They can reflect some dimension of yourself back to you that is of value to you.

The time comes when you no longer distinguish that much between one entity and another entity. The time comes when all that you see and identify with and all that is that is important is one state of being of empowerment and that is unconditional love. All other perceptions end up that way.

You do not lose your identity by others going on, you going on or parts of you going on. You gain identity. You gain understanding about more of what you are. You gain that understanding in many ways, but one way that you understand that is you are like a particle of the Creator that has separated away for the purpose of exploration. Some of you might think, for example, that the Creator is all knowing. No. It is not. It is always expanding and knowing more. I might add it is significantly more knowing than you are at this point. However, it is always growing, expanding and transcending itself in a dimension that is not quite time. It does not grow through time. It grows through another dimension of experience not describable by any human language of which I am aware. The way that it grows is through aspects of itself, us, which become creative in new dimensions and through interactions with other parts of it.

Right now, you may identify yourself as a certain self, but in fact, you are much more than that which you have identified with as self. Every time you are more than that which you have identified as self, it is called growth, and sometimes it is called a challenge. Sometimes it is called pain. Sometimes it is called struggle.

All that I am saying is that time and again you will have trouble with that exact same principle in many different ways until the time comes when you do not have trouble with it anymore. That is that you are not who you think you are, and you are going to continually find that out through your existence over and over and over again. Every time you will be surprised to find out you are much more. People are not who you think they are. You will find out they are more than who they are over and over again. The only way it gets is beautiful.

Sun Bear

Who is ready now to connect to a Guide very fast? Close your eyes. Let your neck relax. Relax your shoulders. Tell your body to go moderately limp, just comfortable. Feel your breath comforting you. Feel it as though it is so pleasurable, so easy, so gentle and so peaceful. Tell all the tension to leave your feet. Inside of you say, feet, relax. Ankles release. Calves release. Knees release. It feels very comfortable in your lower legs, like all the tension of the day is just leaking out and a warm comfort is coming in. Feel it going up your legs, your thighs, your genitals and buttocks, your stomach, warm and easy, your spine. Your solar plexus becomes very comfortable, very relaxed and your shoulders.

Do not go to sleep. Keep hearing. Feel yourself, imagine yourself floating on a cloud or gentle softness, suspended without gravity. Feel your shoulders ease, your arms and elbows, hands, fingers, everything feels so peaceful and gentle. Feel your throat relaxing. You gently swallow any time you need. Your jaws become slightly unclenched and relaxed. Your eyes are gently closed and your scalp is at ease.

Let your spirit remain gentle for a moment, breathing easily, feeling very receptive. Do not look for anything. Just feel gentle. Enjoy the gentle.

Now focus with your eyes closed. Become aware of your third eye, between the eyebrows and above the nose. Visualize there. You will see a hazy light like a fog. Perhaps it will be bright. Perhaps it will be dim. Maybe it will be bluish or orange. Maybe it will be misty. Do not look at it too hard. Just be aware of it. Be aware of it. As you are aware of this, remain gentle.

Ask one of your higher Guides please to come and give you a little sign or signal that it would like you to have. Maybe you will feel a pulse of energy. Maybe you will think you feel a pulse of energy. Maybe the light will grow a little more intense. Maybe your ears will become filled with silence. Maybe you will feel your Spirit Guide as though it is surrounding you. Perhaps you will sense a form in front of you, behind you or to the left or to the right.

I am now going to be silent for a moment. I would like you inwardly to talk to whatever presence you sense or think you sense. Ask it questions such as do you have a name? For what are you here? Is there anything I need to know? Speak up so I can hear you better. These things are good. I will be silent now.

Okay. Begin to close and ask whatever presence you sense for assistance in whatever you believe you need assistance in and thank the presence.

The practice comes in learning how to stay gentle enough to see with your awareness rather than with your eyes. How do you do that? It is very easy.

Nobody will ever see pitch black when closing the eyes. You will have to see something, color, dust, speckles, light, movement, energy, something. Therefore, if you want to see more light, the next time you see any light, just say ah, there it is. Do not say, where is it? It is not enough. I am frustrated. I wish it would be more. The way to see more light is to acknowledge the light you see. Say, ah there it is.

That is also the way to see more Spirits. However, people do not want to do this. Do you know why? They think they are going crazy, but you will find you will not go crazy. You will only get inspired messages if your intention is to get higher guidance.

If you are willing to encounter your Guide frequently, we will find ways to make it easier and easier and easier for you. However, if you stop at the point of your disappointment, there is no way we can make it easier and easier until we find a way to use the world around you. We have to put things in front of you, and sometimes you do not like these kinds of answers.

Psychic Development
Merlin

Everything you do with consciousness is a psychic act. Visualization is the psychic act of receiving an impression. Realizing is creating something and moving to some place. Clairvoyance is receiving. We want you to be able to distinguish the feeling between when you are creating something psychically and receiving something psychically. They are both psychic acts, both psychic functions.

To create a picture oftentimes requires more energy than to see a picture unless what you see is a memory you do not like. You will learn to distinguish the difference and you will get very good at it.

What we are doing here is not so much psychic reading. It is learning how to translate messages or symbols that are coming through your consciousness into useful messages. We will show you certain techniques. You have to refine the messages that you get so you can get as specific as there is to be gotten. However, in order to be able to get specific information, you must first get used to translating, to bringing through ideas, consciousness, visions and feelings.

We have a little assignment we would like you to fulfill, two things that are very simple. One, acquire a journal. It must be very special, something that you like very much, attractive to you, good looking, appealing to you. In addition, acquire a writing instrument that you like very much, something that when you look at it, you want to touch it and you want to write something with it.

The second part of it is record at least one dream that you can remember. It may take two or three attempts before you remember a dream successfully. If you do not remember your dreams very well, on a night prior to trying to remember the dream, write in the journal I intend to remember my dream. Then when you wake up, you must write whatever you remember. If you remember nothing, then write I remember nothing. Do not just say I remember nothing. Write I remember nothing and write whatever it is that you are feeling emotionally. If you are feeling excited, sad, confused, whatever it is, write that.

What you are going to do is write down one dream, which may take two or three attempts. Sleep with a flashlight, your journal and your pen right near your bed so that when you have a dream, you are inclined to write it down. It is a very important suggestion to have the journal right there with the pen because that suggestion will help you remember the dream. If it is three o'clock in the morning and you say, oh, I will remember it in the morning, it will be gone, no matter how important because dream is a different sphere of consciousness.

We are going to work a little bit with dreams and consciousness. Dreams are the key to learning how to journey beyond the body. Journeying beyond the body is crucial to create realities in other dimensions that then come to pass in the physical dimension.

For example, you could go on a journey to find out what you shall be doing for your right work. When you learn to dream lucidly, you can go right to that place and say, oh, that is what I have been doing. Well, why do I not go and find out how to do something else now? Then you can find yourself absorbed in the dream doing that. The next day when you awaken, something will happen in that day toward making that happen, whether it shall be a telephone call, whether it shall be something that comes in the mail. By manipulating what goes on in the other dimensions, you can create your life here and now. This will be the beginning of that. It is also the key to learning how to be in two place or five places at one time, which will be very convenient for some of you.

You need some step-by-step guidance with lucid dreaming. Your next step is when you have enough dreams, see what some themes are. What you need to do is go through some of your dreams and see if you can get anything in those dreams about what the themes are and write down the theme in one or two sentences. If you have a whole drawn out scene that takes pages to write about how you met with this person and that person, what was the point? The point about a particular thing was being shown. You need to read the dreams and see if there are recurring themes. Those one or two sentences about the theme, are they similar? You may need to categorize them.

The first step is learning how to draw through and translate information because it is a very important key to understanding messages from your Guides. Many more messages shall be coming to you other than through us in this manner.

Telepathy
Merlin

Everything you can imagine and more exists. Every reality you can conjure is not conjured because it already exists somewhere, and more than you can imagine also exists somewhere. Each of you access that reality to which you relate and it is all real. However, there is a truth beyond all other truths and that truth is not about a particular matter. A place exists where all truths are experienced as one and all things make sense, no matter how divergent. You all have touched that place. Remaining there is another issue. When you are in that place, you understand everything and all things make sense.

In order to come to that place you must come eventually, and you will, to understand that the world that you focus in through your physical body is not real. It is not real. It is such a tiny part of the reality that to use this as the foundation from which to determine what is real will never lead you to find reality. You must start from an expansive perspective and find this place in that expansive perspective, not the other way, and find out what the cosmos has to do with that. If this is the reality, then that is not. That is real and what is this doing here? That is the perspective from which it must be approached.

All the hogwash about conscious and unconscious I do not believe in by the way. As far as I am concerned, there is no such thing as an unconscious or a subconscious. As far as I am concerned, there is only that which one chooses to be aware of and that which one chooses not to be aware of, and it is all conscious. It is just at some times you suppress it.

In order to be the receiver telepathically, you must be a bit of a busy body. You must care about what is going on in people's minds. If you do not care what is going on in other people's minds, then it is hard to be a receiver. If you are a sender, you are usually a very good manger or boss because that means you send thoughts so strongly that people listen to you. If you are not a good sender telepathically, you can yell and scream all day long and no one will listen because you are projecting another message.

Telepathy is the strongest mode of communication there is. It does not matter what else you say, nobody who is a telepathic receiver will believe you if you are not true in your thoughts. Nobody will listen to you if he or she is trying to be receptive.

In order to receive telepathically, you must be more interested in what the other person is thinking then what you are thinking about yourself. You must become obsessed about what they are thinking. To send, you must project and project only one idea.

A good exercise to increase your telepathic skill is to go through a deck of cards. One at a time, hold up the cards with the back to you. Write down what you think each card is. Go through the entire deck like that. When you are done with everything, go back and score what you wrote down. This is a test for clairvoyance when you do not have anybody else to project to you or for you to project to somebody. You are clairvoyantly looking at the card.

If you get zero, you also are psychic. To block totally is unlikely and would have to be a deliberate block. That is not the law of averages, but is well below the law of averages.

It would probably be better if you did it with a couple of hundred cards, but to go through a deck of cards will probably be sufficient. You will probably be tired by the time you get to the end of even one deck, but try to get yourself through this exercise so you can find out.

Deepening Your Connection
Merlin

Let us see if we might be able to help you understand how to connect to the source of your own answers. Our purpose in connecting with you is not so that you might know in fact that there are such things as Spirit Guides. Rather it is so that you can be at one with that same Spirit, that same great Oneness, that which many of you term God, that to which we are connected. It is so that you might learn more clearly what it is that you are, what it is that Creator is, who it is that you are and where it is that you are going.

We are going to talk a little about what Spirit Guides are, what you are and a little about what God is. We will talk about how they all connect one to the other and how to connect to your own inner guidance for being able to receive messages about how to carry on your life in this world, to receive messages that sometimes come from your higher self, to receive messages that sometimes come from us. All that it takes is a little bit of love and openness. Indeed, if you are able to make a connection with your inner and higher guidance, then one of your Guides can guide you into the God experience if you should choose.

Actually, when it comes to methods and techniques, it really is not so much techniques that get you in touch with your inner self, higher self, spiritual guidance and God. Grace is what gets you in touch with it. If you have the intention to get in touch, you shall. That is what is most important. You must have the clear intention. Clear means you must be free of doubt. You might think that is a very difficult thing, but being free of doubt does not necessarily mean believing. It means choosing to lay your doubt aside, to allow yourself to approach as though you were an observer, a scientist and one who is simply waiting, watching, looking and going deeper.

In order to get in touch, we must speak about a few things. What I am about to share with you is some theory and some metaphysics. What I share with you may not be the way that you understand this world or this universe. It may not be in alignment with that which you believe. Prior to my saying what I am going to say I shall tell you, you need not believe anything that I say or anything that anyone after me says. We ask not for your belief. We ask for only your ear, for if anything we shall say rings true for you, then it shall. If it does not ring true for you, nothing we can say shall make it ring true, nothing shall convince you of it. Only your own experience eventually shall reveal to you the truth of anything that we might say or anything that you learn anywhere. Therefore, hear, but reference against your own understanding.

First, you are collected in physical bodies. The physical body is very much like a microscope. That is to say, your consciousness, your awareness lives within the physical body and through the physical senses you become aware of the world, you become aware of what seems to you to be the physical universe. However, through the body you are aware of only a tiny, tiny portion of this universe. You can only see a very small range of the frequencies of light available to you. Some of the instruments you have developed may have allowed you to perceive into the ultraviolet and the infrared ranges of light. In terms of how far your vision can see through your eye unaided or any of your instruments, there are a certain limitations. There are certain bands and frequencies of light you are unaware of and distances you cannot see. You cannot see beyond a certain size of smallness. You cannot see beyond a certain size of magnitude either. Living in the human body, you are seeing through a very limited range.

The same is true with hearing and sound. With sound, you only hear a certain range to certain levels of decibels, certain levels of frequencies. Above or below certain levels you are unable to hear while many other creatures are able to hear. An elephant, for example, can hear sounds so low it can hear the mutterings of other elephant miles away that you who stumble right in front of the elephant and would have never heard a sound, so low are they able to hear. Dogs are able to hear very high pitches.

Naturally, as human beings, you have developed some sort of extension for all of your senses through your instrumentalities that are able to perceive further than your physical human organism. Even so, you are able only to perceive a limited range even with those instruments. Most people who are able to understand the instruments that can see into the macrocosm and microcosm are able to see that, but most people are not able to see that. For most people that is not even in their awareness.

However, none of that is important because human beings have another way of seeing. Human beings see through the eyes of consciousness, through the eyes of thought. Human beings can become aware of much, much more than that of which they recognize themselves to be aware. We are going to attune to that aspect, that dimension of your being.

You, housed within these physical human bodies, are a collection of a band of frequencies called thought. Maybe you do not know this or maybe you do. Little particles of consciousness have banded together to become an entity and have become aware. These particles of consciousness, of awareness, when banded together, one becomes identified with those. One calls it self. As you live your life here in this world, those particles of consciousness expand and grow. They collect new understanding, new awareness. The entity you are expands with every idea, with every realization, with every breakthrough.

Sometimes those particles of consciousness you are that are banded together do not function so well in an integrated fashion. These are the many different aspects and parts of self that sometimes people feel. There are other times one can feel rather unified. At other times, one can feel rather fractured within themselves. A part of life is learning how to negotiate successfully the integration of all of your particles of self so that you are at one.

When you leave this world and you lay down your bodies, the particles of self undergo a kind of reassessment. The successfully integrated dimensions of self, those particles might not need to return to this plane and so go on to some other dimension. They may join with a larger body of consciousness that has the intention for its best interest. Other particles of self not satisfied may seek further incarnation into this world to gain greater experience. Those particles will wait somewhere in the great soup of consciousness, let us say, attracting the necessary particles of consciousness, binding together in such a way as it feels it will be successful to create its intent and then might seek incarnation into this world.

Upon death, to some extent your consciousness fractures or divides. It may not happen so simply as I have described it, for the particles of consciousness are so numerous it is like counting the numbers of cells in the physical organism. It is not one or two. It is trillions. The consciousness may fracture a number of times seeking incarnation. All of those consciousnesses that then come into this world, if they come into this world have some relationship to each other. Sometimes you meet some of the people you might have had a connection with because you might have shared common consciousness with them at some time. We will not talk so much about that now.

Every particle that has come into this world from a larger body of consciousness from which it has separated then is connected to, in the other plane, the bulk of the consciousness from which it has separated. Like from above, little spiny tentacles connect to all of those that are here that are a part of it. That larger consciousness is a Spirit Guide.

Spirit Guides are aspects of you and you are aspects of them. You have something in common with a guiding influence, a guiding consciousness. Will the day come when you will be folded up, having no identity of your own, into a Spirit Guide when you master your purpose? Well, let me put it like this. You are here developing as entities to the point of mastery. Those who are successful in their mastery, in some respects have fulfilled the purpose of their incarnation, and those who have not done so, they perhaps will. In other words, the Creator, which is the source of all of this business, is all that is. That is, every single particle of existence either is a part of the Creator or influenced by it. The Creator seeks to influence all consciousness, all entities and all collectives, such as you, toward manifesting its fullest, most radiant God expression. It is influencing its parts, which are in fact itself, toward evolution.

To some of you, that might sound a little bit odd to hear me say that the Creator in itself is evolving, but that is exactly what I am saying. God, as you term it, is evolving. It is evolving through its parts. That does not mean that there is no aspect of God that is not beyond you. Oh, there certainly is, but God itself is evolving. Give it some thought for a moment. For those if you who believe that God is infinite and eternal, what does that mean?

Does the word infinite not imply that there is no end? If there is no end, then how can it be static? How can it be terminal? How can there be, however advanced, an ending point to something that is eternal and infinite? Must it not be that that which is infinite is continually transcending even its own nature? The Creator, God, is not a stagnant pool that remains the same forever.

Therefore, I suggest to you as a part of your path in this world to come to know yourself as the fullest expression of humanity that you can express. You are here until you realize there is no limitation, until you can surrender whatever identity you now claim that limits you. You are here to come to know yourself as one with all that is.

Does that mean you will turn into a God being who controls the universe? Does that mean you shall lose who you are in the process of becoming that? Whatever it means is whatever it means for you as it unfolds in the course of your existence. It manifests in different ways for different people, for different entities, for different beings. However, eventually there shall be a planet full with human being fully enlightened. That might be tens of thousands of years from now, but that was the destiny, the intention of this earth in the first place.

This phenomena I am describing of entities, consciousness, in this case human beings evolving into their fullest expression until they are at one, is a phenomena that is going on all over existence, not just here on the earth, not just here amongst human beings. It is going on everywhere in existence. Existence is doing that.

The reason you have Guides is to guide you through an existence that is, in fact, infinite. Do you know and understand what infinite is? Dwell upon these things for a moment. There are realms of existence so small that there literally are universes within every cell of your physical body, far below the size of your quantum structure that you believe to be the smallest particle in existence. It is infinitely smaller than that. It gets smaller and smaller and smaller with no end, with no proverbial bottom line. It continues smaller eternally.

The same is true macrocosmically. By the way, your physical universe is not infinite. I do not know if you know that, but your physical universe is not infinite. It is a defined size and is an event of energy that is taking place within a void. Beyond its perimeter, there is nothing but void, an emptiness of all energy for a while, and then another event like this universe. Then sprinkled, you might say, through the void are similar events like this universe, and they number without end.

In fact, the very event you call this universe is but a speck much like, although different from, the particles that form an atom cluster, the nucleus, neutrons and protons that form it. This universe is like a particle of substance. In fact, whether you will accept it or not I will say it to you, your physical universe is a speck, a tiny little speck on the body of another larger being. That being exists in a physical universe not that different from your own. Its universe is a speck on an object in yet another universe. That goes on larger and larger and larger without end.

You might think I am talking to you allegorically or you might think I am making this up, but it does not matter. What I am trying to convey is that your physical universe is with limit in an existence that has no limit to its expanse in terms of bigness, in an event that has no limit in terms of smallness, in an event that is without perimeter. Although your universe has a perimeter, existence has no perimeter. Existence is much larger than your universe. When there is no beginning and no end, when all possibilities exist, because all possibilities must exist if everything is infinite, what is the central theme? Can there be a center when there is no perimeter? Can there be a middle if there is no beginning or end? If there is no center, no singular theme, no singular truth, which there cannot be if there is no perimeter, then what is so? What matters? How do you get from point 'A' to point 'B'? I venture to you that then all truths are relative, relative to another point in existence, but no truth is the same everywhere. You are in that kind of existence.

Human beings cannot contend with that, cannot comprehend that, and they seek to find a singular theme, a singular truth, a singular key.

The illusion must be broken repeatedly until a human being, or any other entity for that matter, can come to accept the nature of the infinite, which does not need a singular theme. One must learn to be at peace with contradiction in order to be at peace with what truth is. One must learn to be at peace with divergent ideas, beliefs and thoughts. One must be free of the need to put everything together to make it fit some notion, some conception or some unified theory. If one can have such a restive place within their being, one can be at one with all there is. So long as you need to conceptualize and form a singular theme, you shall never know truth.

This brings us to the subject of the path, and it is for this reason you are so challenged from day to day by life, by existence because continually there is a desire to set up life according to certain values and principles that are meaningful to you. You must do that. You must relate one point to another point in order to have some sense of support, some sense of stability, some sense of personal center. However, understand, the personal center you are experiencing is a truth of your own invention. That does not mean it is false. It simply means it is a part of the whole, but not the whole of the whole. If it is not the whole of the whole, it cannot be the truth. If it is not the whole of the whole, there must be something wrong with it in a sense that what is incomplete cannot be truth.

You must be willing to surrender what you believe at some point to the direct experience of what is so. It is so, so simple. You only need a moment of it. Any time you suspend your awareness, something comes in. If you intend to have a higher idea, a higher principle come in, then a higher idea, a higher principle will come in. What do I mean by a higher principle, a higher idea? An example would be guidance.

Many particles and pieces of awareness are ambient in the atmosphere, so to speak. Each of you are continually connecting to streams of consciousness that are not your own. I know some of you might think that each of you possess your own mind. I suggest to you there is one intelligence only, there is one mind at work in existence and each of you access a part of it. Your particles, your identity, your thought goes into a great ocean of thought. It taps into a certain part of that ocean where you will realize certain beliefs, ideas and understandings that you think are yours only because you identify with them as being yours. In fact, others can be accessing that exact same consciousness, simply occupying the same common intelligence with their awareness, the same space with their awareness.

People can access many levels of awareness, including the highest kinds of awareness of your Spirit Guides. There are many ways to attract to you specific kinds and frequencies. The way to attract your highest Guide is to ask excellent questions of your own consciousness. That is how you get your highest Guide.

You do not get your highest Guide to respond to you by going to a car lot when you are trying to pick a car to buy and say, oh Merlin, which is the better color of car for me, red or yellow. You will not necessarily attract the highest Guide. What does a red or yellow car have to do with your destiny? We could not care less. It means something to you, so choose your own red car or yellow car. Why do you need us?

Merlin, should I eat according to the macrobiotic plan or should I be a vegetarian or a vegan? Should I fast? What kinds of questions are these? You need to sort these questions out for yourself. Yes, from time to time, we will answer these questions for you, but we shall also get very tired of answering these questions for you. Eventually you have to answer these sorts of questions for yourself. It is your life here, not ours. If we wanted to sort these things out for ourselves, we would come here and live a life. We do not want to live your lives for you. We want to guide you.

Before I go any further, let me just say that we do not become offended when you ask these kinds of questions. You just do not necessarily attract our attention when you ask these kinds of questions. Yes, sometimes you might. Yes, sometimes the color of the car may be of vital importance, sometimes, some rare instance here and there. Maybe it catches the eye of your soul mate if it is the right color, something of that kind. However, if we do not respond to a question like that and you demand some answer, and you look and you strain and you force and you push and you pull and you tug and you become desperate, you attract some gamely kind of intelligence to you. They will say, look at the fool here who is so needy, so desperate. One of the things you do not want to do is get desperate when you are trying to get in touch with higher guidance. Do not wait until you get desperate, and I will tell you how you can avoid being desperate.

Many people in this world are very hurt, agonizing, desperate and fearful. It is a very strong frequency in this plane. Unfortunately, people are filled with fear, negativity and doubt so the band, the frequency for this level of consciousness is present and very potent. If you become desperate, you pop into a band of desperate energy and you become more desperate.

You must ask a higher question, a question like what next step can I take to fulfill my life? How might I best achieve the purpose that I need to fulfill? Realms of higher consciousness can be accessed by presuming a positive outcome and asking a question that presumes it. Do not ask a question of your higher guidance such as why am I so miserable all of the time. That will attract all kinds of answers to the question why you are so miserable, but no solutions. How can I take my next step to be more fulfilled? That is a better question to ask.

Yes, it is sometimes important to find out why you are so miserable, but sometimes you will find yourself going around in circles with those kinds of questions. You must see where you want to go and ask how you are to get there. You must decide where you want to go. You must decide. You have to pick your destiny and ask how you can get there.

Some of you say, oh Spirit presence, show me my path. Whatever you say I shall do. I put myself prostrate before you. That is not picking your destiny. Your destiny is very simple. It lies in what you love and in some of your desires, your impulses. I do not mean your every desire or every impulse is the right one. Perhaps it is as simple a thing as making a little list of the things that you feel are important to you in your life, the values you feel are important to you, the objects you feel are important to you, the things and people, the ideas that you feel are important to you. Once you figure out some of what you believe is important to you, then go into a meditation and communicate with us there.

How do you go into a meditation? How do you concretely communicate with your Spirit Guides? Many of you have many techniques and methods, but of course, we shall give you another one. Everywhere you go and everything you read, you shall find more and more techniques. There is no shortage of techniques in this New Age, which is not so new. There are techniques everywhere. However, it is your intention to come to know what gets you there, not the technique.

Would you like to meet one of your Guides? Are you willing to push past anything I have told you and anything you have learned, because you might just need to do that? In other words, are you willing to do your best to be very, very open? Choose to be open. If you cannot choose it, this is not for you. Choose to be open to your Guide. Decide you are going to be open to the highest Guide available to you in whichever way it wishes to make a communication with you.

Some of you have heard wonderful tales about what it is like to be contacted by your Guide. Some of you have said, oh yes, I closed my eyes and a brilliant light brighter than ten thousand suns suddenly appeared before me. I went deeper and deeper and folded into it infinitely. There seemed to be no end and I merged with the infinite God of all creation. Then I was back. Some of you say I never experienced anything like that. All I experienced was where is my Guide? I do not know. I thought I felt a little itch on my ear. Some of you might have heard tales of the Guide manifesting itself, appearing before someone. Others say they hear voices in their head quite distinguishably different from their own, some indistinguishably different from their own.

Being open means that you will be willing to receive whatever comes. You will be sensitive to that and then deepen that connection. You deepen the connection by asking your Guide a question. This is what we are going to do.

We are going to do a little guided meditation to get you a bit relaxed. I shall direct you as to how to open your awareness. You are going to have a question prepared, a few things prepared, and I will go over this more specifically with you. There will be a time when I suggest that you ask your Guide to give you a sign. The sign might be a name that comes into your awareness or a vibration of warmth that comes over you. It might be a thought that occurs in your head or a physical response that occurs somewhere in or on your body. It might a peace that comes over you. It might be a foggy light behind your eyes when you get still. It might be a sound like a vibration, like a humming when you become quiet.

Whatever it is, all I want you to do is simply choose to become super sensitive, very conscious, remain relaxed and open and feel a presence. You are not even going to look for anything. You are just going to become a feeling instrument, as though your entire body is a nerve, a sensory instrument. You are not going to look for anything. You are simply going to become aware. You are going to become awareness itself. Once you simply become awareness, not looking for the Guide, but simply becoming awareness, you are going to ask a question into that awareness. Then you are going to receive a response.

You may need to translate that response later. It may come like an actual thought in your head or it may come as a symbol you do not understand. It might come in the form of a face before your mind's eye. Whatever it is, you are simply going to become sensitive.

I want to talk a little bit about this before we guide you through this. Sometimes you become aware of a Spirit presence. You might see the Spirit floating or traveling in the corner of your eye while you are doing some business. Perhaps you are in the kitchen cooking or walking in the park and you think something catches you in the corner of your eye and you look. You thought something was there, but it seems to be instantaneously gone when you look at it.

Indeed, you noticed a Spirit presence. It happened because you either became very focused in the inner realm because you were deep in thought about something or because you were very relaxed and your psychic eye, which is 360 degrees around, was active. You became aware of some activity, some energetic activity. Because you normally see with your physical eye, you thought you saw it with your eye, but in fact, it never was your eye. You became sensitive to an eye you did not know you had and naturally, because you thought you sensed a presence with your eye, you turned your eye toward it. Since your eye did not see it, it disappeared because you turned off the psychic eye that saw it in the first place. That is why you are not going to look for the Guide.

The way to find a Guide is you cannot look. You simply become aware. Until you learn how to focus with your inner eye, your true eye, without letting other aspects of yourself get in the way of that vision, then you will likely close down to the vision. The way to remain open to the vision is simply choose to become aware.

One thing about choosing to become aware is that you must acknowledge, not deny. By acknowledging and not denying, what I mean is this. You are sitting and you have asked a question, what is the purpose of my life? You become very relaxed and peaceful. I am becoming very relaxed and peaceful and the message is to become relaxed and peaceful. No, that cannot be the answer. What else is the purpose of my life? That is denial. Acceptance is, all right, I will become relaxed and peaceful. Is there anything else? You must acknowledge the message.

Here is another denial. Nothing is happening. I cannot get the thoughts of the day out of my head. Do not do that. Here is a better way. All right, these are the thoughts of my day. Is there anything else? I feel relaxed. I am noticing a little light. Thank you. Can you make yourself clearer to me?

In other words, you are going to enter into a gentle dialog with the inner. There will be no room for denial. The moment you deny, you will close down the communication. Denial is like trying to see something and closing your eyes and saying, but I cannot see when my eyes are shut. Acknowledgement is like opening your eyes.

When you are in communication with your Guides, as a novice and until you become more skilled at it, each rejection is like turning away. You cannot see if you are turning away. Each time you receive something, say all right. Yes. Is there anything else? Can you make it clearer? Each acknowledgement is opening the eye more and more and more. There is no room for doubt here. You decide to leave your doubt for later. You can make all the judgment you want later. You can question it. You can take it apart. You can later deny it, but you must not deny it while you are in the midst of it.

How do you know it is not your own mind? The answer to the question is, if you do not know that it is not your own mind, you do not know. If you get a new insight, a new vision, a new idea, a new distinction about a new direction, a new clarity, does it matter if it is your own mind?

I offer to you that there is no such thing as your own mind. It is only borrowed consciousness that you have entered into to access some awareness. Even we as Guides, that which speaks to you now does not exist until it comes here. When I leave this body, I shall no longer exist. When I come into this body, I exist. The only reason I come into this body is so some of you can recognize me. Why? Because if I took the form when I was not in this body, nobody really notices that or only a small few of you notice that. Therefore, we take a form you recognize. That is what we are going to do within your own consciousness now. Perhaps it will be seemingly external. Perhaps it will be seemingly internal. To us it makes no difference. They are the same.

What good are we unless we can take some form that you can recognize? Never shall it be a form you expect, never. We shall always come in some form that heightens your experience. We come in some fashion that gets you to look further than you are looking.

If you wish to get in touch with what we truly are, and therefore also, at some point what you truly are, then you need to be willing to put aside your mind, for the moment, whether it is your own mind or not. Asking if it is your mind or not in the middle of the experience is like going into the ocean and trying to swim, but not moving your arms or legs. It is like wondering if your stroke is correct, and since you do not know, stopping stroking. You will sink. You cannot bother about it there. You must simply accept there.

A little secret for those who are very accepting, you shall go deeper and deeper and higher and higher, perhaps well beyond the question you have asked. Be very accepting. That is what leads you though the levels, leads you through the planes. So long as you do not accept, then you must study whatever plane of consciousness you can accept or appreciate. If you want to move through the planes, acceptance is the key. If you want to stay in a plane, let us call it a denser plane, then stay there and study it, look it over very well, learn its lessons, go in your circles and spirals until you are completely satisfied with it, and then move to another plane.

When I say a lower or denser plane, I do not mean a worse plane. Let me make that absolutely clear. This plane, this circle plane that you are living in may be a more dense plane, but it is a beautiful and wondrous place to be, wondrous. Besides which, you are not really living in the plane in which you think you are living. The plane you are living in is the plane of your own consciousness. That is why some could be living in a very ecstatic plane right now while others can be absolutely miserable right now, because even though you are in the same world, your worlds are very different. Every thought, every idea, every belief, every understanding creates a different plane or vibration of consciousness that you grow in, so even though you might think you are in this world, you are for all intent and purpose in your own world, a world of your own creation. It is up to you to find these higher dimensions and live in them.

Enough talk about these higher dimensions. Let us now come up with a question that you would like to ask. I would like you now to take a moment to form a question that you would like your Spirit Guide to answer. Perhaps it is a question of how you can make your next step in life pleasurable and easy. Perhaps it will be what your purpose is here in this world and how you can achieve it. Perhaps it shall be a question like, how might I resolve this matter, whatever that matter is, so that I might be free to move on to higher things?

That is a very good question for us if you want to get us to answer questions. In order to get into a higher plane, you might ask how you can resolve a concern. That will get our attention. You will get the answer exactly in the way you ask it, which means to say you will see how it is in fact a part of a movement to a higher plane by resolving some of the concerns you may find yourself in sometimes from time to time. Take a moment now and formulate a question.

A good question might be what steps can I take to support myself in my new career by summertime? In order to draw the highest Guide, you must presume a positive outcome. Then your highest Guide can come and reveal something to you.

Some might have the question what if it just does not work for me. Things go wrong for me. They always have. They never will go right. That presumption is what will create that reality. That is why you must get past that presumption.

How could anybody feel such a compelling desire to fulfill some destiny enough to ask for guidance on it if it were not meant to be? If it were not meant to be, believe me, you would receive a resounding IT IS NOT MEANT TO BE. You will know. However, when you receive answers like keep going, and do this, perhaps when that happens, what we hear then in return is this. I already tried something but, but, but. When we are talking about your life path, let me put it this way, did you eat your lunch or dinner yesterday? Then why do you have to eat it again today? Did you breathe every day sixty thousand times? Then why do you need to breathe sixty thousand more times today? If we are talking about your purpose of life, you keep moving toward it. If it is a struggle, it is a very simple thing. Ask of your higher guidance, how do I make it easier? It is simple. Keep asking higher questions. Keep getting higher answer. You may want to ask about what is the next easy and simple step you can take.

Before we do this, I am going to go over the steps. I am going to give an induction so that you can become very relaxed and sensitive. I am going to introduce you to your Guide. You are going to ask your Guide a question, and I am going to guide you through the whole process. Then you are going to come back.

Find a very comfortable spot, and I suggest that those of you who want to change your positions to walls or floors, please feel free to do so, but do not leave this realm entirely. Please stay with me. I have bothered to come here, so please do not go off into the ethers from where I come. I have come here. In other words, stay awake.

I would like everybody simply to take a deep breath, tense your body, and relax. Let your head rotate a little bit. Tense the body again, and relax. Tense the body again, and relax.

Become aware of your physical body, the flesh from toenail to the tip of each follicle of hair. Imagine that there is a beautiful warm sun. It is your own personal sun, warming your body, gently warming your body, relaxing you, soothing you, comforting you. The chairs you are in, the floor you are on somehow becomes an instrument of comfort and peace. Every movement deepens your level of comfort. Every noise sends you into a more relaxed state. Become aware of the warmth in your feet. The sun shines on your feet, a tingle and warmth. Imagine it. Imagine the warmth slowly crawling up your body, your ankles, shins, calves and knees, the warmth of the sun seeping up, peace, a gentle glow. The warmth moves upward, your thighs, genitals, waist and stomach, soothing warmth, your arms. Warmth, a peace, a calm, a gentleness fills your spirit, comforting as I count from three to one.

Three, even warmer and more peaceful, two, even warmer still and more peaceful, down, down, deep warmth, one, warmer, so comforting. As the warmth moves upward toward your solar plexus, arms and shoulders it relaxes and comforts you, captures you and causes you to swallow gently and unclench your jaws, feeling, floating warmly, gently, so comforting. Your ears relax and your nose, mouth slightly open, eyes gently closed, brow unfurled, feeling and floating so warm and beautiful.

You are now in a gentle, peaceful, wonderful place, stillness, gentleness. You are so relaxed that every sound, every sensation sends you deeper into comfort and relaxation. You are so relaxed that every pore of your body and particle of awareness is alert, so alert.

You grow more calm and alert as I count again from three to one. Three, two, one, quite alert, quite still. Ask of your Spirit Guide to give you a sign of its presence. Look into your mind's eye to the field of vision. With your eyes closed, there is a field of vision. Perhaps there is a smoky light, brilliant light or colored lights. Ask for a sign one time and then just be alert. I shall be silent for a moment. Ask for a sign that the Guide may have already come. Just remember it and sit quietly for a moment if you have already received it. If not, remain alert. If you have received, but you are not certain, ask the Guide to make it clearer.

If you are not still within, ask for stillness. If all you are getting is stillness, ask of yourself if this is the sign, stillness, and see what self responds. If the self responds no the stillness is not the sign, then ask what is. Perhaps the voice that you are talking to is the sign.

All right, remember, remember what you did or did not get, fix it in your mind and tell yourself to remember. Now let go of that and ask into the quiet or into the sign, ask your question and await an answer or a response. Ask your questions now. If it is not clear, then ask if it can be made clearer. I will remain silent for a few moments.

Remember the response. Fix it in your mind. Now gently, slowly return your awareness to the room in which you sit. Gently return, remembering the response. When you are ready, write down the response that you received.

Merlin

First, let us just explain some basic cosmic law. There is a law operative in the universe. Law is the understanding of how Spirit, consciousness, self and all things function in existence in relationship to other things. Cosmic law is not to be mistaken for truth, for truth is merely that which is which may or may not be a constant. Law is something that is a constant within certain parameters. Truth is an alive, vibrant, functioning Spirit that evolves, changes, regularly transcends its own nature.

God is truth. God is love and God is truth. There is a God, which is a truth, and that is what you are. All entities in a cognizant relationship in any way whatsoever with themselves, meaning any entity that is aware of itself and aware that it exists is in a relationship to some extent with Creator or that which you term God. Some connections are very, very weak, while other connections are realized fully. By fully realized I mean there are some that completely know in every aspect of their being that they are one with the Source of this existence and are completely surrendered to it and it is surrendered in them.

For different kinds of entities, different kinds of beings, this manifests in different ways. For human beings, this reaches its highest point in the phenomena that some have come to describe or label ascension, the ascended state, the Christed state, the God conscious, the nirvanic awareness and many such terms. This does not represent the highest consciousness that there is. This simply represents the highest consciousness available to humankind, after which humankind goes on to other kinds of experiences.

The ascendant consciousness, the ascendant awareness is a spirit entirely free from struggle. Simply put that is probably the best way to say it where within one's own consciousness there is no more room for struggle. It means the end of the fight, the beginning of peace, enlightenment and empowerment.

That is not to be mistaken for freedom from challenges. There will always be challenges. Challenges are eternal, but no challenge needs to be a struggle. The only struggle you can have is a struggle that you invent in your own mind, in your own consciousness. Struggle does not come from the world. Struggle does not come from the universe. Struggle comes from your perceptions, the way that you perceive life.

For example, do you have a struggle with love and love relationship? Do you intend to see that end? Do you have a struggle with yourself? Do you have struggles with others, conflicts? Does the world not cooperate with what your needs are? Do you have a need for the world to fulfill you in a certain way, for people, for life to fulfill you in a certain way, and does that create a struggle for you? Do you intend to see that struggle end? That struggle is entirely in your perception.

We would like to help you unfold many things. There are many gifts that are the nature of the human spirit, gifts that have been tapped by all too few over too long a time. The gifts we speak of are meant to be very natural human gifts that are so rare that when they appear, to some extent in one or another, the gifts that are natural seem instead to be rather extraordinary.

That is to say, when you come across a clairvoyant and they are a good clairvoyant, you might think how extraordinary. I wonder why he or she was chosen as though such a person is chosen for such a destiny. When you come across an historic enlightened Master or a living one amongst you in your day, you might say how extraordinary. That was an exceptional, gifted person. I say to you, no, it is not a gifted person. These gifts of the human nature, part of the human spirit, are suppressed for any number of reasons and any number of fashions and ways that you shall come to understand and then learn to bring them forward.

I want to talk a little about mastery. When something is missing, when something is not enough, doing the same things repeatedly is not going to make it work. That, by the way, is a form of insanity. When somebody takes the same thing that never works and keeps expecting it somehow to produce the unexpected, that insanity is very popular in this world. I do not say that because it is a condemnation of this world. I am saying it because it is a very strong frequency, a very strong vibration in the world to become involved with that cycle of energy, with a flow of things and wonder, wait a minute. What is going on here? Then look around and saying, well, everybody else is doing it, and I am doing it too, so I must be doing what is expected. I will keep doing it.

People attach to particular vibrations and frequencies that are very popular in the world. Human beings tend to go with flows of energy. If many people like the entertainer Michael Jackson, then many more people will attune and tend to go along. If people think, in the year 2000 Nostradamus predicted the end of the world, then people will tend to go along with that vibration. People tend to go along with those who have strong influences. If you do not establish what your own influence is, if you do not mark what is important to you and commit to it, then you shall find yourself a part of some other stronger vibration that is not in your own vibration. That vibration may not have your best interest at heart. You may want it, you may pray for it to, but if you are flowing with that vibration that is not your own, then you are at the whims of fate. You are at the whims of whatsoever vibration is all around.

Mastery is about carving your own vibration into the world with such love, with such devotion, with such light, with such wisdom that you are the sovereign entity in your existence. That entity you are is one with the highest vibration in existence. It is a very wise choice to make.

One of the most difficult areas for spiritual people is to translate all of that spiritual awareness into functional physical existence. In order to do that, the only thing that prevents that on any level is some blocks in perception on your part, blocks that simply are not there, but ones that will have been created and that you may not be so willing to take down. This may be quite the challenge, but we shall see if we can relieve these things so you will have breakthroughs.

I would like each of you to find a candle, light it, and sit and look at it. Then close your eyes. I would like you, with your eyes closed, to remember what the color of the candle was. I want you to imagine or remember the color. Try to imagine and find the shape of it with your eyes closed. Imagine how high or low the wax of the candle was. Imagine that you reach out to touch the candle with your hand and feel the warmth around your hand as you grasp the candle. Imagine you see the color of the flame and its flickering.

Now open your eyes. Did you remember the color of the candle? Did you remember the color of the flame? Did you have difficulty remembering the height of the candle? Did anyone have any difficulty with any of those memories?

The reason I had you do this is to show you that you do not have trouble visualizing. You just did it. That is what visualization is all about, imagining. It is as though there were a picture there. When you use your psychic senses, it is like that. You have a psychic impression. Sometimes it is hard to know the difference between visualization, imagination, hallucination and a creative endeavor. We will get to how you can tell the difference between all of those things.

If you will, close your eyes for a moment. I would like you to think of a pine forest, a very thickly treed forest in its later states. There are very high pine trees all around and browning needles on the ground, spongy to the step, so thick is the ground with orange and brown pine needles dried all throughout this thick pine forest. You are walking amongst these trees. I would like you to imagine a rabbit there that you watch bound across the pine needles. It is a white rabbit with pinkish eyes. It is looking through the side of its eye and it sees you there. It is startled and becomes still, and then it starts to bounce away. You can hear its movements as it jumps. It stays in view. It is not too afraid of you. You are not moving. You notice the air filled with pine smell. You become aware of other sounds, perhaps birds and wind as it whistles through the needles and stirs the trees. You can almost feel a breeze blowing across you. The smell of pine is so fresh and strong you can almost taste it in your mouth. The rabbit bounces over to you and nibbles at your shoe trying to connect to you.

All right, come back for a moment. Did you have any difficulty with that imagination? It was simple, was it not?

I would like you to try to decipher where that activity was going on inside of you while you were imagining, visualizing. I would like you to think for a moment about what place in your head it was happening. Was it above you? Was it out in front of you? Did it seem like it was in your skull? Was it in the back? Was it to the side? Did it come and go? I would like you to try to define where that image was for you. Try to define it exactly. Was it in and out? Was it backward? Was it projected out front? Were you inside of the picture? Was it all around you? Did the picture go in and out from the perception of your being inside of it to it being a projection? Was it going back and forth? These things are important.

Some people will be inside the picture. Sometimes you cannot tell if it was half in your skull or half out or whether you were projecting it or you were inside of it or if it moved around. Some of you might also have found yourselves doing a few more things than I mention.

I would like you to deeply inhale and sigh. I would like you to close your eyes and relax your bodies. Tell your muscles to relax and feel a bit limp, easy. We would like you to think of the first place you can remember where you grew up, the house or apartment building, whatever it was, the first place you remember. Think of that place. See it or imagine it, remember it.

All right, if you will come back immediately. Was that inside of you? Was it projected? Were you in it? Was it in front or back?

Because this was a memory, you may have found yourself becoming more involved with it. However, what was most important was what happened when it first appeared. Some of you may have gone into the homes, but what is important to me was where you were when it first appeared. Were you instantly in front of it, and then in? Was it in front of you? Was it behind you, in the back of your head? Was it in a different place than you described for the other?

What I am trying to distinguish here is that a memory takes place in a different way than a creation. You should have had a different experience about a memory than a creation. One might come more quickly and clearly than the other might. You might have an emotional response with a memory. Sometimes memories are stronger, but a positive response emotionally might also make a vision a little bit clearer.

The reason this is important is that psychic impressions tend to come in the same fashion as memories rather than visualization. Visualizing is an active, creative act. A psychic impression is a flash. With either one, you can end up involved. Depending upon how good you are or how good you get, the involvement may be a concoction of your imagination or a further detailing of what you are actually seeing psychically.

The thing that we want you to be aware of is that when you are going for a psychic impression, however faint or strong, it is the first impression that comes like a memory. It may come in your head. It may come in your body. It may come in your ear. It may come in your feelings or emotions. In most cases with most people, psychic impressions are like watching something outside of you as opposed to being inside of it, in most cases.

Dream Work
Merlin

First, we are going to discuss dreams and the themes that appear in your dreams. In order to capture the direction of your dream, you must capture what is the theme of the dream. Most often, the most important part of the dream or the theme happens just before you wake. The consciousness desires very much to have present on your mind that which is most important. Therefore, you will usually dream the most important just before you awaken. If you can capture the last few activities and see what the theme is, you will be able to see what to do with the dream, and it may go several directions.

One direction is you may dream about a theme that is going on in your life that makes you clear as to what you are involved with so that you can choose more wisely what to do beyond that. Another way is that you may have literal dreams. In literal dreams, persons appear in dreams exactly as they are in your waking life. In that instance, you can accept that your communication with that individual did indeed take place and you may have telepathically contacted that person. However, if the person in the dream looks like someone else or looks like someone you know, but presented a little differently, it is very likely that person represents you or a part of you that is expressing in that way. That person in the dream can present perhaps a little older, a little younger or perhaps they look a little like two people you know fused into one or somebody you do not know. In this instance, there may be two of you, one that looks like someone you know, but not exactly, plus you. These represent different aspects of the self.

You may have a wish fulfillment dream. A wish fulfillment dream can also change so as not to be literal. Quite often, many elements to a wish fulfillment dream are out of place. When you have a dream about the future or something that you can make the future, there may be certain things that are out of place, but it shall also come with clear directions about how to achieve what you desire. If your dream is pure wish fulfillment, it will simply show you in the manifest stages of that wish. You will not see how to get there and there will be no hint as to how to create it.

If it is a fearful projection rather than a prediction or a warning, a fearful projection shall be very imposing, threatening and harmful to your being with no solution as to how to solve it. If it is a warning, no harm will come to your physical being in the dream and you will be able to avert the action upon waking. However, if you find yourself actually in some way very harmed, then this is a fear projection, especially when no offering presents as to how you might avoid it. If you feel threatened in a dream and there is no offering as to how to avoid it, when you wake up there should be a way that you can avoid it if you choose to avoid it. If it seems inevitable, it is a fear dream and not the truth. An inevitable fearful outcome with no solution as to how to resolve it offered is not a real prediction or a warning. It is simply a fearful projection.

Once you understand the various themes of dreams, you can then become lucid. It takes practice, which means you have to be willing three to four times a week to leave ten minutes to half an hour before sleep doing nothing. That means no television, radio or anything like that. You can either read or meditate, but read material that helps establish your consciousness in a higher place. Your consciousness needs to be unaffected for a while before you go to sleep by any external stimuli other than what puts your mind in a condition to be conscious. You will need to be able to do that.

Then you will need to write down that with which you intend to get in touch. It might be for you or for another person that you might seek help. You might want to heal somebody or reestablish a better connection with somebody you know. You might have an agenda, a few things. Do not give yourself too many things to do. You might focus on the schools of learning and you might intend to go there. You might make that intent. You might intend to visit one of your Guides, and so on. You can use this time to do that. There are other aspects involved with this, but we are going to work on this aspect.

You must then be willing, when you awaken, whether the middle of the night or early in the morning, to at least write down one theme of one of your dreams every night that you do this meditation. All of the conditions are necessary. If you are unwilling or unable to fulfill any of these conditions, then perhaps this is not a practice for you.

If you make love before going to sleep, you will still need after that to disconnect for a moment from your partner and get in touch with an expanded consciousness. That may include your partner and it may not, depending upon that with which you need to get in touch. It is not that there is anything wrong, harmful or negative about sex. Sex is a very wonderful and necessary experience, especially when it is loving.

What you are trying to do is find direction that exists in service and exists beyond your partnership, which at times may include your partnership and most times will not. It will only include your partnership in the most expansive of ways, but your path is yours and your partner's path is your partner's path. While you may walk parallel, you certainly do not intertwine in certain ways. There are times you may be closer together or in common. At times, you may have to go the distances and build bridges across those distances. However, rarely is it that your partner, whether in marriage or in other forms of relationships, is walking exactly the same path as you. If that is true, you can rest assured that that relationship shall be terminal.

In other words, at the point where people are in totality and in union and one with each other, they then complete. There is no need to be together in order to be together. No matter where you are, you will be together. No matter whom you are with, you will be together. As long as you have a need to be with your partner, that means you are not yet at one and you are relating or in a relationship. When you are one, a very different dynamic happens. You do not need to be together to be together. Usually that is another kind of path. If you are one in your partnership, having exactly the same path as each other, than it is very likely your path will only include service in this regard for a while, and then you will go on to other things.

Some people imagine that what they want is a partner that shares in the work with them. That is very likely to be another kind of a partner than a romantic one, for if you become too much one, you have no relationship. You are one. You are no more relating. However, so long as you still feel a need, and it is a positive need to be with each other, to be together in order to experience your togetherness, you are in a relationship and your paths are different. They may have many elements in common, but they are different paths. So long as the paths are harmonious, it is a beautiful thing. If they are not harmonious, you can build bridges and make it work beautifully anyway. At the point it becomes one you shall find sooner or later you will need to go on to what the oneness has created for you. You will always be together, no matter what the distance. You will also have the understanding that it is all right to let go of your partner at that point, whether it is at death or before death.

People complete. Relationships end. They are not eternal. You complete, finish your business with each other or you become one and elevate to a different plane of consciousness and seek out another one with whom you can relate and create a new evolution.

That was a bit of a digression. What I was saying is that you have to interpret the theme of a dream for yourself. If you do not know or understand the theme of a dream or if you cannot relate to the theme, then write that dream down and the next time you go to sleep, say I need more clarity on this theme.

It is an effort to get in touch with what your super conscious or your highest consciousness is trying to tell you. You will find you absolutely must listen to those messages. They are who you are. If you do not listen, you will likely learn in a more trying manner. You must listen to those messages or you will become increasingly unhappy until you do listen. This is the 'you' speaking, and if you do not listen to your 'you', to your highest 'you', sooner or later life must demonstrate in more material and dramatic ways why you ought to listen to the 'you' inside of you and overcome your fears and doubts.

One who does anything like this will no longer be able to play ignorant. If it makes you happy to play ignorant, very well, because you ought to do what make you happy. What happens when you do not play ignorant? You become knowledgeable or knowing, a gnostic, a mage, a magus, one is a knower, rather than one who is ignorant. Ignorance is what leads to fears and doubts. Sometimes, if you are unconscious and therefore ignorant of what is going on inside of you, there is much room for many fears. It is only from ignorance that fear can spread. This will remove ignorance and reveal knowing.

After writing down your dream and finding the theme, the next step would be to ask what you could do about this. Write that down. What can I do about this? Go to sleep and answers will come. Let go and answers will come. Answers cannot come from not letting go.

It is important to write it down so that you practice becoming conscious about what is going on inside of you. You will find that you are getting in touch with your Guides in that way. They will communicate to you in that way.

Our real goal is to get you to speak our language, which is a universal one, one not based upon personalities and not about language. It is for you to receive direct injections of truth, about which there can be great clarity.

Dreams are like little messages from God. They are messages from the God you have found within you to reveal to your ego, your consciousness, your identity, the truth about the nature of the creator you are. These messages are important to receive, and this is going on even when you are not dreaming. It is going on all the time, right now. However, you are a little over stimulated by physical phenomena, the environment and anything else. Because of that, you do not always pay as much attention to what is going on in your consciousness as you do to the very stimulating effect of the physical plane. Your body, remember, is designed to dynamically experience the physical plane, so sometimes you must experience the spiritual one to give a little clarity about what is going on in the physical one so you can better move through this very stimulating physical plane.

In a dream, if you are with someone who has passed on, you will know you are with that person and you will not have any doubt about it. They will usually find a way powerful enough to make it clear to you that you are with them. They will use some kind of special touch, some kind of special gaze, some kind of special words, some type of thing that grabs your attention so that you wake up with a profound feeling you were with them. There is no doubt about it. You maybe have doubts by trying to rationalize it away, but that is how you know how real it is because you are trying to get rid of it. If it was not real, you might try to rationalize why it is real, but if it is real, if you do not understand it, you may try to get rid of it as real. When it is real and you accept it, it is a very powerful experience, very, very powerful.

If you would, make a great circle of light all around you using your hands as though trailing from your fingertips was a light encapsulating you in a golden circle. With arms up in the air and hands facing toward the sky, the circle fills with a golden light, and then breaks open and merges with all the other golden light of all the other people in the world until there is one giant circle.

Now let your hands fall to a comfortable position. Visualize a light in the center of the room where you are and allow it to expand to be all encompassing of the room in which you sit. The light expands to fill the room and expands to fill all of the house, all the of the street, all of the neighborhood, the city, the state, your nation, the globe, the solar system and the galaxy, and you explode into light filling the entire universe.

Now stay connected to universal and the immediate here and now as though you were aware of both at once and just be at peace. Now you are a focal point for the universe and all of its light and power to manifest through you. From this place, ask a Guide to present to you in your mind's eye a signal or a name, a symbol or sign. Ask this Guide to work with you. It matters not if the Guide is one you already know.

Write down the name of this Guide. Stay connected. If you got no name or no symbol, write down that you got no name or symbol. Write down anything positive that you got when you asked the question to work with the Guide. Write down the response.

Those who did not get a response, ask one more time. Will you help me with my spiritual work and development? Be still and feel the question, just feel and breathe. Do not look for an answer, just meditate, relax and feel. Feel your body. Does your body feel good? That is a positive response. Did you get a chill? Did you get tense? How did your body feel? That is a response.

Now write down a question that you need answered. You are going to ask for some guidance or some revelation that is important to you, some idea or thought.

Now I would like you to find a comfortable position to either lay or sit comfortably for a moment. Lie back for a moment and watch your breath. I would like you to focus on the rhythm and the sound of your breathing as it journeys up and down, letting the rhythm capture you.

I am going to speak to you for a bit, and then I am going to be silent. I would like you to follow my direction as I guide you safely into leaving this plane. After I finish, you will journey. You will drift. When you return, I would like you to recall wherever you drifted, but I am going to let you drift for a while. I am going to guide you into deeper relaxation, and then I am going to be silent.

After I am silent, if you are still conscious of your surroundings, I would like you to focus again on the rhythm and sound of your breath. What I will say will only be to relax you deeper. If it has not relaxed you completely, then afterward focus again on the breath.

Feel your feet muscles. Feel them there, and feel all the tension leave them as you become aware of your ankles. The tension in the ankles dissipates now. Your calves and your shins, all of the tension drains away like a fluid, like a blue delicate fluid drifting out of you. Become aware of your knees and tension drifting out like blue delicate fluid. Become aware of your thighs and tension drifting out like a blue delicate fluid. Your hips and your sexual organs, all the tension drifts out like a blue delicate fluid. Your sphincter muscle relaxing and your stomach, like a blue delicate fluid all the tension releases.

At this point, you are going to become increasingly more relaxed as I count from five to one, with each number more relaxed. Five, four, more relaxed, three, two, one, very relaxed.

Now in your solar plexus area the tension releases like a slow and delicate fluid. Your chest and pectoral muscles and upper back, all releasing like a slow blue delicate fluid, drifting. Become aware of your neck relaxing, the blue gentle delicate fluid drifting out. Your cheekbones relax and your jaw and mouth gently falls open just a small delicate fluid drifting out. Your nose and eyes and eyebrows relax, a delicate fluid drifting out. Your brow relaxes with a slow delicate fluid. Your fingertips, fingers and hands, relax and drifting out like a slow and delicate blue fluid. Wrists and forearms, relaxing like a slow blue delicate fluid. Arms, upper arms and shoulders relaxing, like a slow delicate blue fluid.

We will go deeper into relaxation, becoming less aware of the physical and more aware of consciousness with each count from ten to one, going deeper and deeper into the state of pure consciousness. Ten, deep, nine, deep, eight, seven, deep, deep, six, deep, five, very deep, deep, four, deep, deep, three deeper, two, very deep, one. Breath, rhythm, sound, answers. If you fall asleep and wake up, you will immediately recall your thoughts. If you fall asleep and wake up, immediately recall. Breath, sound of the breath, the rhythm of your breath just relaxes you. I will be silent now.

Begin to come back now. Coming back and remembering, remembering and coming back. I will count from one to five coming back and increasing in memory, one, two, three, four, coming back now, five, come all the way back. Wiggle the fingers and the toes. Begin to come back, wiggling the fingers and toes.

Some of you had contact. Some of you had dreams. You saw pictures given to you by the Guide you asked to help you. Some had thoughts about what is going on in your life. Write these things down. Write them down now.

If you were not aware of what was going on with your body for periods, you were gone. Your consciousness was elsewhere. Write down whatever you have gotten.

I would like you to write down the theme of your thoughts, dreams or visions during this excursion in a sentence or two to the best of your understanding. More detail may come, but write that after you write the theme. In a sentence or two, describe the actions that went on, the trend of the action.

It is a very important thing that you must go with the Guide that appears to you now in your inner consciousness because you do not want to hold onto your Guide as they were in the past when in fact your Guide has gone on long ago to some other state of being. They may simply recollect that past persona for establishing a rapport with you now. When you go into the inner plane, they are showing you more true self and more and more until you are joined entirely with the light. You must go with what is revealed to you from within.

No matter what Guide or God itself, you must not hold that or even yourself to one definition. Your Guides do not want an identity or a definition any more than you do. They assume that identity for the purpose of connection so that you can go beyond it. They must take a form you can recognize. Do not become too attached to any form of Guide other than that which is revealed to you from within. Rest assured, you will get changing definitions. Everyone has many Guides. The idea is that if you are going to work with Guides as a worker yourself, you are sent a Guide who is most able to work with you. Work with the worker Guide that is revealed to you.

If you are not willing to accept your Guide who comes to you, that is all right. You will have to wait until another time when there is another Guide willing to work with you. However, you can expect and almost count on that they will never present as you want, but as you need. For this reason, we cannot be held to a definition you project onto us anymore than you can be held to a definition we project onto you. You must allow us to be as we are, as we appear to you for the sake that you will be able to let go and go on as well.

I will say one very important thing. Hardly anyone's Guides, guidance or God will show up in the way that you expect, but you will always see it in a way that you can recognize.

Kathumi Singh

You are living in a beautiful incarnation at this time, for life is a very beautiful experience. However, it is only a beautiful experience to the extent that you allow yourself to experience and be filled with love. You have been taught love is only available to you under particular circumstances and some of you have not even been taught that it is love you are seeking.

Ultimately, what you are seeking is the love that exists within your very being, for each of you is a shining, radiant soul. Right now, you are filled with all of the radiance with which you will ever be filled. Do you understand the beauty of there being nothing you must further do to become more beautiful because you already are beautiful? No lack of beauty or love exists within your being, but perhaps only an inability to access all the beauty of the life force that exists within you now.

Perhaps you are aware that to one extent or another you have allowed yourself to experience the beauty of your being and that you are seeking to unfold or to give yourself permission to experience the whole range of your being, in this very moment, no longer letting it be conditional. Each of you, for at least a moment, has touched the beauty of your being, and each of you has touched the beauty within each other from time to time. If you will not be distracted, if you will be focused, if you will be devoted, then you will be able to consistently unfold the very experience of your being. Whatsoever lessons you must encounter and whatsoever challenges you must face, you will be able to face them, dear ones, in the knowledge of your true self.

It is not meant that in the pursuit of that which is important to you that you lose your love or misplace it. It also is not meant that you find your fulfillment in that which you pursue, for the fulfillment is already with you and it is a matter of you being conscious enough to remain in touch with it or to return to it when necessary.

That is why it is so important to create for yourself as many circumstances and conditions as possible where your awakened self and awakening self are supported. It will never be that those circumstances you place yourself in will be equal to the experience of your true being. It shall never be that those circumstances ever can be arranged perfectly so that you are totally supported externally at all times and in your highest inspiration with your aspiration properly placed. Nevertheless, if that is a part of what is your love, then Spirit will guide you. Your Spirits will invite you into the realm of the fourth dimension and beyond.

In coming, we wish to share with you another opportunity to enter into a collective awareness of that which exists beyond your individual identity, that which exists beyond you. If you will let yourself be free, you will be able to join us, if you have not already. If you are able to let go right now whatever else grounds you, if you have not already entered into your true and higher self, then invite your higher self to be present here and now. Let your mind, feelings, heart and spirit shift, and feel what is present. Feel the divinity that is within you. Feel the divinity that is around you. Allow yourself to enjoy the pleasure of being, the pleasure of your breath, the pleasure of your heartbeat, the pleasure of this moment. Feel the tingling energies of pleasure, the pleasure of your love for each other, the pleasure of us, the pleasure of your path, the pleasure of your focus, the pleasure of your efforts, the efforts that have brought you here out of the intention to again unify with your truth. All the revelation you need is here right now with you.

Let us move forward now into our newer dimension. It is time for another step. In order for you to be able to take another step, there must be an intimacy between you, in your self in its true form, and us in our true form.

It is time for it to go far beyond it being a connection you make with us in this manner. You must choose whether you wish to let go to a level far beyond what takes place here. Will you let us become your friends and your conscious companions? Will you let us, in our way mingle with your lives even more than perhaps ever before? Will you trust us to enter into your dimension, as we trust you to enter into ours? Will you put aside all that is not love to embrace lovingly an eternal embrace, which no longer holds fear and suspicions, which embraces your true self as your true power in your sovereign nature?

You will see yourself as that which we are and we as that which you are. Will you see us together as a part of a great and potent good of energies merged and molded into a wonderful unit that does not deny you your unique expression, your unique access and does not limit us and deny us of our gifts that we would share with you from love and that which we would receive from you in this holy and divine exchange?

This level of a step is an invisible step. It is far beyond any practical application of time, efforts and energies, even though it shall involve that as well. It is far beyond simply doing something to produce a result, but becoming something in full cognizance and letting go of denying of all aspects of true self and the embracing of your original nature. Will you allow the formless part to be experienced through form at this time? Will you let us be that which we are sent to you for, to be your Guides?

How do you access this assistance? You have already begun. Each of you listen to different parts of that which we say, whether it is through this channel or any of the many channels that are around you, friends, family, teachers, life experiences. However, the primary key is through your appreciation of life, your willingness to choose to appreciate life again and again and again, every day, no matter what. That is where you let us assist you.

Some of you have to give up your confusion. Some of you have to give up your cynicism. Some of you have to give up your insecurity. Some of you have to give up your self-doubt and self-hatred. Some of you have to give up your anger and rage. Some of you have to give up your self-pity. Some of you have to give up your attachment to unhappiness. Some of you have to give up your relationship. Some of you have to give up your former self. Some of you have to give up your belief systems. Some of you have to give up your attachment to being right. Some of you have to give up your attachment to fear. Some of you have to give up your attachment to teachers. Some of you have to give up your attachment to ego.

Where are you stuck? Honestly and ruthlessly examine where you find yourself stuck over and over again. What have I just said that rings a chord in your being? What 'stickum' grabs you over and over again? Where do you find yourself experiencing more obstacles? Offer that up. Give that up. Invite us to lift these things away from you. That is our gift. That is our talent. That is our joy. You are not here alone.

When you go to your rest, it is crucial that for those of you who are not already meditating, you meditate for a time last thing before you sleep. It does not matter if it is sixty seconds or twenty-four hours of meditation. For a while let it be important. Then, in your journals, for those of you who are not doing this a maximum of four times in a week and three times minimum, state your intention in writing to become in union with your higher self and to be shown some important lesson for your growth and happiness.

It is important that you let your consciousness orient itself toward learning regularly while you are journeying in the realms of the unconscious, that you put your consciousness to work on these levels intentionally and that you take this seriously and capture upon awakening whatever it is that you can remember, even if it is just a feeling. We have said this already, but we will say this over and over again, for we see that it needs this reminder to do it.

It is important that you not only capture the dream, but also write what you believe it means. Be never accepting that you do not know, but remembering, interpreting to the best of your ability what you believe is the meaning of that dream in alignment with the question you have asked the night before, trying to link the two things.

Upon awakening, write whatever dream you had. If you had no dream that you can remember, write whatever segment you can remember. If you can remember no segment, then write the emotion you are feeling, confusion, happiness, sadness, joy, excitement, depression. Whatever it is, write the emotion. Keep working on the same issue night after night until you get some reply. Even if it takes three or four weeks, stay with one question or one intention. Even if you had the dream, but you cannot remember what the dream was, you ask the next night for the same thing and this time ask to be made clearer or to remember better, working on the same thing every night until you get some insight.

In one or two sentences, see if you can write the theme of that dream. Not what it means, but a statement of what happened in one or two sentences. I do not want a meaning for the dream, but a statement about what happened in that dream, a theme of one or two sentences and not what it means. For example, it might be a dream about receiving information from teachers and friends, and questioning the validity of those teachings. That is what I would say is one statement. The dream is about questioning the validity of information received.

What really matters is the way that the writer of the dream sees it. What you are doing is taking the elements that seem important to you and making a statement about it. The first step is to assess the dreams direction or momentum in a sentence or two. The second step is to understand its meaning.

After you have the message of the dream, if you wish, you can begin interpreting the symbols in the dream. Symbols are either direct statements or symbols that seem to carry other meanings. Symbols can be objects, actions, persons or states of mind. A symbol in consciousness is an encoded message of some kind. You look for things that seem to be messages. Make a little note about what you think are the symbols, not the meaning of the symbols, but the symbols. It is very important to make your own distinctions about what is a symbol and then what it means.

Keep it simple. You simply first make a statement and then you understand what it means to you. Then if you wish, you can interpret the symbols and determine what the message of the dream is.

When left with a question not answered, you dream again. You write your intention before sleep that this is what I intend to have answered. Your consciousness and your Guides will design another dream that will help you further understand the meaning of the message.

You really are not trying to understand the meaning of the dream. You are trying to understand the message. If the message is not clear, then you say the message is not clear. Can you design another one that has the same meaning? The consciousness will keep you dreaming of the same message in different formats. Once you get the message, you stop having the dream.

You may have an entirely different kind of dream that is nothing like the last one if that is what it takes to understand the message. Many times, you cannot interpret the messages of your life. That is why you dream. A dream is a way to get understanding that you could not get when you are conscious. You will keep going to the dimensions from where this understanding is trying to come.

Eventually, you will see that your waking life is also a dream, also a symbol. The way that you see things and interpret things in life is also symbolic for lessons. That is why it is important to appreciate your dreams, to learn to interpret your dreams. You will soon end the differentiation between waking life and dreaming life, and that is when you begin to see clearly. This is a very difficult border for human beings at this time, for human beings are terribly afraid they may lose the distinction between reality and unreality.

Every dream, because it is a function of consciousness and a telepathic message between you and the universe, you and self, you and understanding, has many levels on which it can be perceived. You will see all the appropriate levels if there is more than one level to be experienced. Many dreams have different kinds of messages.

Communication of telepathic understanding is so beautiful and so perfect because many things can be communicated telepathically that never can be communicated verbally or that will take forever to communicate the same thing. That is the beauty of telepathy.

It is our intention, the intention of Spirit to have all teachers and all receptive people at this time in this world come to understand the language of telepathy. It is essential to the survival of the human race at this time. It is part of why we have you study dreams. You can unravel years and lifetimes of karma of not understanding the messages of consciousness by studying your dreams. When you understand the messages of consciousness, everything becomes very clear and simple. Your intellect does not need to translate everything for your mind to be able instantly to become prescient about telepathic messages communicated viscerally and telepathically.

There is a synchronicity of events between consciousness, physical world and astral world. All are integrated into a cosmic braid. The reason some people do not recognize the support of the universe is because they separate themselves by their beliefs and ideas from the ability of the universe to support them in what they wish. The reason they are separating might be defined as ego or separated consciousness. The reason one does that is fear, fear of losing self, but in fact, they will find themselves. People develop an ego because they are afraid of going insane. Their grip upon reality and the boundary put between themselves and the universe, people believe that to survive they must make that distinction.

There is always a period where someone needs to do that at many different junctions. However, they must be willing to let that go because all egos, like all boundaries, must be challenged. Boundaries are not there to contain you. They are there to help you grow secure so that you can branch out farther beyond them. Without boundaries, at first there is a sense of total loss and confusion. However, the idea is not to build up excellent boundaries and then live within them. You make boundaries so that you can have a branching off point for further exploration into understanding of life and of self.

The ego is an identity or boundary one repeatedly relates to so much that you cannot tell the difference between that with which you have become identified and self, what you really are. You come to think you are boundaries and all that is within it, when in fact you are not that. That misperception leads to suffering. Identification with that which you are not leads to your pain. Letting go of that identification, those associations is painful. Embracing that you are in fact something larger than that many times is also painful, but it does not need to be a traumatic process.

If you are able to understand the messages of the universe to you, if you are willing to understand the messages of the universe to you, if you are looking for the messages of the universe to you, the universe will not have to create through dreams and life experiences bigger and bigger messages that are more and more intense. The more you ignore the messages, the bigger they must get.

Therefore, attune and listen to your highest consciousness. Invite the presence of your most expanded self. Get used to inviting that into your life. If you then do not feel any different, fine. If you feel greatly different, fine. However, invite it, please.

All of your dreams not only have inner meaning, but outer meaning. There is no difference between the inner and outer plane in truth. They are exactly the same plane. This, if it is not evident to you in your life, shall increasingly become more and more evident to you. Everything in your dreams, no matter if it is utilizing the past or about the future or some combinations of that and some alternate realities that never existed, is always about something going on now. There is always an element about something going on now in your life. Whatever is going on in a dream, it is always going on now. That is another way to begin to try to interpret a dream. What is going on in my life right now that is like this dream?

If you list the symbols, you may be able to attach significance to each one. If you do it one at a time, you will then be able to relate one symbol to the next and the next and the next. You begin to get clearer. It is not necessary that you interpret every single dream you capture in this way. This is how to take it apart, however, if you are stuck. The main essence is what is the message of this dream for me? What is the message to me? The message becomes clear when you begin to understand the theme related to is there anything in my life going on like this now. Capture the meanings of the symbols and then it begins to get clearer.

The more you are able to capture the messages of your consciousness, the more you begin to see the order in the universe. Capturing the messages of your consciousness is the tool development skill that it takes to be able to interpret your Guides. If you are able to capture and practice capturing the messages of your dreams, you will increasingly be able to understand the messages of your Guides to you. Part of it is being willing to understand, because remember, a great deal of not understanding life, your messages or your help is the desire not to know, the desire to be in denial, the desire to tune out, the idea to let someone else, something else take responsibility. There is tremendous resistance most people have to taking responsibility for their life. It feels too burdensome. Many are engaged in letting others take responsibility. The opposite is trying to take ultimate control, take control over everything, even things you have no business trying to control. Control and not taking any responsibility are exactly the same issue.

The universe is intelligent. You are intelligent. All consciousness is intelligent. Guides are that aspect of conscious intelligence at work in the universe that is, shall we say, clear and full of light. You are a miniature universe, your being is a miniature universe with all levels of awareness, from ordered to chaotic and confused.

Awakening to what you truly are requires you going through a progression of becoming more and more clear or more and more attuned to the meaningful elements in your consciousness, the wiser, kinder, gentler elements of your consciousness. Those elements of your consciousness are connected to like elements beyond your consciousness. Those like named elements beyond your consciousness are simply Guides or a guiding force.

All of the ones who come here and I do not exist in this form. When I leave here, I no longer maintain, if I do not wish to, a separate identity as Kathumi Singh, but rather I become one with everything. I only divide when I come here. There is a subdivision that is a part of the Brotherhood of Light so that when I leave here, I join that subdivision, but that subdivision expands and becomes a part of the All force.

What I am saying is Guides know because consciousness knows. God knows. The God in us knows just as the God in you knows. When you seek to get in touch with Guides, you are actually seeking to get in touch with your more knowing self, your higher self and the part of the universe that is clear. Ultimately, the challenge is will you in fact trust what is you? Will you trust your own higher guidance?

The pain comes from not realizing that you are the knowing force in the universe, so there is difficulty in trusting. You may think that you distrust life, but you actually distrust yourself. Your self seems separate from life somehow. There is a perception that I must guard, protect myself and so I must be very suspicious and very careful or I will be misled. I will be hurt. I will die. This consciousness is not just singularly in you. This consciousness is in every single life form on this planet. It is inherent in the evolutionary process.

In other words, the inherent molecular structure in every life form is very competitive. I must vie for my existence or other dominant forces will overcome me. The evolutionary system is built in survival of the fittest. Survival and struggle is the issue. That consciousness is encoded in every single cell of your body, and every single cell of your body has an intelligence that is motivating you, energizing you, filled with that belief.

What we are speaking about here is taking steps into another way of existence, defining the evolutionary pattern of all of life kind on this planet away from the belief that, even though these are not conscious beliefs, I must struggle for my existence. We want to change that into I am a part of that which is at the highest in existence. One must let go of one's mindset, one's psychology, one's emotional reality, one's visceral reality and embrace an enlightened reality. Those who have taken those steps in history have been relatively few. It just so happens that at this time more and more will take that step.

Everything inside of you and everything inside of everybody will fight taking that leap. It is history in terms of lifetimes encoded in every single cell of your body, the entire five billion years of evolution encoded in every single cell of your body. Everything that has ever happened historically is like a code in your body. So that when somebody says to shift into another mode of consciousness, you are fighting five billion years of not only your history, but also everyone else's history. It does not matter, if you come in for the first time into human body, the moment you get to the human body, you suddenly possess the history of five billions years of earth history.

You also possess the memory of twenty billion years of universal history because the earth history is simply an aspect of what has unfolded in the universe, and that is encoded. In that encoding, is not only the history of the universe, but also the potential of all life kind. That is what you are seeking to find. In the mass of data that is encoded in your cellular and psychic memory is also the infinite possibility that you are. However, it just so happens that the predominant ideas humankind has embraced, however many ideas that is, are shared like a group consciousness. At some point, it is easier to identify with some ideas over other ideas simply because so many other people believe in them.

Therefore, some things that are agreed upon by the mass of humanity, but that are completely false, will seem more real to you than what is really true, but with which nobody agrees. The mass of human consciousness is not focused on the reality. It is focused on something that is decidedly unreal. It has not woken up to what is truly real.

The only thing that is real and true and the only support that is real and true does not come from within the confines of the consensus belief structures. It comes from outside of that. Those are your Guides. That is your true self. True self always comes from outside of what the consensus mass beliefs are. It is not meant to be like that. One day, when human beings are all in their light, then truth will come from within the human consensus mentality. However, the human consciousness is now still so primitive that everything that is true comes from outside of the consensus beliefs. That genius comes into and is accessed by many people in different ways in the sciences, arts, music and spirituality, those ones have been able to see beyond the consensus mentality and be like lights that introduce new ideas and experiences into this plane that opens up human consciousness to that which existed outside of it.

When you ask how do the Guides know? We know because knowing exists and it can be known, and you can choose to know it. What you will find is when you know it, you will see that it is yourself, and that you are a part, and that Guides, that higher consciousness is not separate from you. That is who you are, except that you have identified yourself with something else. You have made the associations over and over and over again that you are something else other than that.

Why would you do that? It is simply because you have not learned yet. It is ignorance. Are you responsible for being ignorant? You are responsible only if you choose to be ignorant. However, all consciousness goes from one point to the next, starts from darkness and goes into greater and greater awareness.

What you are doing is getting the highest part of your consciousness that is available to you. When you have a dream beyond your ability to grasp the meaning of it, this means some light is trying to come to you that you just cannot understand. That is a point of consciousness, a point of awareness beyond your understanding that is trying to reach into your understanding. The more you simply ignore it, the more you are saying I do not care to learn. I want to be blind. The more that you seek to know, the more you open and the more you see. This eventually brings up every single fear and resistant you have because it must threaten your current identity. It must threaten your current belief system, no matter what it is.

Survival, for all of you at some juncture, has been a very scary thing. You did not know that it was scary. Someone had to teach you that survival was scary. When you were born or got older, you could have slept on a bed, fallen off the bed and been hurt and never known why you were hurt. Never known why you were hurt means you could do it again and again because you had not learned to be afraid. You had to learn to make an association about these kinds of things. You had caretakers who taught you all the things that are dangerous about life. So rather than getting hurt every single time for yourself, you began to observe. Now let me get this straight. I get hurt. How many different ways can I get hurt in life? You begin to go around learning how to survive. This means now I am smart. Now I understand. I know about life. Life is about survival physically, emotionally and every other way.

What happens if you do not have to fear? What then is intelligence based on beyond survival? There is much more to existence than survival and that is in the level of joy. You are born in joy from the zero point and the zero point is joy, but many times, you learn to go backward. Each of you has had lifetimes like that, born in joy, went backward and never went past that point. Next life even went farther back and farther back.

You do not need places like this when you have done that enough times. Nobody is going to stop you from going forward this life, nobody. I do not care who is there, who gets in the way. I am doing it no matter what. I do not care how silly I look. I do not care who believes me or not. I do not even care if I do not understand all the time. I am just doing it.

Then you begin to develop keen eyes and you begin to recognize your bothers and sisters with keen eyes. You do not care what mask they are wearing, you can identify them in a moment. They can be open. They can be cynical. They can be different types, different races, different religions and you start to recognize who your brothers and sisters are. You start to recognize who your teachers are. You start to recognize the vibration of truth and that becomes all that matters. You begin to understand that it has very little to do with words and has more and more to do with feeling that begins the shedding of the old identity.

Eventually all of that identity that you made up that was so smart, so wise, so clever, you realize that has very little to do with your life. By that time, you are very invested in it. You are very much attached to it. Letting go of the identity is like peeling an onion. You may think you are letting go, letting go and letting go, and you will wonder when you will let go all the way, but it is like an onion, a cosmic onion.

You are so careful, so judicious, so jealous of how you let go of each little bit of identity, not certain if you will be safe as you let it go. Every place where you took on that layer of identity was based around some fear or some pain, so every time you take off that layer some fear and some pain is revealed. Sometimes the path of truth, for many, feels like a path of endless revelations in their pain. Some say, until I found the path of truth, I have never experienced so much pain. There is not a way at this time for human beings to embrace their lives without hating God at least once. There is simply not a way of doing it because there just is no way around it.

Much that masquerades as truth must be undone, so much of ego, so much false identity, but it just seems like the pain for some people at some junctures will never end. It can be pain. It can be confusion. It can be loss. It can be sickness. It can be disease. It can be suffering. It can have many forms. It can be confusion. It can be madness. It does not matter. It can truly seem endless.

The solution is very simple if you are smart or fortunate enough to invite something beyond yourself to participate with you. You must at least give up that much ego. You must have at least that much humility. The moment you can ask something greater than you as you know yourself for its participation to work with you, that is when your journey begins. There must be at least that much humility. Then the ride gets very beautiful.

Security is recognizing that that which is greater than you is also part of you. That is real safety. Some make the mistake of thinking that that which is greater than them is separate from them. There are those people that say, yes, there is that which is greater, and I am it, so I am everything. You are nothing. Forget about it and come with me. You must be careful of that. Then there are those that will either tell you that they understand and that no one else can but they or that they are so great and you are so small, so forget about you and focus on them.

You are the greatness that you discover, even if it does not feel like you. The only thing you have not discovered yet is that you are a part of it. There is always one more paradox. Be prepared to be a part of everything and everything itself. You are never all of that alone. That is to say, the only place you may get in trouble with the expansive side of negative ego, and there is a diminutive side of negative ego, but expansive side of negative ego thinks I am God and nothing else is and therefore, I must control everything. It does not always think it in those exact words. That is where people get into trouble.

You are everything and you are a part of everything, which means you are not everything. You are everything and not everything. You are both extraordinary and ordinary. You are great and small. You must be prepared to accept either one at any moment. I am absolutely tiny and I am absolutely extraordinary and infinite at any moment, just like that. Either identity is acceptable to you. You feel good in it.

Your experience is just a reflection of your own consciousness. Accept it. It does not matter what it looks like. All you are seeing all the time is a reflection of your own consciousness, a projection of your own consciousness. If you think it is anything else, that you are the actual and objective observer of what happens to you, you are mistaken. You are seeing your consciousness projected.

Once you realize it is your own consciousness you are witnessing, that you are projecting and that you are experiencing, you realize that the key is to be in that place that you most prefer. What is that place you most prefer? What is that like? What are those dynamics? The highest place that you most prefer is not what some might imagine, a flawlessly crystalline perfect existence where you are always smiling full of energy and light, where nothing ever affects you, where you are perfectly asleep and nothing affects you, oblivion. That is not it. The highest place to be is in such acceptance that everywhere you look, you are at peace and everywhere you look, you see love. Everywhere you look, you see support. You see lightness. That comes from acceptance.

Acceptance does not mean anything that maybe you think it means. Acceptance is that state where you are in total self-acceptance, where no part of you hates yourself anymore, no part of you condemns anymore, but rather that you are in a state of love. Pain is judging yourself and your experience of life.

You can wish a lesson were over as much as you want. That is not what is going to get it over. The way out of the trap is simply accepting that you are seeing a projection of your own consciousness and accepting that it is right to see that. Acknowledging the way that you feel is the first step to moving into more empowered energy.

Astral Projection
Sun Bear and Chief White Eagle

We now start a new aspect of a journey. This is going to require some work on your part. I hope that you will be ready to work. We are going to begin with projecting the consciousness, learning how to project your awareness to where you want it to go.

On one hand, you can call it astral projection. On another hand, you can call it time travel. You will see why in good time. On another level, you might call it meditation. On another level, you might call it dreaming. On another level, you might call it falling asleep. We hope we will have none of that here. The key is to be alert when you go where you want to go.

Astral projection is you emitting or projecting the astral substance to one place or another. If you will, close your eyes for a moment. I want you to think about Paris, France for a brief moment, even if you have never been there. Okay, return for a moment. What did you think of when you thought of Paris, France?

The place you just went, that is the astral plane. You visited that in astral plane. What is the difference between what are your thoughts and the astral plane? You just now projected a small piece of your awareness as though it were ejected like a bit of gas to that place, in either the physical or the astral, and sent a part of your sensory equipment to that place. You saw something and returned.

You may have mentally viewed that place, but if you send more of your substance to that place, it becomes more intense. It begins to be a little more sensual. You might see more colors, hear more sounds, smell more smells, taste more tastes. If you focus on that place for long enough and if you have a strong enough emotional attraction to that place, you will send enough of your essence there so that you lose consciousness of what is going on here. You would not have enough essence, enough consciousness to function in your body operating your sensory equipment here. Whatever is going on in the room where you are, if you are there enough, you will have no idea. When you are dreaming, that is in essence what you are doing.

Who has noticed that in order to fall asleep, you must let your mind dwell somewhere else? If your mind is in the body, all you will notice is the discomfort of where you are sleeping, the noise from the dripping faucets, that you are too cold or too warm or something along those lines. Only when you can send your spirit, your thoughts far enough away can you lose consciousness and go to sleep.

Who are deep sleepers? Do you have very vivid dreams? Who are moderate sleepers? Who are the light sleepers? Light sleepers and deep sleepers usually dream vividly. Moderate sleepers usually never remember their dreams because the light sleepers are usually very, very alert and the deep sleeper usually are very involved. Lightness and involvement are the two ways to be conscious of where you go and how to direct where you go.

It is possible to project the astral body into the physical world rather than the astral world. I must explain a few things about that. You are in the so-called physical world. The physical world is just one big agreement. You are in no such thing. You are not in the physical world. You are somewhere that you are in agreement with others to some extent or another. What would happen if you did not agree to be in relatively the same place as each other? You would be judged insane.

For example, let us just say you were in a room full of people and there were four candles on a table in front of you. Most of the people would agree about the four candles on the table. At least on one level of reality they have no problem with that. Let us say I was a guy named Joe and we were all sitting around in that room. Suddenly I say, oh, I see fifteen fairies hopping in and out of the candles. You would look at me and say he is crazy because I am not in the reality upon which everybody has agreed. If maybe children were in the room and they were all between three and five and I said there were fifteen dancing fairies, they might say, oh, but do not forget the little pixies. Do you see them? Somebody else would ask where are the pixies and fairies? Everybody would maybe participate, but some would say, where are those fairies? They have not learned yet to agree on the reality. Maybe if they said that in front of their parent, I see fifteen dancing fairies, the parents would say, no. There are no dancing fairies there. The children would say, okay.

Little by little, you are taught to focus on a certain aspect of reality, and that is no accident. Each culture and each time period is taught what is acceptable to focus on as real and what is not. By the time you get to be adults, if you happen to be growing up in the same culture, you may agree upon what a reality is.

For example, in your culture, the one you are living in right now in this land you call America, you are allowed to walk around if you wear a certain amount of clothing. If you wear too much clothing, you might look strange. If you wear too little clothing, you might look strange. If you go to the ocean and bathe, you are allowed to wear a little less clothing. If you take off all your clothing, then something is wrong. In your reality where you are here in this place, it is considered inappropriate. If you go over maybe to many countries where you can bathe in Europe and many other places, everybody takes off all their clothes. Not everybody, but if you decided to, you would be all right. In different cultures, different things are acceptable.

Agreeing on what is reality is like agreeing on reality by consensus. That is to say, if you get enough people to agree with you, it is real. If you do not, it is not real. Mr. Albert Einstein discovered that time is not fixed, but it is relative. He was going in the right direction, but nobody agreed with him, thinking he was crazy, he had lost his mind. Now get enough people to agree and he is a genius. That is reality by consensus.

If you wish to take the journey to discover what is real, you must be willing to put aside reality by consensus and begin to accept that everything is real. That means that your thoughts, your imagination is real, everything here is real and everything everybody else thinks is real. By the same token, nothing is real. Why do I say nothing is real? It is for this reason. If you are not experiencing the whole, then you are experiencing a part of the whole. If you are experiencing a part of the whole, it is incomplete. A picture that is based upon something incomplete is not a complete picture. It is a false picture. However, reality is not important for our purpose as you might define reality because what is important is what is going on in the universe of your own creation, not what is going on in an objective reality, because remember the objective reality is not a reality. It is just an agreement. If you try to make your experiences fit into some preconceived consensus belief, then you will invalidate your piece of the puzzle. You will invalidate your reality. You must be willing to accept your piece of reality as valid.

Sun Bear

Who has been in an accident and found yourself ejected from the body, floating above the body, seeing the body or been on an operation table asleep and seen themselves out of their body, but in a physical dimension, what you call the physical world? Who of you has been out of the body? We will not call it out of the body, but in an extremely real seeming experience like dreaming, but more than dreaming it felt very lucid, very real. In that lucid state, who has experienced while in that very lucid state that you knew consciously that it was a dream? When you knew it was a dream, what did you do? Do you remember? Did you force yourself awake? Who has experienced a bi-location, as if you were in two places at once? It could be like being awake and asleep at the same time. You can be in a dream, but you feel the bed on your back. You might be walking around and inside of the dream, but there is something on your back at the same time, which is the bed. Who has had that experience?

Dreams repeat so that you can understand the message of the dream. Dreams stop repeating when you understand the message of a dream. They repeat because there is a message that you need to get. Once you get the message, the dream ends and you move on to the next place. This is why we want you to write down the themes of your dreams so that you can make sure you get what these themes are so you make sure you get the message.

One of the best ways to get lucid in a dream is to write it down. When you get the message in the waking state, then the next time that message comes in a dream, you will get lucid.

You must see if that dreams theme relates to anything going on in your life right now outside the dream. That is one way to find out. The dreams always relate to something going on right now, but I do not want to focus on dreams so much, but more on astral projection first.

We feel astral projection and being in touch with your dreams is a very important part of your ascension. As most of you know, even when you are in the physical world, you can relate to the non-physical pretty good. Probably most of you can relate to the non-physical more than the physical. We will focus for a while on the non-physical, but all this spiritual business is useless if you cannot apply it to the world where your physical body lives too. That is very important.

Each of you journeys to different places in your favorite part of the realm where everything is going on. Let us describe all that is as a globe and everything in the globe we will call the entirety of everything that is going on. You find maybe the tiniest of a percent in that reality and go there for lifetimes. For you, that tiniest of a percent seems like infinity. You may journey to different places within that infinity for lifetimes just trying to understand that small part. When the time comes for you to leave this world, you will go to the realm that you can relate to based upon what you are familiar with, based upon what you have studied, what you have learned from your journeys.

There are many ways to journey in spirit. One of the ways you can journey is through meditation where you are not so much projecting the consciousness. You can journey in the astral body, like when you are floating outside the body, and you can float, you can journey in the physical world in the astral and you can journey in the astral world like in a dream. You can go through a dream in an unconscious state or in a lucid state. Then you have the realms beyond the astral. The ones beyond the astral, depending on what culture you are in, are called many different things.

The ones you are most familiar with probably are the mental, causal and spiritual planes. In each of those planes, it becomes less and less sensual. That means you are in realms that do not have as much sight, taste, touch, smell. You go beyond the astral and there are not so much visual things there and sensual experiences, people, circumstances, buildings, activities. In the mental realms, you may occasionally come across shapes, geometric shapes, triangles, circles, squares, objects and numbers. The causal, you will not even come across that. It is even more subtle, like impulse, no vision, no touch, no feeling, and in fact, most of the time you will only know that you have been in the causal when you come back from the causal. You only know that you have been somewhere, but you cannot seem to remember where. Then there are the spiritual dimensions. Well, all of them are spiritual, all of these planes, including this one. They are not stacked one on another. They all actually interpenetrate each other. In other words, right in the room where you are, all of the planes that I described are all right there. You do not have to go flying high out of the body, astral higher, etc. It is not a physical thing. They all interpenetrate right here.

The spiritual planes, by this time you are not traveling anymore. What in fact has happened is you in a sense have osmosed. You have become one. Awareness has interpenetrated thoroughly all of the dimensions. The highest of the spiritual is where you might say that you feel you are one with everything. Hence, no need to travel anywhere. Why do you need to travel if you are here and in the center of existence at the same time, here and penetrating dimensions at the same time? You are simply everywhere, everyone and everything. You have osmosed into everything.

Astral projection is learning how to target where you want to go. Some people, when they die, just keep going to heaven. Ha, ha, ha. They cannot seem to get past heaven. The funny thing about the heaven worlds is you cannot stay there. They are like resorts. They are recovery places. They are like hospitals. They are places for the sick and the tired. When you finally are restored, you are booted out and you go on to other things. People think, ah, I will go home to the light where I will rest forever, but that is not the case.

There is work to be done in the heaven worlds too. However, everybody rests, and everyone is shocked when the cosmic foot comes flying through the ethers and they must go out and do something worthwhile. For everybody who thinks that is where he or she is going to be eternally, it is very abrupt. When you go into the light, it is to get communion, to get oneness so your intention as an entity and the Great Spirit's intention can become linked and aligned with purpose.

People get in their heads that the end goal of life is death. The end goal of existence is nothingness, zero, completion. That is entirely to have misunderstood everything. The nature of infinity by definition means never ending. Anything that ends is stagnant, is ended, is finite. If it ends, it is not infinite. If you are the Great Spirit and you are at the core, then it never ends.

We often say people are not seeking eternal rest, as they believe. They are seeking eternal aliveness, eternal energy, eternal enthusiasm, eternal awakeness, eternal spiritualness, not death, not stagnation. Let me put it like this. Have you ever known anything, no matter how beautiful, that if that were all you could have, that you would be satisfied forever? No, that would be prison.

The beauty of your true self is that it never ends. It is never finished. It never ends in perfection. It goes on forever. To project consciously means that you can live out what you need to live out and learn.

I have an assignment for you. We have explained some things. We would like you to notate in your journals. We would like you to have either meditation times or dreamtime where you will notate where you believe you have gone. Note whether you have gone into an astral place, into a mental place with the figures, numbers and geometric shapes. Note if you have gone into the causal, which will feel like blankness, nothing, just charges and impulses. Note if you have gone into one of the heaven realms, which often are marked by lots of lights and sounds, like harmonies and music and so forth.

Try to find twice in one week a time other than your sleep time. If you have to do this at sleep time, do it differently. If you are laying on the bed when you are about to do this, lay across the bed, turn upside down, lay in a different direction or on the floor or on the sofa. It is best if you can do it at a time other than sleep time twice in one week, and do the following method.

You are going to pre-designate two or three important destinations. You are going to pick one. The places can be any one of these three kinds of places, a physical place in the physical world that you have already been to, a physical place in the physical world that you have never been to, a person in the physical world that you want to visit. I will put in one more kind of place to choose from, somebody in the non-physical world, a Spirit or a relative, if you wish and if that person or Spirit is available.

What you are going to do is very simple. You are going to hold that place or person in your mind as you lay on your back and focus on them until you fall asleep. You are going to hold them in your mind as best you can. You are going to keep putting their face in your mind. The best time is late afternoon, if you can, four, five or six in the evening. Sometimes in the morning, four, five, six in the morning. If you have to wake up at that time, remember to turn in a different position. You need to be in a different position than normal so you do not fall into the same pattern of your normal sleeping. You want to be a little more alert. On your back is the best way.

If you lay there awake for more than twenty minutes, that is enough for that time, but you will likely pass out before then. If you fall asleep, then as soon as you awaken, try to remember where you went. Even if you do not go to what you were thinking of, just by holding a target and trying to do something in particular, wherever you go will be very vivid. Try to do this two times in one week.

Pick somewhere you have always wanted to go. There needs to be some emotional charge and not just a place in which you have no interest. When you astral project, emotion is the power to target the place. It has to be a place you have always wanted to go.

You can contact a relative in the non-physical world if you want and if they are available. They may not be available. You may go and meet somebody else. You hold their face in mind. If you are picking a place, pick a place, a specific kind of target. Like if you have never been to France, you might want to hold the Eiffel Tower as a target or some popular place that is easy for you to focus. That is what pulls you there. If you are targeting a person, you may not want only to hold their picture in your mind. You may want to start waving to them, try to touch them, pull yourself in and shout to them. Become involved with them mentally. As you start to leave this world, you will gravitate there.

They will have action perhaps if you really get there to them. It depends. If the person is asleep when you are doing this, you are likely to meet them on the astral plane. You will have a dream about them and they may have a dream about you. It may not be the same dream that you have because you will not be in their world, but you will find you mutually dream about each other. If they are awake, then you may get them, but they may not notice you. If you shout to them, touch them, you may see them startle and say what is going on here? They may later have a feeling about you. They may start thinking about you.

You may get startled and you may startle them. Do not worry because if they do not want you to be in touch with them, whoever it is, you will not be able to be in touch. You will feel a psychic shield. Even though they may not know that you are trying to contact them, if they do not want you near them, you will just find that you cannot get to them. In that case, you will find you cannot hold their image in your mind or it is too frustrating or your mind keeps wandering.

When you project on the level you call mental, it means most of your essence is here with your body and a tiny bit of your essence is there. The mental essence is a very thin essence that can journey to more places than the emotional and the physical. It is a finer vibration. It is less sensual, finer. In fact, the emotional and the physical will get in the way if you carry that into the higher vibrations. It will keep you from going there. There will be a ceiling. Only if you put some of that aside can you get into the higher realms.

It is important to know how to work with all your levels. Your emotional self, I have difficulties using these words, is not bad or dense. It is just unrefined. When it gets to a certain level of refinement, you cannot take the energy called emotional into the upper realms. It must refine. It is too crude sometimes to go into the upper realms.

For example, you can have feelings in the highest realms, but if your feelings were the kinds of feelings that many people have that are raw in the physical world, they would never get there. By the time that you project your most spiritual self into the highest spiritual realms, you can move some of the other levels up. As they come up, they come through a refinement process where you are not as reactive, impulsive and compulsive. There is no shock, no terror and no fear because what has happened is you have raised the levels of all of your energies. All of the different levels are now vibrating at a different rate.

Everybody has multi-levels of frequency let us say. Everybody's spirit, mind, emotion and body are vibrating at different levels. However, you have four levels that can operate on higher and higher frequencies. Those four levels must all be raised eventually so that all of those four levels are in the higher frequencies.

This is all much more complicated in description than it is in experience. All of you have been there. The problem is you cannot always get there when you want to and you cannot always stay there if you wish. That is because you have not learned how consciously to choose to vibrate at the frequencies you want to vibrate at because you are pulled by too many kinds of unrefined thoughts. This is an exercise to refine that.

Channeling

Mataare

One reason I am teaching part of this class is so that I can understand it a little better. Every time I teach something, my understanding of the matter deepens.

I am unconscious during channeling and when I first did this class, I channeled it and allowed the Guides to teach it. I consider the Guides experts on channeling because they are the ones who have been here during the process. However, the Guides have asked me to do part of this. They feel that my experience will be very valuable for people because you will also need to understand some things from my perspective about channeling.

I call this a getting in touch with your Guides and beginning channeling class because all getting in touch with your Guides is a form of channeling. It may not be channeled information that you give to somebody else, but you are in a sense receiving messages and insights that come in the form of energy and translating that energy into useful ideas that you can understand and from which you can take some guidance.

One thing about channeling is that it is not appropriate, I feel, to be slipping in and out of a trance state all the time. You need to have some sense of control over when you want to be in trance and when you do not want to be in trance. In addition, it is not better to exclude yourself as unimportant and the Guides as all important. The Guides stopped me from doing that with them very quickly.

I realized that my fears about the whole psychic and spiritual realm were based on many things, including things like the *Exorcist*, my Catholic upbringing, some of the things my guru said about it being bad to be out of the body and all of these kinds of things. It occurred to me at one point that I am not sure my guru exactly knew what he was talking about because everybody who falls asleep is out of the body. There is nothing bad in being conscious rather than unconscious when you are out of the body. In fact, I think it is better to be conscious than unconscious when you are out of body.

I want to talk about my first few experiences going into trance because some of you may have had or may have some of these experiences. To learn about what someone else experiences will help prepare you so that you allow the trance to develop and that you do not either fear it or interfere with the process, not realizing that it is trance.

One time when I was present during channeling, it felt like I was very drunk, talking like blah, blah, blah. Really, I was saying things, but that is what it sounded like to me. Another time, I call it backseat mediumship where you sort of hear and see yourself talking, but you are somewhere in the back of your head saying oh my, I do not believe this is really happening. Is this really real? While you are thinking about this, your mouth is just talking away and all this energy just going. Sometimes you may be a little merged with the experience, where you are perfectly aware that it is you speaking and yet there is a different energy. There is a little bit of an etheric feeling, as if you are mildly intoxicated. You may find yourself speaking differently, a different speech pattern and different feelings, different emotions in your body, different states of being and consciousness, different ideas running through your head.

It is not necessarily better to be unconscious when you are channeling. The reason this happens, and I think this is important to understand from the outset, is that all consciousness is like a grid of energy and thoughts that people access all the time unknowingly and knowingly. What we are going to talk about is getting in touch with your Spirit Guides and channeling, which just means tapping into that grid of energy and allowing the grid of energy to expand upon what you know and move into other regions of thought, of energy than what you already understand.

When we talk about Spirit coming through you, there is the need to identify you as separate in that grid. You need to be an identifiable and separate kind of energy from that grid for Spirit Guides to focus their energy on you and to come through. One thing that makes you identifiable to the Guides is your affirmation and your intention to have them come through and the intention of other people around you to have them come through you. That isolates you. That marks you. That sets you up to help complete the circuit.

Once the Spirit Guides do come through, and they come through when they come through, they will use whatever energy exists in your part of the grid that is useful to them. This is very important to know because some people say that they cannot clearly tell the difference between when they are channeling or not and if it is indeed a Guide that is coming through them. Some people will even feel that they do not want any part of their own consciousness to be a part of what the Guide is channeling. That is absurd because the Guide needs your energy. To exclude your knowledge, to exclude what you understand is to rob them of vital information they need to be able to communicate because the Guides themselves also learn. They also grow by the process just as you grow by the process of having them come through you. They learn about you. They learn about the world. They learn about what is important to be able to help you and to be able to help others. Therefore, it limits them if you want to exclude yourself. The Spirit Guides will exclude the irrelevant aspects of your knowledge that they want excluded. You do not have to worry about controlling what they will say and what they will not say. They will eliminate what they do not want used.

Sometimes it helps to set up a way for the Spirit Guides to get in touch with you beyond having them come through you to talk to other people. Sometimes it helps to develop a relationship with the Spirit Guide first so that you feel safe with the Guide and the process and you know that it is safe to receive their energy and information and translate it into meaningful information to you.

We are going to go over one of the ways to do that, a way that I have developed with my Spirit Guides over the years. They have given me many, many ways of learning how to be in touch with them. What we are going to do is use one of the techniques for getting in touch with your Guides and find what I call a control or doorkeeper, one that will help you get in touch with Spirit Guides and help the Spirit come through you.

What a doorkeeper does is helps you go in and out of other dimensions or other states of consciousness. A doorkeeper for a channel also helps other Spirit entities that want to come through, helps make sure that only the right kind of entities come through and that when they are done they go completely. That is important because every Spirit that comes through or into a consciousness will leave a little bit of their energy, but you need to have your own consciousness restored to some integrity that you can relate to that belongs to you rather than belongs to that Spirit.

Your consciousness, your body is your gift and you are the owner of it, even if it is only a temporary rental. It is very important to adopt that particular attitude. Your body really does not belong to other Spirits more than it belongs to you. You are the owner of the body and you are the leaser of your consciousness. You are the one whose integrity must remain inviolate, except when you invite another entity in and out. The control or doorkeeper helps you make sure that that is what is happening. Therefore, it is good to develop a relationship, a connection with your control or doorkeeper.

If you have met your doorkeeper already, you may find this process a little redundant, but I would like you to go along with this. Those who have not met your doorkeepers, just follow along when we do this and meet your doorkeeper.

When you meet the energy of your doorkeeper, it may or may not be anything that you expect. You are going to need to be very open and accept whatever it is that you get as a signal from your doorkeeper.

In order to meet your doorkeeper, it is necessary first to become very physically relaxed and that you have a very, very open mind. We are going to create a space between worlds, somewhere between our dimension and their dimension that they will then come into and introduce themselves to you.

The introduction may be a physical sensation that you get, like a brush across your hair or your face, or it may be a feeling of tingling that comes over your body. The introduction may be a manifestation that appears before you. It may be a vision in your mind's eye or a voice that comes into your inner ear. The introductions may be your own voice that you hear saying I am here. It will be whatever it is.

What we are going to do is a little process and you are going to watch whatever happens when other comes. You are going to ask the presence to identify itself and ask if it is your doorkeeper. If it is your doorkeeper, ask its name. I will guide you through this. I am just telling you what is going to happen. Once you connect with your doorkeeper, this will be our first step, and then we will go onto the next step.

Contact with any Guide or any consciousness beyond your own has to make a contact through your awareness. It is always through your awareness. Even if you want to disown it and say it is not through my awareness, it really is. If a Guide comes out and appears before you, stands outside of you and says yes, here I am, that communication is still perceived through your awareness. Nobody else may see that, but because you have made a definition of inside something and outside something, which may be a different line of demarcation than another's inside and outside, you may think it is from outside of your consciousness. What I am telling you is it is all inside your consciousness. It is irrelevant whether you think it is your own thoughts or you think it is not your own thoughts because it is coming into your awareness, into your consciousness.

When contacting a Spirit Guide, you have to let the question as to whether it is you or a Spirit Guide become completely irrelevant. You can make all your questions and judgments after the experience, but while it is happening, you cannot allow yourself to be caught up in whether it is your consciousness or beyond your own consciousness. That is what channeling is about. When you hear, for instance, to channel you have to get out of the way, it means letting it happen without interrupting it with questions about what it is or is not. Is it real? Is it not real? Getting out of the way does not mean trying to eliminate you. It means letting whatever happens happen.

The quality of the channeling and the quality of the experience will improve with practice. It is going to be a dusty channel if the channel has not been used frequently. After you get the dust out of it, it will definitely surprise you how powerful what comes through that channel is, but let that not be a question for the time you are doing it.

It could be that it will come clearly as separate, such as I have heard my name called sounding as if it is external. I have heard all kinds of things. One of the clearest messages I ever got that seemed external to me was once when I was very depressed. I do not remember what I was depressed about, but it was probably some relationship ending. I was just sitting there and Donna, my doorkeeper, came and asked can I be with you for a while? That came clearly outside, as if somebody whispered it in my ear in the most beautiful voice I have ever heard. That I would say was outside of myself. It was not outside of me, but it sure sounded like it to me. There are many other times when I constantly hear the Spirit Guides through my own thoughts. I can now separate what I call my thoughts and theirs, but there were time I could not.

A common experience for people, and they may be unaware they have been in touch with Guides, is they drift off into another space and find themselves in conversations. You come back, snap back, and you realize oh, what was I just saying? It may happen while we do this exercise.

You do not realize that it is happening while it is happening, but as you come out of something that is very much like a dream, you realize something was said, but you do not remember the content of what was said or you find yourself talking to somebody who is not there. That is another very common experience of communicating with the Guides. In the middle of talking to somebody who is not there, you think, oh, I am talking to somebody and there is nobody around me. A lot of getting in touch with your Guides is very automatic because they come right into your consciousness.

The first stage is just to be able to get in touch with the energy. Let us just call it the energy until it identifies itself and we familiarize ourselves with it. Then you can ask it if it wishes to be known by a name and ask it if it is your doorkeeper or control, and dialogue with it to develop a rapport with the Spirit. After we get to that, then you can have it come through a little bit.

By the way, one of the very common things about when you start to channel is you start humming, singing and swaying, all these sorts of things. The Spirit Guides will often do that to get used to your body, get you used to them and lighten and loosen you up a little bit.

For this exercise, we want you to try to remain awake so do not lie on the floor. Try to remain conscious. The idea is not to slip entirely into trance. You want to keep in touch with my voice.

Get comfortable. Loosen your belts. Take off anything clinging, watches, rings, anything around your neck. If you have anything around your neck, if it is tight around your neck, even if you are used to wearing things around your neck, take it off if it is tight. If it is loose, it is okay. Sometimes when people slip out of the body, they have a gagging or chocking kind of experience. Things around the neck cause people to cough and they feel like they are going to stop breathing or choke if they are slipping into trance. The idea is to have nothing constricting on your body and to feel comfortable and natural. Especially if there is anything tight around your neck, take that off. Loose things around your neck are fine.

Close your eyes and feel yourself sink into the floor or the chair where you are sitting. Feel your body relaxing, becoming easy and gentle, quiet. All the noises around you seem to relax you even more. Every movement seems to relax you even more deeply. The air feels like the perfect temperature and gives you a warm and comfortable radiance. You become aware of your feet and feel the tension ease out of your feet. With waves of energy, the tenseness just wafts from your feet. Your feet feel a warm, cozy, nurturing vibration that comes over them, like a warm, thick liquid that massages and heals.

This warm, comfortable liquid eases upward to your ankles, shins, calves and knees. It feels so good, so relaxing and so peaceful. The warm liquid moves up further to your thighs, moves around your pelvis and stomach, your back, calming you, relaxing you, comforting you, feeling all the tension pass away from you. All the thoughts of the day ease away, all concerns, doubts, all ailments seem to be floating away.

You feel the warm, gentle liquid moving up through your stomach and around your middle back, solar plexus, chest, shoulder blades, upper back and all through your spine and neck and down through your arms, shoulders, elbows, forearms, wrists, hands, fingers, fingernails, so soothing as if they were in a safe, soothing, warming, light and liquid. The liquid light and warmth moves upward through your neck, chin, jaw. Your mouth gently opens, your eyes comfortably closed, your brow, your eyebrows, the forehead become relaxed, your scalp, your ears, your hair follicles. Your body becomes completely relaxed, completely at ease.

With every count, your physical body goes into a deeper and deeper relaxation, but your consciousness remains alert. In fact, so alert, so aware that you can hear into the silence. Your consciousness becomes receptive, with every count becomes more receptive.

From five to one I will count, and with each count your body grows more relaxed and your mind, your awareness more alert. Five, deep, deep, deep. Four, deep. Three, three deeper, alert, deep. Two, two. One. So gently deep, alert.

In your mind's eye, imagine a palace, a castle or a mansion. Notice its color, size, shape, the windows, if any, architecture, depth, height, the substance of which it is made, the environment that surrounds it. Stay with me. Hear my voice. Remain alert. Get closer to the building, right up to the doorway, right up close, closer, and through the door. Go through the door.

There you are in a great vestibule, a great hallway, great reception area. Several doors lead out of the reception area off into other parts of the palace. You see one door amongst all of those doors. This door seems to shine more brightly as though you are being invited through this particular door. You feel as though behind this door you will meet someone, something very special, a special friend, a special helper, a wise, kind, loving special friend and Guide, a keeper, a gatekeeper, a doorkeeper.

Move closer to the door, but not through it, and feel its radiance, the light coming from it. You find it is not a door at all, but a doorway. What appeared to be a door was merely a consolidation of light. It is a somehow perfect light, a more beautiful light than you have ever seen. Go through the light and feel the light coursing through every part of your being, cleansing you, healing you, making you more receptive.

You enter the most beautiful space you have ever seen. It feels beautiful. Whatever you imagine ought to be in this space appears. Notice the colors, the shapes, the textures, the materials and the sounds, notice the sounds. Perhaps there is music. Perhaps there is the wind, birds or instruments. Notice the smells. Perhaps the fragrance is rose, gardenia or honeysuckle. Perhaps it is frankincense, copal or sage.

You look to the doorway now. Look to the doorway, the doorway you have entered. Through the light of the doorway comes something, something wise, something strong, something wondrous, something gentle, something magnificent. It is beautiful. It is very beautiful. It is magnificent. It is subtle and yet powerful. You feel it about to speak. This is your doorkeeper. Ask your doorkeeper for a sign, a name. Ask for a name. If you are not certain of the name, ask again if it has a name. You can almost hear it like a thought, maybe stronger. Ask of this presence, whether it has given a name or not, if it will guard and keep your door. Hear and remember the reply. Feel the reply.

Ask now if it would have you know anything in particular. Is there anything you need to know, any message, any word of advice, any guidance it wishes to convey?

If you are not clear, ask if it can make it clearer and notice if there are any signals, messages, words or feelings that come to your physical body or to your awareness.

Now ask the Spirit to blend with you for a time, to give you the experience of blending with it. Ask the Spirit to blend. Let go to it blending with you. You might feel a tingling around your body. Relax into it.

Perhaps as it blends with you, you may feel impressed to move a part of your body, your head, your hand. You might feel not to resist the intention that is the will of the Spirit. You might feel to sway, to hum, to sing, to laugh, to move, to twist, to turn. Allow the intention of this Spirit blended with you to interact with your being.

Now let go of the blended feeling. Let go of the blended feeling and feel and see the Spirit as again separate from you. Ask the Spirit to help you return to this gentle place at will when you wish to and notice its reply. Ask the Spirit to return you to this gentle place when you wish to instantly.

Let the Spirit exit now through the doorway. Let it exit through the doorway. Turn around and look at the room, the space, notice it one last time and exit through the door. You are again in the reception hall noticing all the doors, and now you exit the palace. Now you come back, present to the room where you sit.

I will count from one to five and with each count you will grow more present here, more energized here, more alive here. One, coming up and back, letting go of the other place. Two, three, four, coming all the way back, letting go of the other place, retaining your memory, letting go of the other place. Five, coming back here.

If you got a name, please write it down. What happened when you asked for a name?

Paramahansa Yogananda

There are times when we come here and speak much of the other planes, the afterlife, higher consciousness and the spirit of love and communication with God, communication with Guides, all of these things. Some of you have touched those experiences from time to time and others of you perhaps have not knowingly touched those experiences. However, in order for you to have enough interest to even be in a place like this, you must have communed with the Most High on many, many occasions, even if you do not remember, because otherwise you would be unable to relate to anything that goes on here.

When a person touches the experience of something far beyond the ordinary that is spiritual, many times a soul may not realize that they are in fact touching the spiritual dimension, for the spiritual dimension is that realm, or at least in the way that I am speaking of it now, that comes from beyond the mind. Which is to say that all of the experiences you remember having that are other than your spiritual experiences are experiences of something that goes on in your mind, in your awareness. However, when we speak of the spiritual experience, at least the way I am speaking of it, I am speaking about that aspect that is beyond your normal awareness, beyond your normal mental state.

When you touch into that experience, there is nothing to relate to that experience. When a person is in a very open state, perhaps through meditation, perhaps because they are particularly relaxed at the moment or perhaps because they are very near to sleep, in these very open and expanded states sometimes people tend to lose consciousness or lose awareness. The reason is that what keeps you conscious is having your brain, in a sense, stimulated by sensory perception, sight, hearing, taste, touch, smell, or your thoughts. Your thoughts usually are based upon experiences of things you have heard, touched, seen, felt or smelled. However, when you touch the realms beyond the senses, there is nothing there in a certain dimension, which we will call the spiritual realm or the heaven worlds. There is nothing there to see, feel, taste, touch or smell in this uppermost dimension. So that when you, as a consciousness, you as a spirit touch beyond that, the natural instinct is to go unconscious from under stimulation. Therefore, most people who touch this dimension are unaware they have touched anything at all because it is nothing, yet it is everything.

On the way to this dimension, there are many things to taste, touch, smell, hear and see. It is for this reason it sometimes has been said that the world is full of illusion and one can find oneself trapped in karmas or actions and reactions for eternities before ever reaching and resting in that place that is beyond everything.

That is not to say that other dimensions other than that one are unimportant because all dimensions are important, the uppermost and any place beneath those. They all have valuable experiences where one can gain much understanding, much joy, much love, much insight and much growth. Yet in those same dimensions, there is a great deal in which one can become lost. Not that being lost is so terrible because if you are lost long enough, you get to know the territory in which you are lost. However, one can spend a great deal of time in life indulging in the realms of the senses, never knowing there is anything more than that.

If you believe in past lives, you can spend many existences never knowing the value of what comes from above that. You can even be deeply spiritual people and have touched that realm of existence beyond the physical senses and go to sleep for lifetime after lifetime once touching that place.

The time comes for a soul, at whatever point it is in their existence they become awakened in that dimension, where they stop going to sleep when they touch the Supreme Consciousness. Sometimes it is entirely appropriate to rest in that Supreme Consciousness. Sometimes when people die, that is what they do. They go up above all the realms and dimensions, the astral, causal, mental, and spend a part of their existence in those dimensions and they go for something that many have described as eternal rest. It is not eternal, but in that state, everything is eternal. One minute is an eternal minute. Ten thousands years is an eternal ten thousand years. One millisecond is an eternal millisecond. As soon as one touches that dimension, there is no more time. Indeed, there are places where there is no more time long before you get to the highest dimensions, but sometimes when people die, that is where they rest.

Sometimes people who are alive touch that dimension and all they really want is rest. When they touch that dimension, they simply take the rest they need to nurture their need. However, more times than not, when a person touches that dimension, it is so filled with power, love and energy that human beings are not used to experiencing at that level of energy. It is gentle, but it is not subtle.

For example, can you imagine the power that it takes for the earth to rotate around the sun? Yet to all of you, you do not even notice it. It is very gentle, but it is an incredible amount of power. The same is true with the Creator, with the God experience. The earth going around the sun is not a subtle thing from one perspective. If that could be harnessed, you would have no energy problems. In fact, you would have too much energy. It is more energy than human beings need to harness, much, much more.

When you communicate with the Source, with the Creator, with the Beginning, with the Source of all the beginnings, it is much more powerful than the power of an earth rotating around the sun by far and it is not subtle, but it is gentle in a certain sense. However, at some juncture, when an entity such as you touches that power, sometimes you also become aware that it is more immense than anything you have ever known and you are about to come alive greater than you have ever before come alive. At that point, sometimes the spirit, you, can shut down, not because you need to rest as in some other instances, not because of anything else other than the power is too much for you and you black out, go unconscious or might become afraid.

I am talking about these things because each of you has experienced that. Some of you might remember it and others of you might not. Nevertheless, I am also speaking of this because each of you is going to touch that again many times. At the point a soul can exist in that state of power without going unconscious, that soul becomes awakened or what you call God realized or you might say enters Samadhi.

To enter into that state without going unconscious takes practice. That is why we suggest the practice of meditation, because when you enter into that state without having to go unconscious and you can do that consistently, then you have accessed the highest there is for you to access and your life from that point begins to change.

For those who have touched that, this is why all of this is a familiar place for you because where you have touched is an expansive existence called truth. Truth is not words. Truth is certainly not the words I am speaking. Truth is that state of existence that has long ago left all possible words behind. Truth is that existence that permeates all existence, all places and all times. That place, when you come back from that in your meditations, in your relaxations, in your soul journeys, in your sleep times, in your calm moments or when you are listening to music and so on, when you come from that place, you cannot forget it. Even though you do not know what it is, you cannot forget.

The reason you do not know what it is you cannot forget is because there is nothing else in your mind to which you can relate it. However, one thing you know, wherever you encounter a similar vibration, you will recognize it again and you will search and search and search for those places and experiences, persons and circumstances where you again can have that experience. You will not even know what it is that you experience, what you are trying to match up with, but what you are trying to match up with is truth. The truth is not in the words or in anything like that. It is a memory of the experience of the highest place you have been.

There is a little, how shall I say it, quiet place behind you in your existence that will vibrate in your being. Sometimes it feels like it vibrates in your heart. Sometimes it feels like it vibrates in your mind.

Sometimes it feels like it vibrates in other parts of you. Nevertheless, wherever you go where there is any reflection of the truth where you have visited, you will want to stay there. You will want to return there because, for you, it is another opportunity to touch the highest thing you have ever known.

You will never touch that highest thing in the way you want to in a place like this. Nor will you touch it in the way that you really need to in any other place except within your own beings because until you have found the most direct course that has nothing to do with where you are, you will not be satisfied. Until you know you can open and close that door, until you know you can go through that door any time you wish, your souls will search until either you find the way to do that or you develop the capacity to do that. Again, this is why we suggest to you the practice of meditation.

I wanted to tell you these things so you might see if you can recall, see if what I am saying strikes any memories in you because the more you discuss this, the more you meditate upon it, the more you are made aware of it, the more you can remember this place. To remember it is almost an instant door back into it.

In the country from where I came, it was called remembering the name of God. The name of God certainly is not Yahweh. That is a verbal utterance. The name of God certainly is not a mantra because those things are uttered too. The name of God is not God either, by the way, for those of you who do not realize that. In India, this was called satnam or the holy name, and it was the unpronounceable, ineffable name of God. Because it is a vibration that is so subtle how could the tongue pronounce it? It is so subtle that the mind has to struggle to become aware of it. In fact, you have to put the mind aside.

Remember I am speaking of mind now, which is really like a processor of sensory data. You hear me speak, which is vibrations, but vibrations for which you also have meaning. When you hear me make these vibrations out of my mouth, they might as well be ug, uh, ah, u, because that is all it is, vibrations. However, when I pronounce the vibrations in a certain way, you have meanings for them in all of your vocabulary. You process in your mind the meaning to comprehend what I am saying. You hear vibrations and then you have pre-attached meanings to every kind of vibration I am speaking, once I speak English. In your mind then you concoct some definitions about what I am saying and you have an experience based upon not only the vibrations you are hearing, but also the meanings you carry for that.

It is the same thing for light or for all you see. Light is also vibration, but in waves, much more subtle than the vibrations of sound, but vibrations nonetheless, vibrations you can capture with your sensory organ or the eye. Not only do you capture the sensory vibrations, the light patterns with the eyes, but also you then have certain meanings attached to those patterns. So that when you look at a brown table, it is not just a brown table to you. It might be a beautiful brown table or an ugly brown table. You might see what else is on it. You might have many associations with that. You might wonder if it is a wooden brown table or imitation wood. Whatever it is, there is much more than what you see that you are interpreting, and that all is processed in your mind.

A vibration that is so subtle that no sensory organ perceives it, but instead, some other manner of perception is aware of it, what does your mind do with that? Your mind can do nothing but remember it. Your mind can do nothing but experience it, and if the mind is active, you will not experience it. You must put your mind aside and develop a peaceful mind. That is also something that develops from the practice of meditation.

One cannot unite with God without activating one's psychic awareness. So that by focusing into this highest most realm, you cross into all the other realms on your way, and awaken many things and open many doors. Sometimes accidentally, without intention, people go into these various places within these different realms for reasons they do not even understand. Children do it all of the time. Sometimes people get familiar with certain places within those realms. Once they get familiar with certain places within those realms, they might find they accidentally opened one kind of door or another. They may have opened an intuitive door or they may have opened a clairvoyant door. They may have opened a mediumistic door. They may have opened an artistic door, a musical door. They might have opened an intellectual door. They may have opened all kinds of doors in the realms of consciousness because they project their awareness, through habit or by accident, into one of those places, which are in fact on the way to the Supreme.

When one meditates upon the Supreme, then one no longer has accidental openings. One no longer has to have worry about which door they open. They will just simply start to open those doors that are the most empowered, loving and wise for them to open by aiming toward the highest.

I come here to encourage you to focus your awareness regularly into the name of God, into this vibration that is the highest. You may not know how to do that and wonder what you should do. There are many ways, an infinite numbers of ways to open these doors. A few of them perhaps I will share with you. However, techniques are useless without your desire, devotion and commitment to open them or to put it simply, without your practice. Practice is useless without love because the practice becomes dry.

You must approach the door of any meditation with a loving heart as well as with a peaceful mind. That is why one excellent way is to meditate around a center from which compassion, love and devotion comes, which is the heart chakra. A very simple way is to become quiet and become aware of your heart beating. Try to feel and listen for your heart beating. That will quiet the mind and you will exist in consciousness.

Another way is to focus upon the breath in any number of ways. India is filled with techniques of meditations centered on using breath, in one nostril, out another nostril, in another nostril, out the other nostril, for example. Another is to hear the sound of your breath. Another is a practice a circular breath. Rebirthers are famous for this, but they did not invent it. This was done long before. You can simply listen to your breath in your mind as it rises and falls, following it to the top and following it to the bottom. If you become quiet, you can hear a ringing in the ear and you can meditate upon that.

There are many, many techniques on how to awaken these things. Sometimes you can visualize. Visualize a flame in your mind's eye above and between the eyebrows or visualize a light. Focus upon the light with your eyes closed. The day will come when you do not have to visualize the light anymore because when you close your eyes it will explode with brilliant light, brighter than millions of suns. These are just some things, and I wholeheartedly encourage your own investigation. There are many roads, many teachers.

You do not need anyone or anything in order to open the door yourself. All you need is a little bit of intent and a little bit of love. It used to be said, and still is to some extent, that without devotion nobody reaches God. In India, this often meant you have to have a guru because the guru was one who inspired devotion. However, many times, I am sad to say, my sisters and brothers in India, my fellow yogis, gurus and others have fallen victim to very sophisticated control trips. Rather than becoming empowering to the disciples, they have created a dependency in the disciples, and dependency weakens the disciples. They feel like they are unable to live unless they are in the presence of guru. Their lives often become dysfunctional and nothing else is important. This very much is cultivated by many teachers, and yet that is not necessary. That might be the path for some, but that is not necessary at all. What is necessary is within you. Have devotion for that union and cultivate love for that union because there is power in devotion.

What devotion does is it grabs you and removes the need for discipline. What becomes a forceful struggle and practice for some, once they become lovingly devotion cultivated, they love meditations. They look for opportunities to connect because they love the experience of being in the presence of the most high.

Regarding channeling, the best thing for channeling is to practice channeling with other channels, with other people trying to open or with people or a person who is an anchor. That is to say, make a little connection with your highest spiritual guidance by asking to connect and affirm your oneness with the highest. Then invite an anchor there, somebody who would like to hear, who you feel comfortable with, and let come through you whatever comes through you. The most important thing is affirmation of your oneness with the highest and that whoever is there, you are comfortable with them.

If you are trying to channel through writing, that can be done alone. If you are trying to channel some words, either for yourself or for someone else, it helps to have an anchor there, someone to pull it through you. If you are channeling art or music, it usually helps to be alone when you are doing that.

Channeling is not a phenomenon that is limited to a Spirit coming through. Channeling can be letting in your own higher awareness. Channeling can be attuning to your creativity. Channeling can be an attunement to a Spirit Guide or to God. The word channeling means to access a different dimension and bring it through into this one, and there are a number of reasons for doing that and there are a number of ways of doing that. Some of the ways include doing it with people there and other ways are best done or practiced alone.

Certain kinds of channeling are very helpful, particularly where you channel in a Spirit entity, a Spirit Guide that has lived in a dimension more knowing then your own. That spiritual force tends to electrify or imbue your own aura with very positive qualities. To do that can make your meditations easier to access. It can also make you more familiar with a higher vibration than the kind you normally live in so that you then attuned toward that.

It is when you are channeling spiritual entities that there are the most pitfalls. When you are channeling creativity in the form of music, art, writing, there are no dangers. When you are channeling other kinds of things that come from your own higher awareness, there are no dangers. When you are opening to let actual Spirits come through, whether they come into you as with this medium or whether they are telepathically communicating into your mind, it is very important that you give limited access to spiritual entities, only allowing a quality of entity that you trust. You do that by making an affirmation of what you want to come through. That is the most important thing. Then you are safe. However, there are many other things, and I would not recommend opening to channel Spirits unless you become very knowledgeable from many writings on the subject, from a good teacher on the subject or from the Spirits themselves. It is good to acquire some information.

The best thing to do is if you are interested in channeling Spirits, talk to other people who are channels and get some good advice and guidance on how to do that. Otherwise, where people get into trouble is because people do not know how to open the door to what they want to come through, and even after they open the door to what they want to come through, they do not know how to close the door. They leave the door open, much like an invitation to any presence that passes by your open door. That presence may not be a presence that you want to come through you.

The reason people generally get into trouble from not closing the door is that people have different moods, different attitudes, different philosophies, different belief systems, not all of which are very functional. The time when a person is in a negative place and their door is open, it is like an invitation to a negative presence. When your door is closed and you are in a negative place, you do not have to let in any negative consciousness, any negative entity. Most people who get in bad moods linger in the presence of negative energies, but they will not be dominated or taken over by any negative entities because they have no open door.

A good channel gets in the habit of opening and closing their door. A channel, because they are mediumistic, has to be a little more guarded. One who deliberately opens their door had better know to what they want to open and close their door. Once they start opening the door, they must invite only the highest presences to come. Frequently you will see people who are beginning to channel invite the Spirit Guides, Teachers or Masters they first feel safest with, like Buddha, Jesus, God or a Guide with whom they feel most comfortable. They feel safest with that and that is what the world characterizes as safe to all to come through.

These spiritual forces shape the tone of whatever else must then come through. Then, if they are not able to shape the tone, provided that person is following some good instruction as to how to properly channel, then their Guides will cause them, in one way or another, to encounter people and circumstances who will get them doing it right, if they get off the track.

The dangers are only if people do not shut the door. How do you know the door is shut? You close it. It is done. It is finished.

The most important thing to shutting the door is this single thing. You have your own right to your own thoughts, your own inspirations and your own ideas even if they differ from your Guides, whether they come through you or whether they come through somebody else. You must have your own sovereign nature. When in disagreement with a Guide, it is not better for you to go with what the Guide says. If you are in disagreement with your Guide, you do what you believe is right. If that Guide tries to start forcing you to do what they think is right, that is not a higher Guide. Accept your decisions over ours. We have no need to make you do what we think is right. That is not guidance anymore. That is domination. That is interference.

Guidance, whether it comes from a Spirit or from another person, is not guidance at the point you do not want to do it. If your Guide threatens you that some terrible thing will happen, that is not a higher Guide. It is very popular amongst religions and Guides that are on misguided paths to say, unless you do this, something bad will happen. You will burn in hell or perhaps, you will forever be banded from the truth and things like that. That is how you know right away it is not a higher Guide because we are filled with alternatives.

A long time ago, when Mataare started channeling, we told him the biggest law in channeling is there are more 'do nots' than 'dos'. If you get the 'do nots' right, you do not have to worry about the 'dos'.

There are such things as lower entities and sometimes people are in the influence of lower entities. This happens one of two ways. One, they invite and accept lower entities or two, have been severely broken down to the point where they exist for a long time in a state of being desperate. When one is desperate and powerless, that is where you do not want to be. Those people are vulnerable. Therefore, do not get desperate. Stay away from despair.

Channeling is going to be and is becoming a more and more popular phenomena. When we use the word channeling, it has a certain aura of mystery to some people, which there will not be so much in the future. It will become very commonplace. Whether you realize it or not, you are always channeling something because everything that comes into your mind, everything that comes through you, you do not own it. Your minds are not really yours because there only really is one mind.

There really is no such thing as your mind, even though we use the term repeatedly your mind, your mind, your mind. It really is not yours. I am sorry, but it is not yours. You do not own it. It is more like this. One intelligence courses through all existence like a vast sea, and entities such as you access aspects of that intelligence. People can access it in any number of ways because sometimes they are taught things that allow people to access some of the same regions of thought, some of the same regions of energies, some of the same regions of ideas.

What you are calling you, and therefore your mind, is that you are plucking different areas of the sea of intelligence and gluing them together. This is what you identify with as you, your thoughts and who you are, but none of it is you. You have just borrowed from aspects of a universal awareness, and that is what you call ego, which is neither good nor bad. Ego is completely innocent. Ego is just an identity you have created. Then you give vent to that identity. You give vent to that kind of consciousness. You piece together your identification with who you are by borrowing from the different places in the cosmic awareness, and then you think it is you, and it is you in a certain way because nobody else has constructed it exactly the way you have. Nevertheless, it really is not what you are. What you really are is everything, not just the things you have plucked. You are everything.

Growth is the process of two things, increasingly becoming aware that you are everything and choosing that with which you wish to identify and that with which you do not wish to identify. That is what growth is because even though you are everything, not everything is useful for you. Not everything is helpful for you. Some forms of awareness and consciousness are simply useless for you and some are very relevant for you. One becomes identified with the wisest, most empowered, gentlest and loving forms of awareness they can, releasing other forms of awareness and therefore creates a oneness with all of higher Spirit. That is still manifested uniquely from person to person.

We do not meet in a dimension apart from yours. Our dimension interpenetrates your dimension. That which is our dimension requires on your part both willingness and skill at being able to become aware of that dimension of which we speak. This dimension has many qualities, joy, peace, empowerment, fulfillment, vision, insight. All of these things and more are available to you now.

Know that the oneness with that which one discovers in meditation should not be left just for times when one sits in the posture and mode of meditation. That oneness is able to be experienced in every moment, for it exists in every moment when one will not allow oneself to become distracted or attracted to other things not as complete.

A soul may become distracted many, many ways in existence. Existence is very large, has no limit to its dimension. You are in an existence that has no limit while your bodies occupy only a certain amount of space and live in the experience of a linear time. This helps your awareness focus on matters where one might need to focus. However, your true self is not limited to linear time, nor is it limited to space as your body is, and therefore, your awareness can journey into any aspect of creation without limit. Without the ability to focus one's awareness or one's mind, this that is an unlimited opportunity can become an eternity of distraction.

Therefore, it is important that one knows where to allow one's consciousness to journey. It is important then that your consciousness dwell more and more on what is loving, empowering, wise, gentle and kind, for these perspectives are that which allows your awareness to enter into the highest of available places.

The time will come when you will see many other directions that seem worthy and appropriate. There are times when you will think it is no longer time to be kind. There are times when you will think that the most certain path is not always the wisest one. There will be times when you will mistake love with that which is not empowering. These things are amongst the many distractions and all the ways these things manifest themselves. Therein lie your lessons, for where so ever you come to think your most direct path is other than that, it is there where you may find all your lessons and karmas.

Because you will have many karmas and lessons, it is appropriate that you spend some time in the dimension or state of awareness where you are able to live in a mode of experience that moves faster than this plane, where your lessons can be grasped more quickly and easily. That which takes a great deal of time to unfold in the awareness of linear time does not take as much time to unfold in another state.

For example, the realm of your thoughts moves more quickly. Even as we speak, a flurry of ideas is passing through your mind, so many that you are hardly even able to keep track of all the ideas that have just passed through your awareness in the last five minutes. All of the things that have gone through your mind in the last five minutes are creating realities that you will someday experience. Who knows when that might be. Maybe in the next ten minutes, maybe in the next hour, maybe next week, maybe the one thought you now have you will spend one year living out what you have thought in this one moment.

In these levels of awareness time moves very quickly, and it is in these levels one creates their future and their reality. If you have the perception to be aware of these subtle states of movement, then you can guide your destiny in accordance with only your most desired and hopefully highest intents. If you are unable to be aware of that which goes through your own consciousness, unaware of the movement and trends of your awareness, then you have no power over your own destiny.

As entities become more aware, they cannot do so without also becoming aware of the trends of their thought and consciousness. This is indeed why meditation is important so you can become aware of the motion of your thoughts and redirect them more successfully. Where you are not able to do this, a Guide or Guides shall eventually appear and help guide you in the ways that leave you more in control of your destiny and less a victim of fate.

The Guide or Guides that appear to you can come in any number of ways. They can come in the form of a stranger who, with a passing sentence, changes the direction of your entire life for that time. It can come in the form of a friend or a loved one. It can come in the form of a teacher or an enemy. It can come in the form of an animal. It can come to you in the invisible realms of dream, super consciousness and meditation states or it can come to you through mediums, psychics or each other. There is no limit to the ways you can be accessed by your higher guidance. It only requires your attention, you paying attention for that guidance, and you will see it elevates itself.

Many on this side journey in the dimensions of soul, and their only intention and reason for existence is to love and to serve. By opening to such influence you will receive it, and by attending to that assistance, so long as it is wise, kind and empowering, you shall receive even more and more and more. Soon you will find yourself in the position where you are yourself a peer to that which had come to you and offer assistance and guidance to others.

I have come here to say these things and to say watch for me in your states of dream, if you are consistent with two things. One, that you are intending when you sleep to communicate with me and the others and two, that you are willing to keep a record, a journal of either your thoughts or significant dreams. In this way, you will open the door for the guidance to come.

Merlin

We work with those entities that are in some way like us where there is a certain relationship. There are Guides called universal teachers, which means we tend to a very broad expanse of feelings, thoughts and ideas and work with many people.

In a sense, you choose your Guide. Whether you are in the knowledge of choosing or not, something in you identifies with the Guide. When you identify with that Guide, in a sense, you choose that Guide. There are times when Guides will ask you if they may be a Guide for you. Through that way, you have identified with the Guide and the Guide has identified with you.

Every person likely has amongst their Guides at least one angelic entity, an angel. You may wonder why so many people have angels as Guides. It is because there are so many angels. There are many, many more angels than there are human beings, countless times the amount of human beings. I am not saying that as an exaggeration.

We do not go around saying, well, that one is good enough. Let us take her. That one is not good enough. We do not do it that way. In fact, our relationship to everyone is magnetic. It does not exist in the sense that somebody qualifies to be guided by a certain Guide because of his or her merits. It really is not like that. It is more magnetic as a magnet attracts steel. Guides are attracted to people and people are attracted to Guides. A similarity in energetic may not translate into specific reasons. Sometimes it does have a specific reason and sometimes it does not.

If a Guide is available, all it takes to have the Guide you want is one prerequisite, love. Sometimes someone may want a Guide who is just not available to be a Guide. That is different. However, if you can be open enough to feel loving connection, the love is all it takes. We Guides on this side are unconditionally open to you. We do not need a reason to love you, a reason to pick you or a reason to be near you. Love is not reasonable. Love is unreasonable and it ought to be unconditional.

We believe in unreasonable and unconditional love. If you say Guide, I would like you, we will say fine. We will have you. There is no reason you ought not to have us as a Guide. If we are available as a Guide, we love to work with you.

There are rare occasions when available Guides are not available to you. In that rare instance, the reason is that Guide represents a force that if it were present in your life, it would interfere rather than help. In that instance a Guide will not be a Guide if the presence of that force would cause that to happen.

The only thing that would cause somebody not to have Guides is an extreme rejection of any kind of help whatsoever. It might be a person who wants no association with other people, one who pushes all manner of kindness and assistance away. It would be a person so willful and so hateful of any kind of participation in their life by anybody that they push away help from other people and Spirit.

Sanjuro

If you wish to develop and utilize your trance state, it is very important for you to be able to receive spiritual guidance that wishes to express itself. You must not limit it to specific entities, because what if something other than that entity wishes to express itself. If you look for a specific format, then you will force your guidance to conform to your expectation. If your perception of highest guidance is a particular famous teacher in history, you will then limit it to what that teacher was when he or she was here. Why do that? If you think God or higher guidance should be some specific format, you will make the guidance to conform. Your ability to channel depends upon your willingness to allow the consciousness that forms to express itself as it wishes to provided what comes through conforms to something helpful, wise and loving. That statement is important to affirm.

In order that you can have the right kind of entities, it is important that you do it only at certain times. You must not leave your door constantly open to channel spontaneously any more than you would leave the door open to your house. You open the door to let in a guest. You close the door behind him. You open the door to let them out and you close the door behind them.

When is a guest not a guest? It is when they are always knocking at your door. That becomes an intruder. You are the sovereign owner of this existence. Would you let a guest come into your house every time it decides? Excuse me. I think it is important to hear from me now. If a guest decided that it was important to come any time, is that a guest? Is that someone who acknowledges your own privacy, your own sovereign right to your own separate existence?

Even with the highest guidance, you decide when it is appropriate and when it is not appropriate to have that guest come. What is truly higher Guide will respect your desire to let them come when you wish and will not take offense to it. You say this is when I am available. This is when I am not available. Excuse me, there is knocking at my door. I feel the presence of my Spirit Guide wanting to channel. Do not think you must open the door every time. You say, is this appropriate? Yes, I will let it in. No. Not now, but another time is fine. You must teach your Spirit Guide when it is you prefer to have it come in and when it is you prefer it not to come in.

Understand that our realm is different from your realm. You must get to know us when you channel just as we must get to know you. Do not think you must always defer to us.

When you become open to channel, you must get used to utilizing the trance state, growing comfortable with the trance state. The trance state is different from your normal state. In order to utilize trance well, it is important that you first let certain kinds of guidance come to you.

Merlin

I am not going to spend a lot of time with you talking. I am going to spend a little time with you doing. Let us just shift the modality of our consciousness a little bit by taking a couple of deep breaths. Sit yourselves in a way that is comfortable for you and let me direct your consciousness along certain lines for a moment, for this is how to get into a trance state quickly.

First, think of the word calm. Think calm. Relax your shoulder muscles. Release tension in your stomach. Release tension in your anal sphincters. Let your eyes gently close, but not too tightly. Relax your jaw muscles. Breathe a little more loudly than you usually do, but just loud enough for you to hear. Once you are able to hear it, let it quiet down, but keep listening to it. Stay calm enough that you can still hear your breath. Now with all the rest of your muscles, relinquish muscular control as much as you feel comfortable with, only keeping those muscles active that you feel you must in order to hold your position, but every other muscle that you are aware of, simply relax it and hear your breath. Think of the words gentle, calm.

You have now entered into a light trance state. No particular entity is channeling yet, but this is the light trance state. Can you feel it? As you answer my questions, I would like you to stay lightly in trance.

Open your eyes and stay in trance. Keep gentle. Staying calm and gentle move one of your hands up and down and then the other. Move the parts of your body that you can move and stay gently entranced.

Now I would like you to become aware of whatever higher consciousness means to you, whether it means your own wisdom and understanding, whether it means a Guide or God, whether it means something you do not have any idea of, but are willing to let come through. Become aware. Invite higher consciousness to be present.

While you listen to me, I want you to give permission to higher consciousness in your being. Give permission for higher consciousness to speak even though you do not know what it shall say. I want you to tell the higher consciousness that it has your permission to speak. Staying in trance, I would like the higher consciousness to communicate to you one statement about love. Become aware of one statement about love. Staying in trance, I would like to ask your higher consciousness something. What does it state about love, staying in trance?

Stay in trance. Think calm, gentle. I would like now for the higher consciousness to say to you something about the purpose of your life or the purpose of life, whatever comes to you. Just give voice to it in the entranced state. Higher consciousness, what do you have to say of the purpose of life?

Now I would like you to stay entranced, to think calm and gentle. I would like you to let your higher consciousnesses speak to you. You are going to let your higher consciousness respond in whatever way it does to my questions.

Do you have a name?

Are you often with this one?

What can this one do to be more aware of your presence?

What does he or she need to believe?

Will it be useful for this person to be in touch with you?

In what way will it be useful?

What way do you wish to develop this person?

Which times are best to receive clear communications that this person might know, if there are any?

Do you frequently come to this one?

What is the way this person might best utilize your presence?

Thank you, Spirit.

I invite you, if you have not already, to release the consciousness that comes to your door and simply resume your most comfortable normal self. Let your consciousness let go. If you will, be with me for a moment here and now. I would like you to thank whatsoever presence communicated those things into your consciousness. I would like you to thank it.

I wish to say some things. To bring a Spirit through for yourself is just like that, to ask it some questions that you need answers to and let it speak or to put yourself in the presence of other people who have questions so that it might be drawn through.

What you did here is you trusted enough to let me address a consciousness other than what you normally are. What you let through is indeed the consciousness that spoke as you allowed it to speak. Perhaps in part or in whole, it got through.

If you want it to get through more, you must give it an opportunity to get through more. I have a very strong recommendation. If you have a desire to see what more this consciousness has to say to you, then get together with another who has things to ask of this spiritual presence that do not relate to you. Let them put their questions to the presence and you watch how the presence chooses to respond. Let this presence be drawn through more and more. First, ask the presence that comes to you universal or broad questions because the higher spirit is willing to address things of a broader perspective, things that have to do with more than just yourself. See how the Spirit responds to that.

We know the questions you ask of a Spirit might have two different answers. You have your opinion and the Spirit may have its opinion. They may be overlapping, but they may be very different. You will be surprised to see what awareness speaks through you in a state of trance.

One of the things you might want to do is see if the Spirit can be identified. If it does not want to be identified, then do not make it. If it cannot, then it cannot. Just let it be. Let the Spirit reveal itself as it comes through. Only open the door at special times, designated times.

I have a list of rules that I want to give you about channeling and about channeling Spirit presence. There are many rules.

When you channel for yourself, make certain that you are not disturbed and you take it seriously. There are fewer rules when channeling for self. You can let it flow. It can be very improvisational. However, when you channel for others, when you channel in the presence of others, do at least these things and you will stay out of trouble.

Number one is to know ahead of time that you plan to do it at some later time.

Number two, you must prepare. Meditate and/or do some things that let you know you are in a preparation. You may want to bathe. You may want to change your clothes. You may want to refresh yourself. You may want to meditate. You may want to pray. You may want to make affirmation. Prepare yourself.

Number three, make an affirmation at the time you are about to do it stating some positive intent.

Number four is to ask for protection.

Number five, do not do it too often. Do not channel all of the time or frequently. You must have your own life. Do not channel spontaneously. What do I mean? Someone says, oh, what does your Spirit Guide say about this matter? Well, let me see. Do not do that. Use your own wits most of the time. Get in touch with yourself if you want to get in touch with yourself. Get in touch with your own higher being. Do not get in the habit of getting in touch with your Guide for every single little thing. Use your own wits. If you have questions that you want to put to your Guides or others have questions they want to put to your Guides, refer them to the times when you are available for that. Do not make yourself available to that every time you are asked and every time you think you want to do that. Have times that you do that, and I will tell you why.

You must not cajole or force a Spirit presence to come or you will invite imitators. You will invite another consciousness. If you want and want and want and need and need and need, you will eventually attract all kinds of consciousness other than the one you want. You must learn to stand on your own integrity and own sovereign beingness as much as you can, referring your questions or saving them, writing them down for those times when you do that. Otherwise, you will feel pulled at all the time. You will feel harassed. I do not mean harassed by the Spirit. I mean harassed by you. You will feel as though you have always to refer, as though you are not good enough. You do not want to foster, to cultivate that because that undermines the sovereign integrity you are and makes you vulnerable to other Spirit forces.

Other Spirit forces do not go around looking for people to take over. However, they do find themselves around those who feel themselves harassed constantly. For those who cannot make decisions for themselves, they are all to ready to make decisions for you and for those who spend a lot of time feeing desperate. So do not despair. How do you despair? Inaction, long periods of inactions on whatever you receive impressions to act upon leads to desperation. Inactivity on what you are inspired toward leads to you being desperate, and at that point, you grasp at straws. Being in touch with Spirits is sometimes like grasping at straws, but that is all right, provided you demonstrate or cultivate your own wits and then you also have other times when you cultivate your channeled energy, your channeled wits, channeled consciousness.

You do not have to believe this, but you are not in human bodies for the purpose of constantly being in touch with cosmic consciousness. You are in human bodies because you are supposed to do something that human bodies are a gift for doing. Human awareness is a gift. If you try to be in your human body and constantly leave the awareness of it, you will end up desperate, without power, not knowing why you are alive and very confused, and you will seek exit from this plane. A happy medium is if you find and work on your reason for being in the body and use your higher consciousness to guide you. That is a happy medium.

You have experienced a little bit of channeling, the beginnings of channeling. How you utilize it, which is what this is about, is if you have questions, thoughts and ideas that you need to get in touch with the higher consciousness and/or your Spirit Guides, make a time that you plan to do that. Get into a trance state by calming yourself and keep your questions handy. Answer your questions in writing or channel them aloud and record them.

You can do this when you are alone, provided you have your questions there or give your questions to a friend you trust to ask them for you. Say, here are my questions. Once I get into trance state, I would like you to ask me these things. I would like you to say these questions. Let yourself be asked these questions. Tell them that if they do not get an answer, to move on to another one or let them ask questions they are inspired to ask while you are in trance.

You may be surprised at what comes through you when you are in the trance state with an anchor there pulling the spiritual awareness through. At first always have someone there who is loving and kindly disposed toward you and kindly disposed toward your process. You must first do it in the presence of those who are kindly disposed to you as individuals and kindly disposed to your channeling and development process so that they can draw through you without your own doubts having to interfere.

After you are comfortable with the channeling process, that is when to allow others to begin to filter into it. Not other Spirits, I mean other human beings who may be a little more skeptical or may not be as kindly disposed to the process.

It is important to open the door in a safe environment many times before the Spirit is strongly anchored. Otherwise, you will chase the Spirit away. You will start feeling things like oh god, this is no good and who needs it. You will begin to cut the Spirit off. You need to let yourself welcome the Spirit in more and more often.

Each of you shall encounter many other people, now that you have opened your door, also beginning to channel and utilize the trance state. You will come into the presence of friends, other teachers and other persons offering more insights from many other directions. Take advantage. Your Guides will lead you to these other opportunities and not accidentally. Take advantage of this to cultivate your communication with the spiritual process.

Develop a friendship with your Guides. It is very important. Do not have a standoffish relationship between you and Spirit. Say, I want to talk to you about something that is bothering me. This is what is bothering me. What is your response to that? Develop a friendship with your Guides. Sometimes the channel, the medium tends to have a very parental relationship with their Guides. It is a very patriarchal relationship with the Guides and with Spirit and with God. Have and cultivate a loving friendship with your Guides. That is what is going to develop trust. You have to get to know them and they have to get to know you. How do you do that? Ask questions and talk to them about that. Do not require of your Spiritual Guides that they be patriarchal with you. Let them be friendly, loving, wise and kind.

As far as the information coming through and whether it is genuine, all that I can tell you is it is perfectly all right for you to question your Guides. The way for you to understand is to question. You will doubt the process, no question about it, and well you should doubt. Why? If you are so absolutely certain about everything the Guide says, then how do you know it is not just you? If you are not so certain about what they are saying at first, until you develop a strong relationship with them, then it is important to put what you receive to your test. I think that is very much a part of the channeling process. Question them. We are open to that.

However, how do you expect a Spirit to prove to you that it exists when you cannot prove to the Spirit that you exist? In other words, you will always come up without an answer after asking your Spirit to demonstrate its existence because it cannot. Putting that aside, all you can do is reference it as guidance, for awareness that is intelligent and loving. There is not a way a Spirit can prove its existence to you. Perhaps somewhere along the way you will get this piece of information and that piece of information, this little proof and that little proof, and before you know it, at some point in time, you will know that it is that presence. However, you can never ask any Spirit or any person for that matter to prove that it really is there. I mean, you can ask them, but they cannot prove it to you.

How do you know it is not another aspect of your unconscious? Well, you do not really. You do not, but I will say to you this. Until somebody defined for you your unconscious, you did not even have an idea there was such a concept as the unconscious until it was explained to you. That means that explanation was something invented by somebody who claimed to have an understanding of it and was clear enough to communicate his or her understanding to you about what unconscious was. You looked at that understanding and said, hum, that makes sense to me. I believe in it. In other words, you did not know that there was an unconscious. You just knew that that sounded pretty good. You did not know what it was. That is what has to be put aside to channel. The important thing is to let the wisdom and guidance come through, no matter what form it takes. That is how you get to greater awareness. Channeling is a kind of phenomena that you only understand by letting it happen, and then you understand it.

When people channel spontaneously, it is usually because they suppressed some part of an awareness that they have been getting in touch with and are in denial of so much that it has to protrude through now and then. One should not let oneself get in such a condition where they are suppressing awareness that is in fact for them of vital importance. When someone gets in that position, it must spontaneously break through to get that person's attention. Once they stop ignoring it, it stops spontaneously breaking through.

You will have an easy time channeling so long as you understand one basic thing. There is not a way to prove it yet, not to your liking. So it is simply a matter of you being willing to trust the process. If you choose to do that, that is it. If you are waiting for Spirit to make something happen for you, well, we do not make anything happen through anybody. We let ourselves do what the medium shall allow.

Let me say one final thing. Your Spirit Guides do not want to live your lives for you. Do not ask us to do that. You can ask us for our help and we will help where we can with advice and doing what we can. However, do not ask us to do everything you would like us to do just because you want it done. You can, but understand, sometimes our answer will be no, and we have a right to say that. That is very important. We must respect you, and we will listen to what you ask of us when it comes to keeping ourselves coming through when you like. We will accommodate that. You can say no to us, but also know that we can say no to you. Some things we refuse. Do not think that if we refuse something, we are angry with you. Know that we can have differing opinions, be totally out of agreement and still love you. Know that we can from time to time disagree vehemently without becoming hostile, angry and defamatory.

With a Spirit always be specific about the thing with which you have some disagreement or problem, very, very specific. A Spirit Guide will always wait until you are ready to discuss it, will always say, by the way, are you ready yet? When would you like to discuss the matter about which we have conflict? A Spirit Guide will try to pin you down about it. It is fine if you do not want to talk about it now, but when would you like to talk about it? Then a Spirit will always hear what you have to say and respect what you have to say as important.

A Spirit Guide will always tell you what it sees as the problem and what they think you can do about it. You have the option to do nothing about it if you want, but Spirit will always tell you what its opinion is, how they think is a good way of going about it, what they think you will get and how they think that will improve the relationship. Then you can filter all of that. You can say hogwash, and the Spirit will say fine. Now we have discussed that. That is a good fight. Usually there is some point of being able to negotiate.

A fight should always cease at the point it becomes argumentative. We will come back to it at another time. It is very important to fight and to learn how to fight very well.

When channeling, even the Guides who come through and say something like you are too fat or whatever it is, that is also some kind of Guide. However, do you want that kind of Guide as a Guide? Either that Guide must become schooled as to a few things or you need to shift into a higher guidance. Indeed the criteria and the test must be wisdom, kindness and love. Love must be expansive. Love must be empowering. Loving in terms of sweetness and kindness is covered in kind, but what I mean by love is that which empowers, because to me that is what true love is, not that which tears down, but that which expands, that which causes to grow. Therefore, it must have wisdom, something intelligent, something empowering and kind. That is certainly the test. Your Guides, ask them to communicate through that, then you get the highest frequency of Guide, in my opinion.

Devorah, Elsa, Olga, Helga & Morgana

You can see your own future. Whatever your future is, it is something you are now creating. You did not come to this day by accident. You created this day. Somewhere along the line, in your past, you foresaw this. Maybe you foresaw this in this morning or maybe you foresaw this years and years ago, but something that you foresaw led to this moment, some things you are well aware of led you to this moment.

If you want to see the future, it is very important for you to become conscious of what is going on in your awareness because that is all the seeing the future requires. To see your future means you stop for a moment and watch what is going on in your awareness because whatever is going on in you awareness is going to be what is going on in your future, which is why you are seeing it.

Once you see it, you have a choice. You can await its happening or if you like what you see, you can go out and create it happening even more quickly. You can even do something else. You can do nothing about it, taking no responsibility in creating it and you may miss the opportunity that you foresaw or you may deliberately stop it.

There are times when people have little visions of very terrible, terrible things. People have dreams and they foresee plane crashes and car accidents and things of this kind. People do not see those things because they are inevitable. People who see these things see it because it is a warning and they see it so they can do something about it, which usually means to tell somebody or to do something about it to avert some horrible thing.

For example, some people see the future of what is going on in the Middle East or what is going on in Russia, what is going on in the

United States or what is going on in China. Many people in this country focus on the Middle East. When you see a bunch of people looking into a situation like that and seeing nothing but war, you are seeing that which creates war. You are seeing a bunch of minds that see war as an inevitable event. It is very important, if that is your view, to be oh so much more clever than that, be so much more creative than that and close your eyes and visualize some other way of resolving the situation than through conflict. Visualize it. Give some time to that. Pull it into the atmosphere. Put it into the ethers with your minds.

You might be surprised to find, once your mind dwells upon that, you are not the only one in that place. Once your mind dwells upon that and visualizes that, then you will start to hear other voices. I do not mean necessarily only in your head, which you might hear also, but then you will start noticing the voices all around you in your world that do have other creative means of resolving situations than through that sort of conflict. It will be things you read in articles, people you bump into and things you hear on the news. You will say that is funny. Where were these people before? You have not seen it before. Once you see it, that targets you to be led to the place where that is a reality. Then those forces can join to create that reality, perhaps even very actively. What I am saying is that human beings as individuals must be responsible for their futures as individuals and be responsible for their futures as a collective as well.

Seeing your future is a very important thing. Nothing that you can see in the future or that we have seen in the future is unalterable. Some things you will not alter, but if you wanted, you could alter anything, for the better or for the worse, because it really is in your power. It really truly is within your power.

The more empowered a person you are, the more power you have to create what you see. Sometimes you can see and see and see and see, but if you have no power, it is hard to create it. However, if you see it and see it and see it, and then come to believe it long enough, you will have more power to create it. Sometimes the best thing to do to create your own reality is become empowered persons and then see the future you want to see. It gets very interesting, very, very interesting.

There are people who are extraordinarily psychics. Frequently they are people who do not think they have any psychic ability at all. It is not always the case, but it is frequently the case. The reason they do not think they have any psychic ability at all is because they think they are just very logical. They think that what they know, they know because it makes sense. Of course, it only makes sense to them, but it does not make any sense to anyone else. Their brand of logic may seem very logical to them, but nobody else has that kind of logic. That is because they see things psychically and then they come up with a rational later. Their rational does not always make sense to anybody except them because they never saw it rationally in the first place. They saw it psychically and their rational was just the best they could come up with to define something they have felt or seen on another level.

Those who are very psychic tend to be the most skeptical of things that are psychic because for them, they like to understand what they see and if they cannot find the understanding, they are going to be very skeptical. Even though they are very familiar with psychic phenomena, they are not conscious that they are familiar with it. When exposed to psychic phenomena, they may be very open, but skeptical because they know wherefore they speak, even though they really do not know. They are not novices in that arena and therefore they tend to be a little more judgmental, even though they do not know why they are being judgmental.

Often the people who are the most psychic are some of the most skeptical and in some ways healthfully so. We always encourage people to question because questioning is a very important part of coming to a point where you understand. It shows that you are exploring the area of knowledge that exists. When you have a question, it means you have begun to get an answer that you have not gotten completely. That means you have touched an area of new knowledge. When you have a question, you have a question because you do not really understand all that you are getting, but just a part of it so questions form. If you have no questions about anything whatsoever, you are probably not interested in finding out, although everybody has questions about all kinds of things or we would not be here.

What I started to say is this. If you want to be psychic, it is very important to take responsibility for your life, to take responsibility for yourself completely, to put yourself in as much an empowered situation as you can. You cannot be very actively or helpfully psychic if you are in a situation where you are dependent upon a number of circumstances to do for you because you are desperate in that kind of a situation, therefore, guarded and protected. You will have to guard your emotions and guard your psyche. Being in disempowered situations closes down your psychic sensitivity because if your psychic sensitivity is open when disempowered, you will be in pain, constant pain.

If you are in a disempowering situation that is painful, you will have to close off your psychic sensitivities in order to survive the painful situation and you will never be psychic in that instance. The first thing you have to do is get out of situations that disempowered you. Very psychic people often close down when they are in disempowering situations, even after they have been psychic because they get very protective.

Sometimes people try their best to close down in disempowering situations and just cannot do it. They are just a mess because they would love to be able to guard themselves psychologically and emotionally, but just feel like a wreck all the time because they cannot shut down. People in such situations have a difficult time if they want to be psychic. They first have to get out of disempowered situations.

If you want to see your future, there is an easy technique where you can go to your future, alter it or do anything you want with it. Get in the habit of doing at least one thing every day that you consciously realize you are doing to empower yourself. It does not matter what you do that empowers you when you are trying to be psychic, if you do not realize that it empowers you. You might find you have accidentally done things that have empowered you. That is fine. However, when you consciously choose to do something each day that is empowering for you, that causes you to recognize that you are a power in this universe. You are in charge of your destiny. By getting in the habit of being in charge of your destiny, that is what makes you feel safe enough to open psychically. If you do not feel like you are in charge of your destiny and you might even be fearful of what your destiny has in store, then you will be afraid to open because you will be afraid you will see something that you do not want to see.

One of the steps is you have to know it is important to take charge of your life daily in at least one way. If that is a practice for at least three of four days, then in meditation or just around sleep ask, I want to see something that is from my future. Just watch. Close you eyes, get in a very relaxed position and just watch as if you are watching a movie with your eyes closed. Close your eyes and watch your field of vision. Maybe you will not see anything in the first few seconds. Maybe after a minute you will start seeing things, but you do not know what it is you are seeing. You will know when you start seeing something, but perhaps you will not know what it means. However, it is impossible to ask that question after you have consciously taken a little bit of charge of your life for a few days or more, not to see something from your future. You will start seeing things about what is coming up in your future if you ask.

When you see something, if you do not know what it means, then ask what it means. I suggest that you ask what it means later. If you watch your field for about fifteen minutes, not only will you see one thing, but also you will start seeing thing after thing. Your imagination will become very alive with visions in your field of vision. Then, if you cannot figure out what it means when you are watching it, after you are done, either write down what you see or think through what you have seen asking yourself what could that possibly mean? Watch how you will be able to interpret what you saw. You will see your future. If there is anything you like, you can make it happen faster and if there is anything you do not like, you can simply make it happen differently.

Sometimes you will see things you do not expect to see. That is always the most fun. I know because I was a seer. It is most wonderful when you are watching the visions and you do not know what they mean because those are always the most exciting ones to watch how they come about for you. That is why it helps to write them down so that when they come to pass you can say, oh, I saw that. I have news for you. Since you are creating your future all of the time anyway and it is going on constantly, even though you are not aware of it, why not see it, since you are creating it? Why not look in and see what you are creating these days?

One other thing I have to say about seeing and creating the future is that some of you have heard many things about ascension. The way that most people think of ascension is the body turns to light and goes up into heaven. I do not know where they got that idea. That is not ascension because heaven is not up. If heaven were a planet, then there would be a purpose for rising up in the physical body. Since heaven is not a planet, why do you have to go up anywhere?

Ascension can mean that a body becomes a body of light, but your bodies are already bodies of light and they just might not be shining as brightly one to the next. Ascension is a process by which the body becomes, in some instances, so charged with energy that sometimes it does seem to glow. Sometimes it does seem to have a special energy around it. That does not mean that someone with a lot of energy around them is an ascendant being, but every ascendant being also has a certain charge around them.

There are many purposes of ascension, but what ascension means truly is that the awareness, the consciousness rises to be in the highest place it can find. The highest place a consciousness can be, a human consciousness, is to see everything in such a way where there is wisdom, kindness and love. The highest place is where the moment the universe intends something, a person wants to do it and can do it instantly.

The process by which a soul gets to that point leads to people manifesting their intentions more and more quickly. As a being becomes more wise, kind and loving, they are able to manifest their intent more and more quickly until they become totally that, and then it is instantaneous. The only thing that keeps your intention from manifesting instantaneously is the elements of consciousness that are struggling and in futility, which causes reality to slow down for you. The more it becomes wise, kind and loving, the less futility, ultimately no futility and you consciously manifest intent in a second. That is ascension.

Ascension is something attained and it manifests differently for different people, but a part of ascension is being able to get in touch with what is going on in awareness so that you can see what is creating the struggles. Then you can let go of that, so you can align the consciousness with the things that remove the struggle and so that you can dwell in the highest frequency and therefore be one who manifests instantly.

If one who is ascendant does not manifest instantly, then things come to them that they do not have to create. It is a very funny thing about ascendant beings and it is almost a paradox. Until you find your own most ascendant nature, in a sense you have to create your own reality for things to come, but once you are in your ascendant nature, strangely enough, you have no desire to create anything at all. Instead, you just happen to be in the flow of everything that is right for you so there is no need to create anything at all. Whatever you happen to intend is so much in the flow that you are just very near where it is about to happen anyway.

I just want to say that part because sometimes people try to get into their ascendant nature so that they can make the table rise. Some people who gain in their ability as they go on in their ascendant nature will find they can do things like that. In fact, sometimes people who gain an ability to manifest realities stop at a point where they just want to prove things to people and remain there for a long time. Some people use it in the wrong ways. Some people use it in the right ways. However, anyone who gets all the way there stops at some point having to do anything because there is an understanding that comes at that point. The understanding is that everything already is worked out perfectly so why expend energy doing things you do not need to do. There is already such a perfect flow and one can align with that perfect flow.

If somebody who was not ascendant wanted to align with the perfect flow and not do anything, they would not get very far. They would find they would have to do something fast. Part of the ascendant nature means being completely responsible for the creating of your reality not abdication of responsibility, but the claiming of responsibility because that is what makes an empowered being.

Merlin

Channeling, mediumship is something very dear to our hearts. We have something to do in this world because of you. Because those such as you are willing to open yourselves to another dimension of consciousness, Spirit can infuse that which we wish to bring into this world, light, in anyone of so many of its manifestations in this world.

There are many aspects of information relevant to the subject of focusing the force of Spirit, the energies ambient around and within, in a particular manner such that they might be able to express themselves. More important even than that which can be done that is functional, which is helpful to us and to you, it is important that every soul come to know the full capacity of who and what they are as entities. As human beings, you have a very, very vast capacity. You have capacity to unlimited resources of consciousness, of awareness, unlimited. As you know yourselves as human beings, a very beautiful ascendant experience is available to you as human beings.

First, it is important to know you are not really human beings, none of you. You just are functioning as human beings for the time being. You are spirits. You are consciousness. You are energy. You are awareness that has in a sense, inhabited some physical form. Indeed, you have manifested your physical form on some level. Some of you, I venture to say all of you, are so good at manifesting the physical bodies in which you are living that you do not even really think about it and you do not even know how you did it anymore. Nevertheless, every element of your consciousness, every cell of your body, every thought, every idea, every particle or awareness, every particle of existence is a conscious form of existence to one degree or another.

As entities, you have become aware of everything that you have identified with as yourself and the world. When you identify with something long enough, you begin to think that that thing you have identified with, that thing you have related to is you. At first it starts out like a relationship and then anything you have identified with long enough, you come to believe is you or a part of you. You come to experience it as a part of you.

In the sufficiently aware consciousness, one who is a human being can come to know they are a part of everything. There is a certain value in that. To know yourself as a part of everything, the only way you can attain such knowledge, and by knowledge, I mean an experience, is if you do so in the context of love. That is the only way. As you get to know yourself as a part of everything more and more, you in fact embrace more love in your awareness. Increasingly you are asked and shown how to let go of all other perceptions, all other ways of looking at things, all other ways of experiencing life. Your awareness can only grasp the truth of your true expanded nature in the context of love.

Love is a power. Love is a radiance. Love is the life force. It is far beyond your ideas about it. Sometimes love is limited by ideas. Sometimes people limit their experience of love by their own ideas, but love is not your ideas. It is not your beliefs. Love is not an emotion. The love that I speak of is a power akin to what you might call the life force, and it is intense. There is no limit to its ability, to its form, to its expression, to its manifestation.

When you open your being to consciousness beyond yourself, it is important that you do it in the context of that which is the highest at work in the universe. That is so you come to know your own expanded nature, and you shall come to know your own expanded nature, in ways that empower you and produce the experience of awakened self and love.

When we speak of the subject of channeling, focusing the force, when we speak of mediumship, we speak of opening yourself to forces of greater love than you have identified yourself with currently. We speak of opening yourself to forces of light that are connected with you, that in fact at some level are a part of you, but that reach beyond that which you have identified with as you. Ultimately, you might know yourself and you might know love beyond yourself on an experiential level.

Some of you have had the experience of channeling already and you know it. Others have had the experience of channeling and have not known it. Some of you have had the experience of channeling Spirit and not being certain as to whether it was or was not in fact Spirit. Certainly, there must have been a time when each one of you has experienced very inspired moments, very high energy, where your state of consciousness quickened, enlivened and was made more vital, and you felt an energy move through you. Perhaps it was learning music, performing it or listening to it. Perhaps it was in the creative process, writing or speaking. Perhaps it was in creating works of art. Perhaps it was as you were performing or acting. Perhaps it is any or all of these kinds of experiences or others where for one moment, for one reason or another, you found yourself letting go of the self as you previously defined yourself and embraced and experienced out of context with that identity. Is that channeling? We will talk about that. Certainly, everyone has had such an experience as that.

It is important to understand a few things about the nature of consciousness. We need to talk a little about what it is that Spirit is and what it is that consciousness is, because that is what we are speaking of here, consciousness, yours and others.

Consciousness is a collection of particles of awareness. For human beings, particles of awareness occur as thought, and thought is energy. Your physical bodies are designed to experience the energy called thought as a tangible and symbolic experience. In other words, any time you experience energy or awareness, your physical brain and your physical body translates that into some symbolic meaning.

If, for example, you receive a little twitch of energy and you itch because of it, at that very moment you have made at least a hundred references to beliefs, ideas and thoughts inculcated in your matrix of responses to energy. Therefore, for you that energy is no longer energy. All energy means something, has a symbolic representation, of which you are either conscious of unconscious.

When you have that much response going on inside of your being in response to sensitivity to energy, you are continually forming pictures, beliefs and ideas about reality and about who you are and what life is. Wherever there are these pictures, conscious and unconscious, that do not make sense to you, you have a question going on in your awareness, a need to understand something because that does not fit into your matrix of understanding.

Each person has a different level of questions that are unanswered that they are comfortable with and a certain amount with which they are uncomfortable. The point at which you are not comfortable with your unanswered questions you might call a kind of a threshold level that beyond that you are not willing to test. You may become irritated, uncertain, confused and doubtful. In order to grow you must test your threshold repeatedly. Those who do not test their threshold repeatedly end up forming a very fixed identity, a very fixed belief structure, a very fixed sense of what life is and sense of who they are. At that point, their consciousness begins, until it opens again, to shut down and growth ceases.

When you do such things as channeling represents, you are challenging the boundary of your own identity, your own comfort level, your own sense of who you are, what life is and what in fact existence is.

Consciousness is a collection of particles of thought or particles of energy that are bound together to form an entity. During your physical existence, you gather a certain amount of identity, a certain amount of beliefs, a certain amount of symbolic references, a certain amount of matrix ideas that you relate to comfortably and a certain amount that you do not relate to comfortably. At death, having no physical body, not channeling your energies and your sense of consciousness through the body, whatever you have related to and learned whose principles are beyond that which has to do with the body, to that extent does your consciousness remain in a whole or in a sovereign integrity.

If everything you have related to has simply to do with physical existence and nothing beyond that, when your physical existence ends, your sense of identity and integrity also ends. Your consciousness, in a sense, fractures, for it holds nothing that you can hold into, and you dissipate into the ethers. Well, no one ever does that utterly. Your parts and particles recombine differently with available particles of energy and consciousness and have another kind of existence, maybe human, maybe otherwise, that it can begin to relate to principles of existence in some more expansive ways.

Since most people who are alive on this earth at this time relate to things beyond simply the temporal, some part of most people at this time is surviving as an eternal entity. You, in part, have been surviving as an eternal entity for a while. I say in part because in each incarnation you have kept a part of your consciousness intact, not by ego, not because you could not relate to the questions you could not answer, but because you found enough of the eternal truth, enough of the cosmic law that survives material incarnations as that there was no need to fracture. The experience you had after the departing of the body was something you could relate to as an entity because you had become identified to some extent with principles that were eternal.

However, many particles of energy have symbolic representations that could not identify with that which survived the body. Those parts of your self disintegrated or left, some of them, perhaps most of them. Those particles that could not identify with those eternal principles, but choose to associate with the eternal parts simply because they felt safe enough even though they did not understand, some of those unknowing, unwise, unenlightened particles may have remained with that more eternal part of your collective while other particles went on.

Those other particles may be able to relate to eternal principles that went on, but not the ones of your particular corporate body, your particular corporate essence. Maybe they connected with other particles also combining and recombining. This is how particles of consciousness in the ethers meet each other. Then they incarnate. Usually they incarnate in relatively the same times as each other and relatively the same places, because remember they have had an association with each other in the past. So that you meet people upon further incarnations with which you feel a connection because maybe a part of them used to be a part of you, so that you have different soul relationships in this way. Soul mates occur this way.

It is not as simple as that. It gets a little bit more complex. The parts that also go on, there may be consciousness that has other needs. It may have identified so much with things that are eternal beyond the consciousness of most human beings that the main body of consciousness may not be willing, able or in need of returning to the physical dimension as a human being. However, other parts of it might return because it needs that. Hence, you have a connection with those who are in Spirit. In this way, you have a connection to many in Spirit.

It does not only work like this between Spirit and the physical. It also works like that between people and other people. In other words, some souls come back who may be a part of you, but they may be those of your particles that end up being mentors to you or those who end up being students or those who end up being peers or those who end up being colleagues and associates. Different soul relationships are made in this way from parts and particles combining and recombining.

Perhaps this is very fundamental to some of you, but consciousness is not only contained by the brain. Perhaps it may be a revelation to others of you. Nevertheless, your consciousness, your awareness and your intelligence is not located only in the brain. It is imbued in every cell of your body. The brain is the organ through which the consciousness goes back and forth, in and out of the ethers. The brain is like a transformer or matrix point for consciousness to translate between physical and non-physical. Because so much activity takes place there, the greatest amount of intelligence can be found in the brain, but the center of your intelligence is not the brain, nor is it the center of the mind. It is simply the center of activity of the mind in the body. Memory and intelligence are cellular, and it is in every single cell of your body. It is not only cellular. It connects beyond the body as well.

Higher self is a consciousness that you might call what you truly are. Each of you, the only thing you really are, is your higher self. Nothing else that is not your higher self is a lasting part of you. However, if you are identified with and focused on particles of consciousness that are your higher self as well as particles of consciousness that are not your higher self, as far as you are concerned it is all the same to you because you are continually referencing or making associations with certain particles of consciousness you believe are you. Therefore, your beliefs define who you are and limit you or end the barriers to your limits. Simply put, you become what you believe.

If you eventually embrace the whole truth of who you are as an eternal being, then what in fact you shall embrace is a collection of energies and particles of consciousness that is able continually to transform, that is continually flexible, safe and empowered. If you have particles of consciousness that are not that, they will not be eternal. If you have particles of consciousness that are that, they will be eternal.

You go through life embracing and letting go of energies that then form some beliefs and some energies that do not form beliefs. Some energy is so subtle, you might say, that it does not translate into anything so defined as a specific belief. Nevertheless, it is energy anyway.

When you have a hold of those most flexible and lasting energies, those are the energies that you will find are attuned to love, those things that are empowered, wise and kind. Your Spirit Guides as well as who you really are as higher self represents that more eternal part of consciousness.

Remember, you are in a sea of particles of consciousness, a sea. It is very difficult for us to distinguish you one from the next. To us, all we see is one great grid of consciousness, of which we are a part and so are you. When a certain part of the grid stands out, it becomes identifiable to us. When you walk on your spiritual path, when you call out, when you set an intention to do something, it gets our attention. It gets us to be able to focus on you.

As channels, if you want energy to come into you, you must state the intention that you wish to be a vehicle, a channel for higher energy. This makes you stand out in the grid. Then we can find you. The more you make yourself available to the energy to be found, the easier it is for us to find you and to have that energy come to and through you.

When we come to you, we come to you in such a way that causes your own higher self to resonate because we are in harmony with that. When your higher self resonates, all the particles of your awareness ready to resonate with it will resonate, as it is able. All the parts that do not resonate with it must in effect begin to separate, must in effect need to go away because they cannot resonate. Hence, some people opening up to higher energies, for channeling or not, must sometimes stop completely because they are not ready to resonate at that particular frequency. They are not ready to let go of the particles that they would have to let go of to resonate with that. That does not mean they are lesser spiritual beings. It just means they have to find a different sort of resonance that resonates in such a way as that they are willing to let go.

Sun Bear

It is important to understand some very powerful things. There is much talk about how you can create your own reality. This is very important, especially now where human beings are coming into their own power. It is very important to realize how powerful you are, how divine you are, how you are linked in with something very much greater than what you define yourself to be.

You form an identity, an ego by making associations with life and your beliefs about yourself, your connectedness to the world and your relationship to it. This defines your sense of self. However, you are greater than that, so much greater than that, and people are beginning to understand that you can actually cause the universe to respond to your own consciousness. Many people grow very happy and excited about that, and there is a great deal of truth to it. There is also a great deal of misperception because people think that just because their consciousness affects the universe that they can control the universe. This is purest arrogance. It is like saying that because you first cannot swim, then you learn to swim and go in an ocean you are suddenly the master of the ocean because you can swim. This is ridiculous. Because you can navigate your position in the ocean does not mean you are the master of it by any circumstance whatsoever. You cannot control the ocean.

You can control what happens to you within certain parameters within the ocean. If you understand the laws of the ocean and you master those laws, then you can navigate it quite successfully, but its power is without a doubt greater than you are. You must respect it if you are to utilize how it can support you. If you realize it can support you and understand its laws, a tremendous universe opens up to you far greater than those who do not understand it.

That is what is important to understand about contacting a power far greater than you are. We are going to begin doing that right now, but we must talk about a few laws. Because you are powerful entities, far more powerful than most people know, there are powers about yourself that are untapped that will absolutely astonish you and lift and inspire you.

It might seem irrelevant right now, but we must establish this from the very beginning. With opening up access to this infinite power, there are many more 'do nots' than 'dos', and some of these things you are simply going to have to take our word for and it will be made clear to you why as time goes on. We will explain some of those things.

One of the things we must explain at the outset, which may sound very crazy, but do not save the world. That is very important. It might sound crazy, I know. None of you thinks you are out to save the world, maybe, I hope, but this mistake is one every single master that has come into this world has had to face. It always leads to huge errors, which create tyrannies, self-imposed and imposed upon others. Even for the noblest reasons the world does not want to be saved. People have a right to their own direction, even wrong ones. That is a part of their path. It is not up to you to rescue or impose your perceptions, whether rightly guided or misguided, upon others. You can put it out and those who are willing to receive it will receive.

You are not in this world to make a mark so your egos can be happy. You are in this world to learn who you are and enjoy that. You are in this world to contribute your light and to know a light so potent that it absolutely intoxicates you and fills you with great, great happiness. This will find its way into the world. Do not save the world. I know that sounds crazy, but when this energy starts welling up inside of you beyond your own ability to hold back anymore, you will face that. It does not come all at once either. That is the first thing.

The second thing is you are both extraordinary and ordinary at the same time. You are miracles of divinity and truth with no limits to your capacities and to what you can create. You are also totally insignificant and meaningless. You are both infinite and without measure in terms of your expression, and you are completely insignificant. You are not either one, but both at the same time. You will have the experience of both. It is important to be at peace with that particular paradox because sometimes your greatness will cause you to realize how fortunate you are and that there are no limits, and other times you will say, ha, I am nothing. Whatever I know is absolutely without effect. If you are not willing to be both and at peace about that, you frequently will be very confused about what you are doing in this world.

What I am saying is this. You are going to open further. No matter how far that door is already open, you are going to open a door larger than ever previously. Please, in your beings, have respect for this. It deserves respect because of the size of the force, not because it is something that is your concept of spiritual, religious or anything else, but because of the pure power of the door that you are opening. When you let it in, it takes hold. Love is a very powerful force. There are not limits to it and it does not always feel like what you describe as love.

Love is pure life force. It has many qualities you are going to learn much more about by way of experience, not by any words I say. Each time you open to one particle more of it, you will think you really understand, but you continually will be revealed there is much more than you ever understood. It is a power that is beyond all of your emotions and feelings and all of your thoughts, which are not the same things, but which is all related. Your thoughts are one thing. Energy is another level of it. Feelings are one thing, and the emotions are another thing. Love is none of those.

Love is something that can permeate those things or not, but love is none of those things. Love is not the feeling that you have when you meet somebody who is a balm for your old wounds. That is a healing, yes, and there is a certain amount of the power of love within that, but love is not that because when they are no longer the balm for those wounds or when those wounds get healed, you will find out what love is then maybe. Love is more like the power in you that exists beyond that which enables you to accept yourself and others because you know an energy of life fulfillment, of life force that puts you beyond the need for something else or someone else to fulfill your need or expectation. That is an experience of personal power, and love is more like that.

This love is the love to which you are going to open. It is pure energy and in the doses you can receive, it is very inspiring, very healing and very wonderful. However, it also comes in doses far greater than you recognize and it can be very confronting, extremely confronting. It is the supreme confrontational force because it will raise in you anything unlike it. It will force you to confront either letting go to it or resisting it. That is your choice. You can only let go to it when you learn what that means by having enough experiences and when you feel good and ready. You are the decider of when and how you open up to it. Nevertheless, it will confront you honestly, whether or not you will be honest.

The last thing I want to say before we begin is this. You have a mind, and in the way that I speak of it right now, what I mean is your particular collection of beliefs about what you, the world and what everything is all about for you. This mind, this persona, this identity also has its own beliefs about what Spirit is about, mediumship, channeling and getting in touch with higher self, God and Guides. It is important to understand that whatever it is that you know on a conscious level, you must be prepared to understand more.

A part of you is super wise, super knowing and super aware, and that part of you already exists right now. You do not have to do anything to improve upon it. You do not have to do anything to become wise enough or good enough to know that that is you or to access it. The only thing you need to do is know what it feels like and to go there if you wish to access some of it.

It is said you have conscious awareness of who you are, subconscious awareness of who you are and unconscious awareness of who you are. This commonly is believed. I think there is no such thing as subconscious. There is only a choice not to be conscious and a choice to be conscious, that all unknowing is by choice and all knowing is by choice. You can choose to know. If you wish to know, you must choose to know. If you wish not to know, you can also choose that.

In order to access this place of knowing underneath or beyond that which is in the forefront of your awareness, you continually go into states of what we call trance where you let go of your normal conscious way of being aware to choose to become aware on a different level. If you ever see a child staring off into the ethers, this is how children get smart. They need these periods because they are leaving consciousness of body awareness and shifting into another dimension of thought, feeling and awareness that is going on at a different level where this super intelligence, this super awareness is, where the collective body of awareness is where there is useful information, useless information and states of mind and awareness. If a child goes into these spaces frequently, they will grow wise and intuitive. If they do not, it will be harder for them to grow wise and intuitive.

If you function in the forefront of your awareness, which comes from a conscious accumulation of data received through the senses, sight, touch, feelings, hearing and smelling, you will acquire a tremendous amount of awareness and knowledge you are not aware of, but you will also be limited to what comes through your sensory perceptions. You, as entities, have sensory perceptions that go beyond the physical body. Your physical senses mirror senses you have that are nonphysical. You have these physical senses as physical organisms because your physical consciousness perceives in that way and eventually through time has manifested physical bodies that mirror the kinds of perceptions that also go on in consciousness.

You have an inner ear where you can receive telepathic communication, an inner eye where you can see visions. You have an inner sense of smell. You have an inner sense of touch or feeling. You have an inner sense of taste. These are all different frequencies of vibration of which your consciousness is able to be aware. It accesses a cosmic mind, a cosmic awareness and receives.

When you let go a little bit of your physical sensory perception or when you take your physical sensory perception and focus it acutely, either way begins to have you access a consciousness beyond the body, a nonphysical reality where there is awareness that floats in to you. In this awareness, in an entranced state, you have tuned out all of your outer senses to become aware of inner ones.

The first thing we are going to do is learn how to develop this state of trance and deepen it. This is something that you already automatically know how to do. It is in your instincts already. You will not have to learn anything new. You do it all the time. First, give yourself a nice stretch and a sigh. We are going to first practice disassociating from the physical body in a few different ways specifically that will sharpen your perceptions of the inner dimensions.

For the first exercise, I would like you to get comfortable, open your eyes and do not close them. Keep them open. Open your ears. Become aware of the sounds around you. Keep your eyes open and attune to the sounds. Notice and identify them. Listen. Become aware of all sensory perceptions. Become aware of the feeling of your clothes and the density of the object that supports your body. Keep your eyes open. Allow yourself to feel these things. Become aware of your tasting sense, the smells and tastes.

Now with your eyes open and your senses sensitive, let your physical body relax and become gentle. Think gentle, ease. Remain alert. Gentle. Alert. Gentle. Put your focus into being alert through your senses even if it means rotating through your sense, first vision then smell, and you may not be able to be alert to all at once. You may be aware of a few to some greater degree, but simply be alert, allowing your consciousness to shift if necessary between alertness from one sense to the next. Become aware. Mark the feeling. Notice what it feels like.

All right, let go of the focus for a minute and come back to your normal way of focusing. Shift back now. Come back to the normal way.

Before we take any other step, I would like you to describe this state of consciousness to the best of your ability in writing. What is it like to be alert in that gentle way we described? On another page, write what it is like when you are focused normally. Write the two. This is one level of trance. Write this down. Write what was your emotion, if there was one, what it felt like, what your mind did or did not do. See if you can also describe some elements of your normal state, your normal form of cognizance, which might be a bit more challenging because it may be a bit difficult to shake off completely the trance state. You may want to think of times outside of now.

This is something that is very easy, but it is very important to know, to have identified the space you want to arrive in first, but some other things are necessary. This is the beginning of a trance state. It will deepen and deepen. We will talk about that and we will do that which creates it. One thing that deepens a trance state is when a Spirit comes into it. You will not have to hold it, but what you do have to do is get there first so we can get hold of you.

There are many places to be aware of other than the physical and many places to be aware of other than the place from where guidance comes. All we have done just now is simply become a little more alert and aware of something. What we will do now is something else.

Do one more stretch, and then go to that space with your eyes open. Think gentle. Think alert. Let it be an energy shift now, not the little parts and particles of how you do it. Just let yourself shift. Think shift. Gentle. Now in this alert state, with your eyes open, let your awareness go to your gut, to your navel, a little below your navel, about an inch or a couple of inches below. Let your alertness go inside, about three inches so that you are becoming aware of a place below the navel and inside, your center. Remain alert. Relax your anal sphincter muscle to the best of your ability. If you have to change your body so that it relaxes, then do so. What this does is let you let go of your gut a little bit. Do you feel the muscles in your sphincter and the muscles all around your center relaxing? Now let go of your alertness a little bit, your sensitivity and just focus on relaxing a little right around your middle, your anal sphincter and your center, let that go a little. Put your attention in there. Let that be relaxed for a minute. Keep this relaxed. Do you feel you have something to say? Keep your attention in the center. Do not go upstairs. Do you feel you have anything you want to say? Let your focus be in your center, which means keep relaxing.

As you are relaxed in this place, I want you to take note of the way you feel. Keep your eyes open. We do not want you to go into this other dimension yet. Keep your attention in your gut, relaxed.

We want you to practice being present. We want you not to go into your space too much. We are not going into this space. Get present. See how long you can keep present in one space. You will be very confronted, some of you, with wanting to leave this space. Do not do that. Hold attention in your gut. As you tense up, wanting to go into another space, keep relaxing, keep your attention in your center.

If you get to the point where you just cannot stand it, then stop for a while, get yourself together and come back. Hold your space. Hold your center. If you cannot hold it, let it go and then come back. Keep those eyes open as long as you can, even if you have to relax the focus to do so.

Become aware of your belly button. Become aware of the inside of your gut and relax the physical muscles. Keep relaxing the anal sphincter and letting your stomach relax. Whatever you go through, keep relaxing your gut for as long as you are able. Merlin will now come to speak with you as you hold your center.

Merlin

We have contacted the presence. We have contacted the space. We need now to contact a doorkeeper and messages. This is what we do next.

Some of you have no idea what moves through you, but this moving through you now is love. It is real and it will continue. Those who let it move and are standing in the energy know what it is to be your self. Right now, you do not care about anything. Right now, you are just fine. You can be yourself right now. You are present here. Everything is all right with you. This is the presences of love. This is not an emotion. This is power. This is a presence. It moves all of your physical body and all of your energy to the next place, wherever that place is.

The beautiful thing is, and all of you need to know is, you do not need to do anything. It is all automatic. All you have to do is get open enough to let it move. It is like the ocean. You cannot stop the rest. The door has opened and it is bigger than you are. You have opened the door.

Nothing else is necessary and everything else is fine. It will keep moving. Do not try to do anything, please. It is all already perfect. Later, if you feel any residual, you do not even have to get rid of it. You do not. If you want it all to be gone, to be over, fine. If you want to hold onto it for a little bit, fine. It is not in your hands anymore.

There are things each of you needs to find out about who and what you are. Watch for those things. They are revealed here. These things happen as the energy shifts.

What we are here for is to experience and contact higher self and Spirit. What is higher self? You. You have a gift that unfortunately sometimes is experienced like a duality, but it is meant to be a gift. We in Spirit do not have this gift. You have a gift to be able to live in the microscope of the body, to have the human experience magnified for the purpose of deep scrutiny of yourself and the universe to bring light in here on a level it is not here yet.

In order to do that, you must be able to attune completely to your humanity self, like the way a scientist looks through a microscope to see things blown up that we cannot see, but you can. However, through that, you identify with the experience you are involved in and after a while, you think that is the only thing there is when that is the tiniest part. It may seem like everything. You must get out of the microscope or you must become confused.

Certain aspects of channeling are very important to understand and there are many ways that one can channel Spirit energy. In a sense, there is very little that is not channeled in Spirit. Most of consciousness of one kind or another relating to human beings comes from a common place, a place of knowing to which each individual has access. When it is that an artist draws, a musician performs, a writer writes or any creative activity takes place, one draws upon a kind of body of consciousness that I shall describe as the more directly associated body of consciousness to you and the less directly associated consciousness to you, and at some points totally unrelated to you.

For the purposes of channeling, one need not channel anything that is totally unrelated to anything that has to do with your lives and your experience. If something is irrelevant to you, it does not matter how relevant it might be in some other dimension or reality because if it is not meaningful for you, it is not meaningful. It does not matter how high one might call a truth because if one has no relationship to it, it is useless to you. Therefore, you are interested in drawing in the energy, the information that is useful to you or useful for some purpose or intention of some import to something that perhaps is beyond your knowledge.

Historically there have always been prophets, channels, seers, psychics and such that have traditionally accessed this body of knowledge. Nostradamus, for example, was one seer who accessed a great, great body of knowledge pertaining to just this time in your history. However, he had little awareness of what it all meant. Furthermore, the way he was able to receive it was through a kind of poetry that to him and to the people of his day had profound significance and impact, but if he were to be asked what is the meaning of this you received, he would likely have had to say I do not know. The one thing that he was certain of was that it was significant even though he did not know why.

This is one of the main characteristics of channeling on a conscious level when one receives an energy that is clear, distinct, profound and powerful, and yet one does not necessarily fully understand the meaning. Those who understand the meaning of any channeled message are frequently the anchors, those on the other side of the experience, many more times than the channel. It is not to say that the channel routinely does not understand what comes through on one level or another, but the channel does not need to understand what goes on at those levels. Sometimes the desire to know what is going on interferes with the entire process.

Another important aspect is being able to have some experience of a realm that exists beyond this one. When I say a realm beyond this one, perhaps those words imply that there is one realm common to all beyond this and that we are now all presumably in the same realm as we speak. Well, as I speak, each of you is in decidedly different realms of consciousness. Perhaps only in some of the most obvious of ways you share a part of your consciousness in this one and common dimension, but each of you have a part of yourself in several others places all at once. Those places are obviously very meaningful to you or else you would not be there. Continually you are referencing any new experience against whatever it is that is going on right now in this and whatsoever other dimensions you are presently occupying.

The exercises are designed to bring your consciousness front and center here and now. There is a very important reason why you do not spend a great deal of time front and center in the here and now, and some of that experience you had while doing the exercise. I do not mean that is the reason not to be front and center so to speak, but what I mean is if you were to be fully present all the time, you would need to be able to embrace infinite levels of energy without trauma. Eventually, that is indeed what you will be able to do.

Perhaps when I put it in the terms of infinite levels of energy without trauma, it makes it seem a bit larger than in fact how it is experienced. Receiving infinite levels of energy is a very simple and natural kind of experience. However, if there are impediments to that, if you are holding onto something that prevents you from experiencing greater and greater levels of love, then you must confront letting go of that and embracing greater levels of energy, and furthermore, getting comfortable with that newer level of energy until you are ready to embrace yet another level of energy.

One can open up to these greater and greater levels of energy many ways. One of these ways of opening up to these greater levels of energy is to be able to understand to some extent a bit about that dimension. Before, all you did was you simply made an effort to be present with all aspects of your being, consciousness and senses. Now you are going to use your natural proclivity for journeying beyond the body, external to the body in another dimension of awareness, a journey, which perhaps you all so love to make that simply you cannot wait to close your eyes.

Your consciousness is aware that you can be in many places at once. Indeed, a part of mastery is learning how to bi-locate and be in many places at one time. So go ahead and enjoy that practice. In fact, in the same way that you had brought your entire consciousness front and center as much as you could into this dimension, now what you are going to do is try to bring your consciousness front and center into our dimension, the place of our dwelling.

This is a very simple kind of an exercise. Before we go ahead with it, let me make it sound so much more fanciful because that way you will be very much more interested when you get to do it. The thing that gets you into our dimension is that you must be attracted. You must be compelled. You must be drawn to pay attention to that specific point of reference so much so that you put your full awareness there to perceive what is going on. Then we shall draw you through.

Before we go into this exercise further, it is also important to understand something called a doorkeeper. Each of you exit your body frequently when your mind wanders on one level and you turn off your sensors and put your consciousness elsewhere. You do it when you fall asleep and you do it when you dream and you do it when you do any creative exercise. You do it when you focus and concentrate on any particular point such that you cut off all of your awareness of all other things except that particular point.

Every time you go out of your body and you have a particular aim, by that intention, by that aim you are utterly and completely safe. Every time you go out of your body to wander, to journey, to daydream, you are provided a Guide. When you are not particularly focused, a Guide must attend you as a kind of protector Spirit, as a kind of assistant, as a kind of an influence to get you to be attracted to those dimensions of awareness from which you might draw more positive energy and consciousness.

Occasionally you may find yourself very attracted to some form of thinking or some construct of beliefs or mental paradigm that is in fact undermining to your well-being. Your attraction to that set of beliefs and paradigm and thinking becomes so compelling that even the presence of your Spirit Guides may not be able to divert you from that particular attraction. When you become determined to focus on that, whatever it is, whether it is supportive of your well-being or undermining to your well-being, we who represent a higher influence must respect your sovereign decision to spend your time in consciousness any place you want. However, our job is to attract you, to influence you toward that which we think is in your highest interest whether or not you pay attention to it. However, it is beyond our, shall we say, willingness to force you into those directions or areas of consciousness that we think are right above and beyond your desire to go there. That is not our way.

There is such consciousnesses as that it is not beyond willingness to attract you into those areas where you perhaps would be vulnerable to undermining forces. However, in order to be prey to some of those forces is not ever anything that happens accidentally, incidentally or shall we say by a trickery or deceit. It inevitably happens by being exposed for a long period by choice or by, shall we say, a preponderance of events beyond your own control that is usually the result of consciousness developed, choices made and understandings attained prior to coming into this particular lifetime.

What does all that mean? Are there such things as possession, for example? Yes, there are. How does this happen? Well, it does not happen the way it does in Hollywood. It never happens that some young innocent merrily playfully going about their business suddenly for no reason whatsoever finds themselves in the clutches of a very demonic and evil person. First, there is no such a thing as evil. There is only such a thing as unenlightened consciousness or that that is not yet as enlightened as other consciousness. Some of that consciousness may seem to be decidedly evil for so undermining it might be to your well-being that you may be want to give it that label. However, it is not true that there is an ultimate darkness where there can be no light, but there are certain territories to stay away from because there are places that are in fact undermining to your well-being.

The best way to stay away from such places is to understand a little about it, but more importantly to be focused in a particular way that is useful to you. If you want to touch into the highest realms of consciousness, it is very simple. All you need is simply the intention to do so. When you see or hear of such things as possessions, spirits performing different kinds of trickery and abusing people, it most often happens when people insist that who they are is powerless and a victim and they are seeking to turn their life over to somebody else to take control of it for them. This also happens when somebody has been subjected repeatedly to various forms of psychological, spiritual, emotional and/or physical abuse such that their spirits become worn down and beaten and they lose their sense of connectedness to their natural sense of strength and self-empowerment. Yes, those people can be, at those times, vulnerable not only to negative influences, but also to all kinds of influences.

Frequently, if such persons are vulnerable to that as children, they often are rescued on some level by their Spirit Guides, for they are unable, quite often, to cope with the intensity and level of their feelings, emotions and physical abuse. A Spirit presence will oftentimes come and help them get out of the consciousness of the physical reality and they will live in another dimension while going through the physical plane abuse. Literally, they are not there quite often for the abuse if it becomes intense enough. They create realms or worlds of their own and we can meet them in those worlds of their own and help them, and eventually guide them to such sources as that they will eventually become empowered and/or healed.

You may wonder why such things can even happen or had to happen in the first place. That is because the level of human consciousness at this time simply has not evolved much higher than that. Human beings are very, very new on this planet and there is a long way to go on the evolutionary scale to being in the consciousness of love, a long, long way to go.

A great number of you are a part of that. Many of you have also been great victims of that physical, emotional and psychological abuse, which is one of the reasons you are open to us. It is also one of the reasons there is so much healing to be done. Opening to Spirit is one of the ways to receive an accelerated healing. Your intention to be healed, your intention to know the highest is very, very important. If you have other underlying motives, they really do not matter if your intention is to be connected to the highest.

These abusive forces I speak of never masquerade as positive forces very long if at all. The reason they never masquerade as positive forces very long is they are not very good at acting like positive forces. They act like negative forces, and it is very clear. They have no interest in acting like a positive force because they have no respect for that which you might call a positive force. There is no respect for being attuned to higher forms of energy. They are convinced that the only thing that works is force. No other kind of power is respected except force, manipulation. When you are part and party to that, you will feel the need to manipulate over and above the will of others.

There is a great deal of this lower level of consciousness intermingling with every entity. The first thing to understand about it, strangely enough, is that it is not your enemy because it is a part of yourself. You must eventually learn to accept, learn to love that part, for only in such an integrated consciousness can the entire affair shift into another level. To fight or to hate that aspect of yourself is to create a schism in your being that creates a great deal of pain.

The ultimate purpose of the higher force is to promote unconditional and unlimited love, which certainly involves at some point total acceptance of all parts of all aspects of existence and all parts and aspects of self. So if it is that this part, which is not really at that time a friend and is also not an enemy, how is it that one approaches this? One approaches it like this, that anything done in the direction of the light raises the level of all aspects of self, you and anything that comes in touch with you. In other words, it does not matter if the consciousness that you get in touch with is pure. It simply does not matter. More often than not, if you seek a pure and perfect consciousness without a flaw, without any quirks at all in it, if you seek such a thing as that, we happen to think this is the greatest demon because such a thing does not exist. That thing exists only in the minds of human beings.

Human beings, because of their pain, like to project the idea that there is something the opposite of that pain, which is perfection and something without flaw. A computer, for example, is a kind of construct that reflects the kind of idea and thinking that human beings have about the nature of intelligence and the nature of existence. Meaning, everything must come out consistently all the time in the same manner, and the closer that is to an absolute, the closer that is to truth.

One thing that is important to understand about truth is that because it is infinite, there is no absolute. There is only that which is relative to something else and that may or may not be helpful to that something else. If you seek an absolute, you will find something that is not truth. Quite often, the negative force uses the idea of absolute in order to gain power. Why? Because if there is an absolute and you are not it, then guess who has the control? That is the one and only reason. A divine source respects your own sovereign integrity and does not undermine it.

A divine source promotes your own empowerment and advancement and seeks to raise it even above itself. A divine source is not jealous of your awareness or power, does not posses it and does not seek to put a position into your consciousness or awareness whereby you become undermined or disempowered, but rather where there is a mutual development. A divine source is always ready to embrace its next step. A divine source is not something that is total and absolute because divinity means its quality is continually able to transcend itself. At the point that it is no longer able to transcend itself, it no longer is infinite. Therefore, being able to transcend itself is what makes it without limit.

You are also a part of that dynamic. Do you know how important that is? That means if you are able to transcend your own nature that there is always something further to go. If there is always something further to go, how can one get perfect before one starts in any particular direction? In other words, it is another reflection of the belief of one's own unworthiness. It is another failure to accept that who one is at that time is perfect as they are right now. That is the motivation of the teaching force in life, to get human beings to accept that about themselves so they can experience the nature of their infinite presence.

With channeling, with getting in touch with Spirit, with getting in touch with your higher self, this is very, very important because the contact you make with the inner dimension may leave you a bit uncertain as to what it is you have contacted, its value, your value and your ability at being able to contact it. Because there is always further to go, because you will continue to grow forever, it is important to receive whatever information you can receive that is important to you from such a contact rather than disowning that contact or, shall we say, rejecting your particular contact as not good enough, clear enough or helpful enough.

In order to embrace greater levels of clarity, you first must be willing to embrace whatever level of clarity you have. If you embrace that level of clarity first, then greater levels will come. In exact proportion to your willingness to accept whatever you get as valid and important, to that extent will you be able to open your channel to receive more. To that extent that you invalidate what you get, to that extent will your channel not only not open, but to that extent will it close down, to that extent shall it shrivel until such time you are willing to open it again. Therefore, it becomes very important to make an effort to try to put whatever you get from those inner dimensions into terms understandable to you.

What are these inner dimensions? That is what we shall do right now. There is an inner realm as much as there is an outer realm. There is inner vision, inner hearing, inner taste, inner touch and inner smells. All of these perceptions are available to you. Since it is in the realm of consciousness where there is no time and space, there are no barriers to what can be accessed. When you access this information, you are in fact accessing the Akashic record, Philos's realm, which is the place where all knowledge, all vision is stored, future, past, present and all possibilities and potential.

Just so that we begin being able to sense that, I would like everybody, for a moment, to simply close your eyes. We would like you to find your center again, and this is how you are going to find the center. You are going to place your attention below the navel and inside. You are going to relax the anal sphincter muscle. You are first going to let your attention be focused in that center.

With your eyes closed, we would like you, after first having contacted that center, relaxing the anal sphincter and letting go as much as you can, to become aware of the fact that you are breathing. Notice either the sound and/or the motion of your breath and let your spirit become gentle. Become aware of your entire physical body as you become gentle. Just feel your physical sensation, the awareness of your body, bones and skin.

Focus your attention now above your eyebrows and between them to the place called the third eye. If you wish, you may even focus your physical eyes a little upward and center toward that point above and between. As you look into that space, notice if it seems completely black or if it seems there are colors, shapes or movement of some kind or haze or smoke or activity, but notice that it is not totally pitch black.

Unless you are good at doing this, notice if it is hard to maintain your perception of that activity. Notice that it kind of moves. It does not stay the same. It shifts and changes. It is not really still. If you wish to be aware of it, then relax your focus a bit and be aware. Do not look, but become aware of it or look. It does not matter.

If you will, open your eyes and look into the air. See if you do not see precisely the same movement in the very air itself as though the air itself seems to be a little bit palpable. A fuzziness seems to be in the physical air if you notice it with your eyes open.

All right, enough of this little exercise. If you will, kindly let go of the focus and let me talk a little bit about what this is. It is very important for the next step.

First, did you see totally pitch black with no movement in it whatsoever? No. Let me tell you why. It is an enormous exercise to get people to acknowledge that there is anything other than complete pitch in that place. However, you are at least sensitive enough to have thought, if not know, that you think you sensed something. Who noticed that it seemed to be that whatever you saw or thought you saw seemed to fade in and out a bit? At some moments, it seemed to be a little stronger, and at others, no, no, no, I am not certain. Who had that experience?

What you are doing is a perception of consciousness, not a perception of the physical eye. However, because you have physical eyes, it might seem as though you saw it. Of course, since your eyes were closed, you cannot have seen anything, could you? You must have perceived it. Your consciousness must have become aware of it.

When you opened your eyes, did you either see or think you may have seen a similar kind of movement in the air? Frequently one's ability to see it in the very air and the fact that it also goes in and out in your consciousness are related to the same principle. When you open your eyes, since you are so used to using your eyes, you focus your eyes to look for something.

Who has ever thought they have felt a presence or a Spirit and looked and it seems to go away? That is because you have a vision that is 360 degrees around that is conscious, not physical. In your perception, you became aware of it. Because you thought it was your eye, of course, you actually turned your eye to it. You then turned on your vision and turned on your physical eyes. That is why it seemed to disappear. What if you maintain the consciousness of that inner vision with your eyes open? That is a part of the channeling energy, to be able to hold the perception of energy. You must be willing to be a receiver and an interpreter of that energy.

Who found that their head was moving a little bit or their body wanted to move or anything of that kind? Some of you heard different levels of pitch, tambour, tone, words going on right inside of your consciousness. It could not have been your physical ear. It has to be some other form of awareness.

Your inner vision and your inner ear, we can trigger. We do not need to have a physical stimulus in order to trigger it. We can trigger it. You will become aware of it, and we will show you how eventually. That inner sense, you must be sensitive to in order to become aware.

What of this thing called imagination? Let us discuss that for a moment. It was not entirely your imagination as you understand it, but it was partly your imagination. In order to be intelligent beings, you must be imaginative beings. All intelligence expresses through some sort of inner or outer sensitivity. Imagination means to image, to perceive. Always that imaging is going on in your own consciousness. Of course, you have to imagine it. Of course, you have to image it. If you do not image it, how will you know it?

Some images are better than others are. Some images are poorer than others are. Some images come from clearer places. Some images come from less clear places. Your imagination, if you wish to call it that, is a dimension of your perception of energy and your desire to translate energy into meaningful symbols.

In order to communicate with you, we must communicate through meaningful symbols. If you get a symbol, you can rest assured, it is meaningful to you. If you get a symbol, it cannot be meaningful to anybody else. It must be meaningful to you. You can assume that if you see symbols or feel feelings or get things, that this is your way of translating through your ability to image, through your imagery, through your sensitivity, meaningful messages from life, from the universe. Continually you are translating energies you sense from inner and outer, which become meaningful to you on unconscious levels sometimes, on conscious levels at other times.

Let us do yet another step. For a moment, close your eyes and imagine something. Imagine your particular favorite room at home right now. If you do not like your particular home, then imagine the last place you know of that is your favorite place to be or one of your favorite places to be. Find a place you actually know and think of it.

Open your eyes now. I would like you to try to define precisely, as closely as you can, where that perception was or is. Is it in the center of your head? Is it forward in your head? Did it seem to be projected a bit beyond your head? Was it in back? Was it above? Did it seem to be half in, half out? Was it to the left or to the right? See if you can define now where that image is that you saw when you closed your eyes. See if you can define that. Where is that image? Where is that activity?

I would like you now to create an image of the following kind. Close your eyes. I would like you now to imagine a gray and white horse. This gray and white horse is moving in a field. It reaches down to nibble on the grass. Now it looks up and sees you. All right, come back.

Did you find this exercise difficult? Did you notice if it had some sort of different kind of quality than the memory? Did you notice if it was or was not in the same place as the memory place? How would you describe that different quality?

That is a very important distinction because what I am saying is that the images that you create take place in a different fashion than images you remember. Images that come from Spirit tend to have the same quality as images you remember.

I know the distinction at this point is very subtle. We are going to do something about that. The main value of what we are doing is not necessarily to be able to distinguish between which kinds of things are where. It is to refine your awareness enough to be able to pay attention, to notice this inner space and see if you can get some things like color, placement, depth and even charge, to notice these, to feel, to pay attention to what is going on in you when you are in those spaces.

Messages that come from your psychic self tend to come from the same place as memories. They are quick and easy to access, and you have less difficulty quite often in holding them. When you are creating an image, it requires more effort. When you are receiving an image, it seems to grab your attention. A particularly attractive image you are creating can grab you too, but for the most part, psychic impressions come in the same fashion as your memories. The more important thing is if you will just simply watch that space for a moment as we did, you will notice differences.

Another important point is that we are not in another dimension, as it were, up there. We intermingle with you continually, but you need to become aware of us. Our intermingling is not for the same kind of purpose that you might intermingle with each other because our intermingling is not necessarily to give you messages in sentence structure in your head or outside of it. We blend with your aura so that you become aware of things, that by moving your energy, you become aware, you become conscious of something that is important for you. We do not have mouths and therefore we do not need language. We do not have bodies, so we cannot really create touch of the physical body. Although, sometimes you will feel it in the same way you see some images so strong you do not know whether you are awake or not. If you are dreaming, you can sometimes think you are awake. Sometimes when awake you can think you are dreaming.

We are going to speak a little bit about doorkeepers and so forth. For a moment close your eyes, relax, find that place near the navel and relax the anal sphincter muscle. Relax the stomach and the shoulders. Simply think peace. Peace. Peace.

Imagine for a moment you are walking in a field. It is a beautiful field with a starry, starry night. The temperature is warm and balmy and there is a gentle breeze blowing across your face. You are walking in a very light and lilting manner, pensive, gentle and open.

There suddenly appears in the distance a light as though it was a haze from a city, but it seems to have an especially silvery, radiant glow. It seems far away as though it is near or over a horizon. You move toward it. You notice your steps seem to bounce. You seem to glide. You seem pulled toward it.

There you are in the middle of this silvery place. You peer into it and there is a mansion. You move closer. You notice its size, its shape, its architecture. You notice the windows. You notice a door that seems to call to you.

You enter the door. As you enter the door, there is a different feeling somehow, curious, quizzical. You are alert, but you do not know exactly for what. It seems to look inside exactly as you might expect it to look or want it to look. It feels nice. As large as it is, somehow it feels warm, special.

You look off to one particular area where you see a door. The door radiates the same silvery light. A smile of anticipation comes over you. You do not know why exactly, but you know something is there for you. You feel a sense of anticipation as you move toward the door. You are not certain at first if it is fear, but it seems to change. You know that it is safe somehow. Gentleness seems to fill the air. It is precious and palpable.

You open the door slowly and you enter. There is a wonderful vision. The space seems larger than it did outside and warm feeling. Oh, you have never felt so warm, so nurtured. A voice says, be calm, for I am with you again. You remember me. We love each other. There enters through the same door you did, as you face the door, a form of some kind. What is it? Is it a man, a woman, a light, a movement, an energy, a feeling? It radiates the qualities of wisdom and love, empowerment and strength. You like this force.

It comes to you and tells you its name and you listen for it. It says to you, he says to you, she says to you, they say to you, I am here for you whenever you need me. Come here when you need. We will talk. You and I, you and we, this place is our place and I am yours. I will always help you when you need. I am never far. I shall guard your door and see to it that only that which is like love that you want may enter. Blessed be, dear friend.

You know it is time to release. There is a bit of sadness, but a sense of wellness, for you know that these words are true. You do not know why you know that, but somehow you know they are. Somehow, you know they are. You come from the door and you look one more time as you turn around to look at it, and you look at the beautiful room.

You find yourself outside of the mansion, looking at its architecture again, its windows, its color, its size. You find yourself going back to the field with the starry, starry night. You feel different, secure, as though there is a friend. Then, here you are again, here with Merlin.

We have gone on a little journey between dimensions, and we have used some imagery to find a place between worlds to give Spirit a place to access you. Did you receive a name? What name occurred to you? Were you uncertain if you received a name? Did you notice that whatever or whomever you saw that it was not what you expected? If you did not receive a name, just know there is much in Spirit that does not wish to take on a name and will not have one.

Cassandra

That which we express when we seek to be in touch with you has more to do with movement of light and energy than it has to do with ideas, concepts, philosophies and truths. However, in order that you may understand, since you are also creatures of intellect, the messages we give directly to you through mediums, through psychics and through your own consciousness often must come in word symbols. If you are willing to allow energy to move through you, beginning at whatsoever level you are open to receive it at the time, then we will be able to increase the level of volume and energy until you find yourself in a greater and greater flow to that extent you are willing to allow it to happen. You must be willing to allow it to happen. You can take control to stop it or if you wish to, you can let go to allow us to express in the way we wish.

A part of being able to open that we may come to and through you, if you desire, is your learning to be comfortable with us and also we are learning to be comfortable with you. You may find yourself, at one time or another, uncomfortable with what is happening. You may also notice that that which is present with you may try to help you to stretch or let go and get used to you, perhaps used to your body, used to your vocal range, used to your tongue, used to your enunciation. You may find yourself making strange faces or unusual motions. This is the letting go to us getting used to you and you getting used to us.

You must remember that we are energies and not personalities as we come through in this manner or as we may choose to express through you. Therefore, you cannot look for us as though we are personalities all the time. You cannot expect that we shall immediately take some shape that you may quickly be able to identify and characterize as Spirit. Rather, in order for us to be able to express that which we wish, you must be willing to allow us to shape the energies that we are mingling with as we come and mingle and blend with your own thoughts, ideas, consciousness, feelings, understandings, attitudes and other energies we shall mingle and blend with. We shall, with you, create and co-create a place, a point in consciousness where we find we are most able, if you will, to broadcast, to express ourselves through you. Sometimes we will express in different ways. Words are just one of the ways.

You shall find that as you allow Spirit to come to you and, if you wish, allow Spirit to come through you, you will increasingly find you will let go. You will find that you will let go to things that you would not do or say and things that other than in an entranced state you would not feel as free to let go. In the entranced state, you open the avenue to super conscious wisdom of your highest self to express itself. You also give us an avenue through which that which is outside of your higher self can express.

We come here to do several things, to help your bodies and voices grow loose and flexible, and to help you perceive and understand into the realm of the psychic so that you are able to allow yourself to see and have visions, and to some extent understand them. With the visions that you come to see and with your beings being loose and free, you can allow these visions to express themselves through you in higher self form, in true self form and in Spirit form.

It is important to understand and know what your boundaries are. We know you are completely safe and it is important to know that you and we work together and we can be conscious of the space. We will not bring you into circumstances with which you prefer not to be involved. If you are willing to let go, you can let go just as much as you want physically and/or vocally. It is simply important to have a free space in a sense.

If it is that you open to practice your channeling, we will often take you far beyond what it is you might think are your barriers, not so much your safe boundaries, but barriers that are falsely imposed that you may wish to go beyond anyway. By exploring the range of your freedom, for you and for us, we get to know you and your instrument, and we get to know how to work with you effectively. We will find that place between the most held back place and the freest place where you and we are most comfortable through which to transmit our messages. The place that is most tight and the place that is most loose, we will find the place in between that we are both comfortable and express from that place.

There are several ways, some of which you know, some of which we will invent with you that we can communicate. For example, there is a way to let us directly through to move and speak. However, there are also several indirect methods. One way is to see into the inner dimension as we show you and as you come to see different visions and then tell of what you see. To channel means to bring through. It does not matter if that bringing through is you or we. If you see it and then tell it, it has been channeled.

One way that you can do this is simply as a seer or a psychic and you simply see and tell. Another is you can hear messages as though words are being whispered into your inner ear or your thoughts or mind and simply say, I hear this and this and this. I am seeing this and this and this. Another way is to say, Spirit says this and this. Spirit shows me this and this. Sometimes when you preface what you say with I am moved to say or Spirit shows me, as you say this, the channel opens more and more.

By holding your center in the pit of your stomach, you can stay centered. If you are going to be present, there needs to be a certain amount cleared first. Sometimes, having Spirit move through you can help you to be present or help you be removed. Whatever is most important at the time is what will happen. However, if it is that you wish to channel and you feel blocked, you must first find the center and then open to Spirit.

What do I mean by open? You simply invite the Spirit to come. If you loose the Spirit and you loose the essence, speak to the Spirit and say, all right Spirit, I am ready to receive you again. That is all, and it will come. We come by invitation.

Let us now do a little exercise. Find an object or a point in the room where you are to focus on with your eyes open, a point. The purpose of this exercise is not a concentration exercise. Find an object or a point that is easy or desirable for you to focus upon. Find an object that you can observe.

Notice the color and the texture. Imagine how it is to the touch, the size, shape and dimension. Define or notice the edges, the perimeter. Now close your eyes and imagine that same object or point with your eyes closed. Try to imagine it at the same distance from you as it was. If the vision is internalized, try to externalize it. Try to imagine it is at that distance. Notice its size, its shape, its dimension and its texture, its color. If you cannot see it, then become aware of it as though you see it.

Imagine you going over to the point where it is and touching it. Come back to the point where you originally were and see the object again. Imagine yourself distanced from it again. Imagine the object now being pulled near to you. Imagine now that you send the object back to where it was. Imagine now that you switch places, that the object is now where you were and you are where the object was. Now imagine that you are looking at that object from the perspective of that point where you are now, looking back at the spot where you used to be. See if you can define what everything is around that object where you used to be sitting and where the object now is.

Now come back to yourself, to your position where you are sitting and let the object return to where it was. For a moment, simply sit there and relax your inner gaze for a moment and rest. Find your center point beneath the navel, about an inch or two, and inside the body a few inches.

Now, with your eyes closed, one more exercise. With a part of you, go to where the object is, look back and see yourself. See yourself from the perspective of outside of you. Then come back and find your center. Come back, find your center and then open your eyes.

What we were doing is a few exercises to become a bit disassociated from the physical body and to more clearly define the inner dimensions. Were you able to get outside your perception to look back at yourself? Were you able to imagine it? Did you find it difficult to imagine yourself from the perspective of outside yourself? Did you find it easy to define the object with your eyes open? Did you find it hard? Did you find it easy to imagine it with your eyes closed? Did you find it easier to imagine it at a distance or up close? Did you find it easy to change places with the object? When you turned around to face it, did you find it easy? Did you find it hard? Did you find it easy to imagine yourself outside your body? Did you find it easy to project to the point where the object was? Was it hard to project to where the object was? Did you find it easy or hard to turn around and face yourself? When you turned around to face yourself, could you imagine yourself back there, but could not turn around and see it, could not get the perspective of turning around? When you saw yourself, were you up close or far away?

These different perspectives have to do with the difference between psychically viewing and astral projecting. An astral projection is an experience of projecting an aspect of your substance, your consciousness beyond the body to view from that realm or from the perspective of beyond the body. Psychically viewing is doing so from a consciousness from within the body, but becoming aware of something.

Astral projection is coming out of the body to view the body or the realm from a perspective outside of the body. Psychically viewing or clairvoyance is actually being within the body and viewing something elsewhere from the perspective or point where you are, where your body is. One is in the body and the other is out of the body. You can have both experiences, be out of the body and clairvoyantly view as well.

The reason this is important is to understand something about coming out of the body. If you had difficulty seeing yourself outside of the body by turning around, of all the different experiences that you may have had that you can tell when you are out of the body, it is the strongest sign that you are out of the body. When you are out of the body, you cannot always, unless you are an expert or get better at it, control the perspective. If you could see your face from outside of the body, you may have been out of the body. If you had the sense you were imagining it, you were clairvoyantly viewing. However, if you had the sense of perspective and a distance relationship, you were beyond the body. Not being able to turn around is a perspective or a distance relationship. If you had the sense that you were out of perspective, the world was lopsided, you were smaller or larger or there was some other spatial reference change, that is also an out of the body experience.

In addition, seeing of the self from outside the body confronts whether you are alive or dead. If you have a problem with life, difficulty with living or dying, it is also difficult to see yourself sometimes from outside the body.

When you are in a trance state and you are completely out of your body to the point you are completely unaware, everything I am talking about is irrelevant. If you are not aware of the experience at all, there are several ways you can become aware of the experience.

The reason these experiences may not feel to be powerful astral projections or out of the body experiences is because you kept some of your sensory awareness located at the body. When you are projecting much further away to the point where you are out of the body completely and the consciousness is near the body, then you totally and utterly lose consciousness of the physical body perceptions and your entire sensory organ is elsewhere experiencing that reality.

Your sensory self must be completely in the body to have a total dynamic and intense sensual experience of being in the body. To be out of the body completely means wherever you are, you are having that sensual or sensory experience, seeing, hearing, touching, tasting, smelling.

Dreams are astral projections. They are so much so that there is very little in the physical body to experience the physical world around you in the room unless the sensory stimulus in the room is so strong that it brings your consciousness back to the body. Some of you have the slamming back experience when you wake or the sense that you are sinking when falling asleep or it could be rising when you are going to sleep.

When you are channeling, sometimes you may become a bit dizzy because you may be coming out of the body to go into a trance state. The state of trance is the experience of projecting or letting go of the body awareness to some degree or another. Therefore, if you are in a trance state, you will likely become slightly disoriented. That disorientation is something that we may or may not be able to work with if you are in a full trance state. Let me describe what I mean.

Many of you wish to go completely out of the body. Well, first, you must be good astral projectors in order to go completely out of the body. That means you need to be willing to let go completely of your physical body and the sense of disorientation and dizziness must not bother you. If that bothers you, then you will hold onto the body to some extent for your orientation. That might make it easier for us to work with you or not. We will have to see. You and we will have to find out where that point is that you and we are both comfortable working with each other.

If you are completely astral projected, you will not be in the room to know what is happening. If you are in the room to know what is going on, you will see your body from some other perspective in the room. However, for most people it is too disorienting to be out of the body and near it.

For example, some of you had a little of that experience of becoming very disoriented and perhaps a little mental drain when we were doing this last exercise trying to project, in, around and imagine. If you noticed, by the end of this exercise you were very sleepy. Do you know why? When you want to go out of your body, you want to go out of your body completely. You do not want to be around half awake and half asleep. You want to go completely. You want to leave the consciousness of the body totally and utterly. That is what makes you sleepy. If you cannot leave the body, you cannot sleep. If you are bothered by sounds in the room, that keeps you in body awareness or any sensual experience, discomfort of the thing you are sleeping on, attention to visual stimuli. You must stop sensing because the only thing that keeps you in the body is if your physical senses are stimulated. You must stop stimulating the physical senses to leave the body or you must shut out the physical senses to leave the body. In doing this imagery exercise, you are in effect tuning out your sensory stimulus. Your natural response to that is to leave the body or to want to go to sleep because for years, every time you tune out your sensory stimulus, that is your signal to go to sleep, to leave the body.

Being in between conscious and unconscious is a trance state. Being present is the state of being awake. Usually people need to be in some level of trance until they are completely healed. Once you are completely healed, you can be completely present. However, if you are not completely healed, you will not want to be completely present. When you are completely present, anything that is in the way of being present will surface. Usually some aspect of a person's consciousness is not present because they have to face what they have to face when they are present. Trance confronts all of that. What I am saying is that the more you go into a trance state, be prepared to go through things.

If you are too confronted, you might choose to completely disassociate. That is one the reasons why this medium goes completely out. It is more confronting to be here with Spirit. You do not really know what kind of medium you are until you begin to channel and allow it to develop.

When you go into the higher dimensions, including the astral, it is hard to for you to retain in the same way as when you go into a dream that you may remember when you first awaken and then it tends to fade away. The reason is that you do not spend as much conscious time in that dimension practicing retaining the kinds of experiences that you have there. Here you spend a great deal of time consciously and you are used to the experiences here. They are easier to retain.

The higher and higher you go into the other dimensions, the less and less sensual it becomes and therefore the harder and harder it becomes to retain. I should say transversely, when it is that a Spirit comes into this dimension or any other dimension outside of where they spend most of their consciousness, sometimes that is equally as difficult for us to retain. Therefore, you can meet with the Spirit in many different places and times and a contact of familiarity and a knowing will be there, but perhaps not the details of every meeting.

Merlin

You must be self-referencing. No matter what it is that you receive, no matter what it is that you are told, you must always reference that against your own thoughts, your own feelings, your own ideas. Nothing we do is meant for you to receive without referencing it against your own beliefs and understandings. You must do that. If you fail to do that, you will be duped. It does not matter if you are told the truth or a lie, you must be duped if you do not reference it against your own beliefs. If you fail to reference what you receive from any other person, any other Spirit or any other force that you sense is outside of yourself, whatever that might be, and are looking to give up taking responsibility for your life, you again will be duped.

Some people do not want to take responsibility, but perhaps they do not know that they do not want to take responsibility at the time. Maybe they need to have that lesson if they do not know that. However, some people are looking for all of the questions of their lives to be answered by somebody else, by something else. There are a number of reasons for that, but we shall not go into them. You simply cannot do that.

It is a very important and very delicate point when you say not my will, but Thy will. There is such a place where your will is THE will and THE will is your will. There is no separation between the two. However, when a human being is out of their right balance, it is hard to tell. As long as you have to say there is my will and there is another will, then you have no business saying not mine, but yours. The time for not my will but Thy will is when you cannot tell the difference, not because you are confused about which is which, but because your intention or the intention of the universe greater than you all seems to lead to the same sort of uplifting and ascended experience. You cannot tell the difference because it all leads to the same place. That only happens after you have let go and after there is no duality anymore and not prior to that time. If you have to push aside your will, your will does not get pushed aside so easily. It has an enormous tendency to backlash.

Some of the rules I wanted to talk about are number one, be self-referencing. It means that if you receive messages that you are uncertain about, either hold that in reservation to see if it has some later meaning or reference it against your own understanding. Weigh it. Either accept it or reject it, but you make the decision about whether it is true for you. That is very, very important. Then accept responsibility for it.

You see, there is a very powerful way that people like to avoid taking responsibility. It is a very tricky thing and it is another way to give over your power. One of the ways of doing that is to get a message from your higher self or Spirit, weigh it and say, hum, this feels right for me. Then something does not work out and you say, oh, Spirit told me. If you have accepted responsibility, it is then your choice. The moment that you decide, it is your choice. Once you choose, own responsibility for it if you choose. If you are not willing to accept responsibility for it, do not accept it. It is as simple as that.

Our purpose is not to tell you what to do, even though we will often advise and guide you. Do not miss the point here. Our purpose is to blend with your energies. Sometimes that means getting involved in counsel and advice, but blending with your energies so that you can come to your own determination, so that energy can move, so that thoughts can be jogged, so that your mind can be tossed a bit, and when it falls into place, you are left with an understanding. That is our purpose, to help you become aware of who you are, who you are becoming, where you are going and where you are now. That is our purpose.

When I say, be self-referencing, I also mean that you will need to be prepared to make your own errors too. In other words, one of the reasons people want others to make decisions for them is usually somewhere along the line that they had gotten hurt and wounded and from those hurts and wounds are enormously sensitive to making decisions for themselves, which they may then have a very high threshold again for hurt. Therefore, they want then to make no mistakes, no errors or they want someone or something to rely upon where they will not encounter any particular kind of quirk or oddity in the universe or in their lives.

One of the things about being self-referencing is it helps you gain your power. It helps you find your strength. It helps you learn that you can make mistakes. You will never make such a great mistake if you are self-referencing in the first place and open to get guidance. Any mistake that you make will never be so far from your center that it is not easily correctable or adjustable in some way with a few other notions or perceptions that will then come. You are much more likely to make a greater mistake by not having any source reference, inner or outer, to weigh against your own consciousness.

There is not a way to avoid error. There is no such thing as perfection. If you look for perfection, what you will instead do is increasingly disown your power. By looking for perfection, you will end up pushing away your own ability to take responsibility. You will lose your power, turning it over completely to something that will inevitably be so disempowering for you that you can only be bruised and hurt.

If you give over responsibility for that which you are meant to own, you will become powerless, a victim of something or someone eventually. It is unavoidable and unquestionably true. If you look for some authority, including us, to be your perfection, even with the sincerest motives, you will also end up victimized because we are not that which wants to be the authority in your life. We do not want it. If you are looking for a power that wants to be the authority in your life, you are not looking for us. You are looking for something else.

It is very important to realize that we are not about that. We are not about telling you, forcing you or cajoling you into doing what we want you to do. We are about cajoling into discovering who you are, what your potential is and what your capacity is. We are more interested in having an influence upon you. That influence is done by simply being who we are in your presence and by that, you come into who you are in our presence. We are not looking for students who remain students forever. We are looking for peers to join us in a great land of light, if people wish to come there. That is an explanation of one of the rules. It may become confused from time to time, but that is the principle at work.

Next, set up times. You do not have to do it this way, but we are trying to give you parameters whereby if you stay within those parameters, you will find yourself safe. Set up times to channel, if you wish to channel, that are designated. In other words, for the most part it is best not to channel spontaneously. What do I mean by channel spontaneously? I mean set it up that Spirit can come into you and express through you. It is best not to do that spontaneously. You can spontaneously access Spirit as you wish to go into it if you want to, or access it for information spontaneously, but do not let Spirit spontaneously express itself through you continually.

So long as you are confused in any respect about what the process is, do not channel spontaneously. Do so at designated times so that you can clearly distinguish those times and moments about who you are and what Spirit is so that we can get used to you at a particular time and we can get used to coming through you at a particular time. It also makes it easier for you to go into a trance state. It also helps you more easily distinguish what is Spirit and what is you. You are Spirit too, and sometimes that is a bit hard to tell, but it makes it easier to tell because you clearly set a boundary. It is very important for all of the time you are open to spiritual energies and continually accessing spiritual energies beyond yourself. That is one of the natures of human beings.

Sometimes when you are in a place of, shall we say imbalance, you can channel negative energies just as well as you can channel positive energies. If you are in the habit of opening spontaneously at any particular moment, then you can also be open to channeling negative energies. When you set it up ahead of time that you will channel at a particular time, your frame of reference changes and your expectation is to channel higher forms of energy.

You can create a setting or an ambience that you are comfortable in, that for you represents letting in only the highest available forces. This is the next rule. Set up an environment that you are comfortable in that represents for you letting through only the highest available forces.

Next, before you channel, make an inner or outer affirmation about what your intention is to have happen. Those are the rules. You can change them if they do not suit you, but we would recommend trying them first.

Do not force any particular Spirit that you desire to come through or you will induce fakers. Do not say I only want one Spirit to come and tell me this particular thing. You can invite the Spirit that you want to come and you can invite the kind of Spirit you want to come. You should invite the kind of Spirit that you would like to come. It is a good idea to invite the Spirit with which you are most comfortable and familiar. However, if no one wishes to come, do not force it. Allow it to happen and allow it not to happen. Do not cajole the Spirits.

The more you structure it, the more it helps if you have difficulty going into trance or the more it helps if you have difficulty knowing and understanding what trance is. To structure it gets your awareness used to the idea that when it happens, it will happen at this time and in this way, and I am available for it then and I am not available for it other times. It helps you distinguish between you and Spirit.

One thing is also important for you to know, but is not a rule. You are not the Spirit that comes through. The Spirit that comes through is not you. I say that because it is important to realize that we do not want to become you and live your lives through your bodies for you.

That is not us. We are not asking of you to give up your bodies to let us have one so we can function in the world. Let that be stated clearly here and now. We do not want to live in your bodies living in the world for you. You, while you have a body, do not need to be living with us in our dimension, letting some Spirit take over your body so you can let it walk in and do business here. That is a bunch of utter nonsense.

Let me put it like this. No higher Spirit needs to live in your body to do what it needs to do. There may be an agreement arranged between you and some other Spirit. There may be an agreement arranged between you and some other extraterrestrial if you wish. However, there is no such thing as a higher Spirit that says, very well, if you really wish to come here, come and I will do the business in the world that I need to do. That is not how entities such as you get into higher spirit. To get into higher spirit is a frame of consciousness. It is a state of mind. It is a state of being. Not being able to cope with your existence is not the way to get into higher spirit. Mastery in your existence is the way to be embraced by higher spirit. It is not issued because you have had enough, so to speak. You embrace your higher consciousness when you embrace higher consciousness, by becoming an empowered divine source. This other business about walk-ins is a bunch of utter nonsense.

Let me make this clear, the usurping, if it is not by conscious agreement, is always by a defeated powerless person who thinks it is toward their evolutionary advantage, perhaps, to allow it to happen in that way. That is a false path and it is misguided. It has nothing to do with your enlightened state of consciousness. It is an error. It is not a way to advance. It is something that later will need to be unraveled.

It is important that as you begin to let Spirit move through you that you save all of your judgments about what is going on for after you are out of trance. If a judgment comes about yourself or about others while you are in trance, you might observe it, but do not please, unless you are certain you want to, stop the process by holding onto that question. Instead, let what happens happen for the time it is happening and judge it later, for you may find that what happens while it is happening will answer the questions you have.

What we are about to do is that I am going to do a gentle induction. When you are channeling for yourself or for others, it is always easier to channel with other people there than by yourself because the other people will pull through the Spirit. We sometimes need an anchor to help pull us through, so it helps to have a person or persons around who are serving as an anchor to pull through. It helps if that person needs or wishes to be in touch with some sort of higher insight or understanding. That makes it easier for us to come through.

When you are going under for yourself, what you may wish to do is tell your body to relax, center yourself in the pit of your stomach the way we have described, regulate your breath by breathing loudly enough for you to hear yourself breathing for a while and make an inner invitation for Spirit to come.

What we are about to do is to channel. This can happen in any of several ways that I would like you to know and be aware of so that you can let go to the level of comfort to which you feel impressed to let go. I am going to guide you in an instantaneous getting in touch.

What is most important is to relax the anal sphincter muscle, because in trying to relax that, in letting that open, instantly you will feel your body going into relaxation. One of the things you may need to do before you channel is to eliminate from your body. It makes it easier to relax.

You are going to go into the center. You are going to invite your doorkeeper to be present here with you, and you are going to do either one of three things based upon that you are impressed to do this. You are going to let in three levels of intensity, any or all. It may go back and forth between the three, the Guide or the doorkeeper being given voice, the doorkeeper telling you and you relaying it or your third level, impressions and saying, I feel, I think, it seems or I am impressed to say. These are the three levels, direct, relay and impression. It may come in any or all of these ways. You as the channel may find yourself having an experience of learning with the process as you go back and forth.

Letting go does not mean getting out of the way in terms of you do not affect the message. That is balderdash. You must affect the message. There is no way we can come through you unless you affect the message. We trust that you will affect the message perfectly and we trust ourselves. We like you. We like how you affect the message. We like playing on different instruments. We get different music out of different instruments.

Do not try to go through this thing such as, well, I do not know if I am enough removed. We do not need you to be removed. We just need you to let us move with you. If you are going to get more removed, then we will get you removed. At the times we get you removed, you will know you have been removed. If you are not removed, do not be busy trying to remove yourself. Just let us work with you. That is a part of the experience.

Do not try to fall asleep. Do not try to do anything except center yourself and invite Spirit, and then be a medium. If you want to practice deep trance medium, then get somebody who has the patience to sit with you, after you set it up, and fall asleep with him or her there. When you wake up, then Spirit will come through.

Let us just begin. If first, you will just do a great stretch and a sigh and then another. Find a comfortable position and get cozy. If you need to wrap a blanket around you, do so. Get cozy like a little baby, comfortable, loose and gentle. Let yourself breathe. Find your center, below the navel and in. Become aware of that center. Let your center begin to get gentle, your body gentle. Become aware of the shift of the gentleness. Become aware of your presence. Affirm only that which is of the highest and that which you are willing to allow can happen and only that which you are willing to allow and only that which is of the highest and at all times that is true. Invite your doorkeeper to be present with you and become aware of your doorkeeper. Make a bond with the doorkeeper. Say hello, exchange greetings, love and affection. Let the doorkeeper comfort you a bit.

I want you now to invite your Spirit or Spirit friends collected around you to speak of a particular subject relating to your health. After you speak your reply, you can write down the answer or as you get the reply, you can speak it into a tape recorder. When you are complete, thank your doorkeeper and close.

Merlin

In your awareness, there are many frequencies, many bands much like radio stations. These bands carry a transmission into which your minds are very easily able to tap. All people tap into these frequencies from time to time. In fact, it is so completely normal that most people consider all frequencies that pass through their mind their own. For all intent and purpose, that is in fact your mind. You do not possess it, but you have access to it. These frequencies are not really you. You may identify with them because they are so easily accessible. Because of your continual awareness of those frequencies you ordinarily access through your mind, it may indeed seem like you. Nevertheless, you are not so much the mind as you are the one who perceives that which is going on in the mind.

In the mind there is a great deal that is useful to you and a great deal that is not useful to you. The higher frequencies represent those frequencies that are more useful to you. Amidst what we term higher frequencies, are those of us who refer to ourselves as your Guides. Many times, in an effort to reassure yourself that you are in touch with us, you like to separate yourself from those elements of consciousness in the hope that you might be able clearly to identify, through an awareness of separateness, yourself from others and yourself from us.

We have access to your points of awareness, even as you have access to our points of awareness in those frequencies. We are not those frequencies any more than you are those frequencies. We are simply those who broadcast through those frequencies, even as you access and broadcast yourself into those frequencies.

I am asking you just to accept this as a general explanation. There are various ways to test and develop your understanding of these things and we will get to that.

Naturally, there are certain types of energy that can broadcast at certain levels and certain kinds of energy that cannot broadcast at certain levels. We find some level to broadcast to you that you can receive at a point we think might be useful, whether or not you can identify it as separate from yourself. In fact, it really is not so important at any juncture to distinguish between who is broadcasting, you or your Guides. What is more important is to understand what is useful and what is not useful, what represents a higher frequency and what represents a lower frequency, that which is helpful and that which is less helpful or not helpful.

Since it is very difficult for you to discriminate between what is useful to you and what is not useful to you in every instance being that your scope of all that is broadcasting may be narrower than ours, when you wish to do this work we call channeling, you are provided with Spirit teachers who serve as doorkeepers. We sit at the door, as it were, of these access points, allowing you to go to only those more useful or helpful places and helping broadcasts to come to you, which presumably are only the more useful kinds of consciousness to which you are available.

The more that you make yourself available as a channel, the more tuned your instrument becomes and the more that we begin to be able to play you affectively. At first, having not been able to broadcast through you, but only broadcast to you in such ways as we have previously found useful without you knowing it is us, to that point it is not really channeling. That is just your openness, to that extent that you are open. It is our ability to connect with you and your openness to us.

Channeling is quite another phenomenon. Channeling involves your deepening your state of trance and becoming more available for us to play your instrument and for you to accept our play upon your instrument. You can determine to what degree you wish to allow this to happen. The thing that enables you to do it well is whatever natural aptitude you have and whatever practice you are available to allow us to work with you toward.

In the process of channeling, deepening of your trance and so forth, you will become more and more available to the higher realms to which we have access. Perhaps not to that extent yet that we have access to those higher realms, but the more we become familiar with you and the more you become familiar with us, we create a kind of magnetic effect toward each other. That is, you will take on more and more qualities of higher consciousness, which we represent, and as we come through, we may even take on more and more qualities of you in order that we can better use your instrument.

One of the better of qualities, for example, is your natural human qualities. Humanity is a memory in a part of your being, a memory that is not always useful where we are, but it is very useful where you are. So in order to communicate through you into the world, we must recall those human features that make us able to be understood not only by you, but also presumably by others whom you wish to understand. As we come through you, we will find those affects of yours, such things as your languaging and the things you have learned and studied, all of the capabilities you have and that you allow us to access, and we will adapt, if it is useful to us, and we will expand upon it.

As you open to us, as you get use to us and we get used to you, you may not easily be able to identify a Spirit presence apart from yourself because we will use those elements of yourself with which you are already familiar. As you loosen up, you will become more and more available to us and you will be surprised, if you are conscious, at just what we are able to do through you, if you are willing to let it happen.

With certain aspects of channeling there are ways you can clearly distinguish that we are separate from you. However, it is important to spend less time trying to determine what is us and what is you and more time trying to develop your ability to allow us to work with you and allow your trance to become comfortable. The fruit of that objective will reveal to you later the quality and ability of the Spirit that comes through you. That is, while it is happening you must try to stay away from your judgment about who or what it is, simply allow it and save your judgments and criticisms about yourself for afterward.

We are going to be working at first with entities we call Spirit Guides. However, there is also consciousness worth channeling that is not in the form of a Guide, but simply higher insight, higher mind, useful to someone who is anchoring for the channel on the other side. The anchor is the one who is outside of the body that is pulling that Spirit through. It does not have to be a Guide that brings through that energy. You may simply tap into that. That is channeling as well.

You are not always channeling an entity. Sometimes you are channeling simply higher consciousness, higher mind. Very creative people have access to this higher mind. No one owns it. It is simply there in the Monad and you borrow it. You utilize it. Those who utilize these venues a great deal often are called very creative people. Some of them think it is they and it might as well be them. It does not matter whether you think you own it or not. It is what it is. Most very creative people are oftentimes quite surprised what they are able to access. You will find that actors, writers, musicians, poets, even a brilliant creative scientist will sometimes be quite amazed at the tracks they find themselves unfolding when they enter into a deep enough trance, a deep enough focus that takes them along a certain track.

Each person has access to different sorts of frequencies, and you may not know what your best form of channeling is. Some may find out that what they channel best is healing energy with no words. Some might bring through music. Others might bring through art. Others might bring through who knows what.

You must see what you channel. We are going to aim for that which is the most useful. Whatever is near that which is the most useful will also come through you as a channel.

We are open to using whatever in the Monad is useful. We are not particularly keen on holding our own form of identity that you have come to know, for example, through Mataare. Although we think Mataare is an excellent channel, he cannot possibly channel all that I wish to express because that which I wish to express is far more expansive than what can get through the venues in Mataare's consciousness so I use many different mediums. That which I bring through is not the Merlin that existed two thousand years ago or fourteen hundred years ago, or seven hundred years ago. It is not any of those Merlins alone. It is all that I have become and all to which I have access, so it becomes very useful to me to have different mediums.

When I come to a channeler, I will bring to that channeler anything they are open to that is useful for them as well on their journey. I am not interested in them being only able to access the 'me' that they have known through Mataare. I am interested in opening their door to what is useful to them in their spiritual journey and to those for whom they intend to channel.

This is one reason you must let go a little bit with your own process and worry less about whether you are making it up or not and give yourself a little space, a little poetic license for your channeling to refine. Of course, your doorkeeper helps this and you developing your own psychic ability and developing your trance state helps it.

When you channel and you are not in whatever represents a deeper trance state for you, you are more likely to be channeling your own access points in the universe through your own consciousness. When you enter into a trance state of a deepened meditative state where you have shut down your outer senses to a degree for allowing your consciousness to accumulate other energies and broadcast it undisturbed by your outer sensory stimulation, the deeper your trance can become.

There has to be some disturbance by your sensory stimulation if you are channeling for another because you want to have some awareness of others and you want us to have some awareness of others through you. It is rare when channels go unconscious entirely. Although many channels have at first a desire to be completely unaware of what comes through them, you must be aware that being unaware of what comes through you has nothing to do with the quality of your channeling. You can be completely aware of what comes through you when you channel and be an excellent channel, channeling the highest of information or you can be completely unaware of what comes through you and channel absolute gibberish, meaninglessness. Your level of awareness of what comes through you has very, very little, almost nothing to do with your quality of channeling. The deepened trance has nothing to do with sleep or waking. It has more to do with your accessibility, the willingness to allow the process to evolve itself in its own way through you, given your natural propensity and openness and your willingness to grow. All of those things will develop.

We are going to do an exercise that will help you isolate what is psychic information from what is more imagined information. When it comes to being psychic, this is useful. When it comes to channeling, it is less important. If you are trying to be, for example, a remote viewer, that is you try to develop a scientific skill of remote viewing accurately in three dimensions, then it is very important to know what you are prefabricating, what you are fabricating and what you are actually seeing. When you are channeling, it is a different story because we may send you messages that you must confabulate in order to express it.

In other words, we may send you images and statements that you do not understand completely, but then when put together, the one on the receiving end understands and you come to understand once it is all out. Really, a confabulation of many images leads to a certain understanding. When channeling, you do not have to understand what is coming through. What comes through has to be understandable to the one who is on the other end. It does not have to be understandable to the channel. That is part of the meaning of getting out of the way.

If the channel is trying to understand everything, they are interfering with the process. The channel does not need to understand everything in order to let it come through. The more that a being is able to let it come through, the better channel they can be. If their psychic ability is also honed, then the more useful the imagery we can pass psychically.

You are able to channel for yourself. One of the best ways to do it is through channeled writings. The problem of channeling for yourself is it is very difficult to get channeled or psychic information when you are asking a question about something in which you have heavy investment regarding the outcome. For example, if you really need to win the lottery and you really want to win the lottery, you are desperate to win the lottery, that is investment in the outcome and that investment narrows your openness. It does not focus your openness. It narrows your openness.

If you are an excellent psychic, the narrowed focus is excellent if you are trying to view remotely a number that will appear in the future. However, if you are not a good remote viewer or do not have highly developed psychic skills, then it does not serve you to narrow your focus. It serves you to open your focus. Therefore, when you are very invested in an outcome, your focus becomes very narrow and that will close you off to the answer more times than not.

The way that it is most useful to channel is to have someone else sit for you, you go into a trance state and he or she asks you questions. You simply let it come through you. Having an anchor is absolutely the best way to have somebody pull Spirit through you. Another good way is writing.

Merlin

When you open your doors to channeling, if you are interested in the information that comes through you, you are likely to hold on to some of it or are likely to restrict some of it based upon your ability to identify with it or allow it. Your ability to channel broadens the more that you are willing to cultivate a trusting relationship with yourself and with a Spirit Guide or Spirit Guides with which you have a connection. This relationship develops over time with your practice of channeling because the nature of your experience, not only while you are channeling, but in the course of your life resulting from the fact that you have channeled, will cultivate an increasing working relationship, friendliness and openness to this particular phenomena.

One can access many planes of consciousness while channeling. For example, there is your own expanded awareness, what we might term your higher self. The higher self is not an individuate entity so much as one might think it is because the higher self needs your physiological individuation in order for it to be individual. The higher self, which functions in connection with a human body here upon the earth, requires a human body in order to be individuated. It may require several human bodies to be individuated adequately.

Therefore, your higher self may be in touch with several or even vast numbers of individuations that for you are like twin souls. Twin souls not in the sense of relationship or soul mates per se, but twin souls as though your physical bodies have been birthed by the same, let us call it, mother spirit at relatively the same time so you are as much as twins.

You may or may not be the same as your twin. In fact, very often twin souls, although they may have a great deal in harmony and an affinity with each other in terms of their character, when twin souls of this type come together, they tend not to make good romantic oriented relationships because twin souls need to be individuated separately in the first place in order to exist. If you were to come together with a twin, you would likely have similar kinds of challenges and conflicts as that would have caused your souls to split into two different bodies. Therefore, twin souls are not necessarily the best partners in relationships, twin souls in the way that I am speaking of them.

Naturally, in much of your metaphysical lore twin souls are thought of as perfectly matched romantic partners. However, I am not speaking of your metaphysical lore. I am speaking of twins in the truer sense of the word. That means entities that have individuated as human beings from the same mother or father spirit, so to speak, a larger consciousness that represents the collective and that collective is connected itself to a broader consciousness still.

The way that a being channels is to first access the more expanded self. Through the expanded self, all of your other Guides or other Spirit entities make contact, so that there are elements of your expanded self in any entity that you would channel. Therefore, there is no such thing as a pure channel, as it were. The Merlin that speaks now is not the Merlin I truly am, but rather a sliver of the Merlin that I represent that Mataare is able to channel. That is one reason I prefer to work through many channels. Each channel is like a different instrument on which I can play different music. You must consider yourselves, if you open to the channeling of Spirit Guides, that you are an instrument that any higher entity welcomed may play their particular music through you.

When you channel, it is not necessary that that which comes through you be as highly personified as, for example, that that comes through Mataare. You may get in touch with different kinds of comfort levels with the particular entities that come near or come through you. In fact, some may find themselves more comfortable to allow themselves to channel other entities if they were once or twice removed from the entity. By that I mean some channels will say when they are in touch with Spirit I am inspired to say or Spirit is saying or my Guides are showing me or I feel or I sense or I am given to see or they are showing me or I am feeling.

For many people, particularly for those who are opening to channel, prefacing what you are about to say with any one of those statements helps you give verbalization to what the Spirit is trying to say. Just as a moving vehicle is easier to turn in one direction or another, a speaking channel is easier to get something out of than one waiting for Spirit to actually motor your throat or your tongue and put words into your head. You may not get moving so much like that. It would be easier to channel if you utilize that which allows you to tap into the expansive or higher self. It is like a third person description of what is going on in the experience of the medium. You will shape it and correct it and you will feel different notions and inspirations.

You need to understand some things about the Spirit world. The Spirit world is very vast. It is infinite, and yet since you are human beings, it is easiest to access other human beings not because you may have a preference to channel human beings necessarily, but because you are a human being. That means you are the equivalent to many more human beings, much more than you are an equivalent to higher entities that may seek expression in this plane. Higher entities that may seek expression in this plane, you must understand, do not need a channel in order to communicate because we are perfectly happy communicating with you on levels of awareness that do not require you to know with what you are in communication. That way you do not necessarily become dependent on us, so to speak. You become more likely to rely on your own more expansive consciousness and more expanded higher awareness not knowing that such as we come into your higher awareness. Just because higher entities exist does not mean they may wish to speak through you or even to you.

If you give the higher entity reason to speak through you, such as your dedication or service or a wish to be helpful to someone else or yourself, a higher entity given to the sort of awareness you seek to access will always come to you. If the information you seek is of no interest to higher entities, you may not get a higher entity to address such a matter. It is much more likely that if you are open to one who can see more from a higher or more refined dimension, you will get another human being who has a greater access to things human than perhaps you have. Therefore, it may be more useful to you to get other human beings than certain higher entities.

For example, if you are looking for the special blue necklace, you may not get Philos to respond to you. You might get another Guide, an Indian Guide perhaps, who may be helpful to you in the physical plane who comes and says to you here is this. You may get your grandmother or a long lost great uncle or you may get no one, for example. Therefore, if you are interested in getting in touch with higher entities, you need to seek higher sorts of information.

It is good to start with a high intention. When you are first channeling, rather than to try to have some specific kind of information you are trying to get in touch with that you deem is higher information, you can let higher Spirit determine what higher information is if you do not target any specific information that you believe to be higher.

Your own higher awareness can target clairvoyantly specific information from the ethers that is also available to you if you are psychic or if you wish to cultivate your psychic ability. However, when we speak of channeling entities, you do not want to force or conjure entities to come that may not necessarily wish to respond. In other words, you cannot demand, Merlin, Merlin, Merlin, I only want Merlin to talk to me about the seventh plane of violet on the sixth dimension, or something like that. You cannot demand a Spirit you prefer to come and address you on a particular subject if that Spirit may not wish to do so.

You can request such a Spirit to come, but you do not want to get into conjuring or trying to make something happen. You do not need to worry about conjuring or demanding if you take a certain few steps we will share with you. Then you will not have to worry so much about whether you are conjuring.

When you work with Spirit, intention is everything. That is, if you treat Spirit and the process with respect, with love and with reverence, then you will attract respectful, reverent and loving Spirits. If you treat it like a joke, you will attract joking Spirits. If you do not take it seriously, you can attract less serious Spirits. If your approach is cynical and negative, you will attract cynical, negative, even malicious Spirits. If you approach it like a game, you will attract gaming Spirits.

It is important to set a higher intention and higher means a respectful, loving, reverent aura when you address Spirit and only that which is respectful, reverent and loving will present. That is the whole of attracting higher Spirit right there. No other thing can occur, but I will give you some other things that will also help you to attract only the right kind of Spirit.

One important thing to understand is that there are planes of consciousness closest to your planes that are easiest to access and that are worlds just like your world. In other words, Spirits of the departed may come and many of them will have jobs, relationships, families in the other plane. If you speak to them of death, they may not know what you are talking about, even if it is your dead relative, if they are in a certain plane. You may speak to some who are in a higher place in the hereafter and you may ask them was it difficult for you when you died? The Spirit may respond to you I am not dead. I am alive.

You must understand there is no death and what you may think about an afterlife may not be exactly what the afterlife is. Some places may be like it and some places are very different. There may be, for example, a Spirit present itself to you who knows you by a different name. The Spirit may say I am not dead. You are just dreaming or I am dreaming.

Consider for a moment where you are. How do you know that you are not the dead ones and they are the ones that are alive? You might ask how it was for them at the time of death. They will say excuse me, you are the one who passed away some fifty-five years ago, and you may be forty. You may be contacting a Spirit entity who is in fact in a place like yours, but who may be clearer than you are about what is really going on.

One reason it is important to work through your Spirit Guides and to have some connection with a friend on the other side is so that you do not wind up very confused. It is very important to understand that as a channel all manner of peculiar things might occur. That does not mean you are making it up. Everything you can imagine and then some exists, but what you want to do is orient yourself with a higher intention relative to something important for you here in this plane. That is something that is helpful to yourself or someone else in some way, setting the higher intention by being of service. It is as simple as that. You will not get into any trouble and that is how to safely channel.

It is some people's work to help certain caught souls move on. Therefore, not everybody channels or gets in touch with Spirit Guides. Some souls of the dearly departed may be in some dimension in which they do not want to be. They are stuck there because they need to deliver a message to someone here on this side. They find an available medium and spend time around that medium trying to get that medium to get that message to the one they need to get it. That is the service of some people. It is some people's service to be musicians or artists or writers or movie producers or director. You do not know what shape your availability to Spirit may take, but you can rest assured that your channeling will always occur if you set the intention to channel and you set the intention to have higher Spirit come through.

One way is to set the intention for a particular time that you intend to channel and to practice your channeling regularly at that time. One thing you may wish to do is to ask your gatekeeper, are there any other of the higher entities your gatekeeper feels comfortable to introduce to you. Your gatekeeper may bring another entity into your awareness.

The purpose of your gatekeeper is to regulate the Spirits with whom you are comfortable. That way you might expand, if you wish, the entities that communicate. You might even want to ask if anyone else is there. If there is, ask if they would care to introduce themselves. After a certain time close the door and close it down.

I would like to show you exactly how to invoke your Spiritual Guides to come to you and through you and I would like to do it here with you and I would like you to prepare to channel. If you would, have at hand a tape recorder.

One of the most important things when you intend to channel your Spirit Guides is to have a comfortable warm environment that is given to trance like states. For example, it is good that you let your consciousness go to alpha and beta. That is, to have dim lighting and if you like, an incensed room. If incense makes you choke, then of course do not have it. Have candles because some Spirit entities may wish to come through and open their eyes. If they do, it is good to have at least some lighting in the room. It is also good to have an ambience of gentleness and quiet.

After you have that, then it is helpful if you do an invocation. An invocation is a prayer you make up that invites the Spirit to come and sets a high intention. I want to pass on a prayer to you passed on to Mataare that is a prayer of protection. That is the chief way you stay out of trouble with your channeling. Say this prayer aloud or to yourself. If there are people that you do not know that you are channeling for, say it aloud. This is a prayer of protection extracted from the Kabala.

Holy art thou Lord of the universe. Holy art thou which nature hath not formed. Holy art thou the vast and the mighty one, Lord of the darkness and of the light. Oh Adonai, Elohim, Tetragrammaton, Allah, Brahma, El, Yahweh, Yehovah, Muter, Mut, Quan Yin be with us. Amen. Selah.

These are some names of some of the deities according to some different cultures and languages, the Father and Mother God.

We are going to do some intoning of the breath or the breath syllables, A, E, I, O, U. A, E, I, O, U, which represent the unspeakable name of God because they are vowel sounds, no lips required and they come from the breath. When intoned collectively, it sounds very much like Yahweh.

You can put this all on your recording. You can continue to go until you feel to stop. Once you stop, you may begin to feel continuing utterances and movements. If your voice goes away from A, E, I, O, U, it is all right because you may end up singing a song that is channeled. You may end up talking. You may end up feeling a little giddy or breathy or feel movement. You are going to set the intention to hear from, through your own higher consciousness, your higher Spirit Guides. You are going to see if you can get in touch with any of your higher Guides. That is the intention.

You are going to intone for a few moments, and then you are going to channel. I want you to let your body be flexible and move. You are not going to make yourself stiff. You are setting the intention to have your higher Guides come. You are going to ask your higher Guides for a message for you, an important message for you, and you are going to accept whatever comes. After that, you are going to ask if there is anything else.

You are going to do the invocation. You are going to say the prayer for protection. You are going to intone, and then invite the presence to come and move you in any way it wishes, having the intention to get a message that for you is important. Then ask if there is anything else. Make sure to have your tape recorders on the entire time.

Begin intoning now, and then I will ask some questions.

Who is here? Speak the name, if there is one. Thank you. Why are you here? Who are you to your medium? Have you a message for your medium? If so, what is it? Thank you. Are you comfortable with your medium? Is your medium comfortable with you? What can be done that you are more comfortable with each other? Thank you, Spirit. Spirit, do you sense any message from relatives? If you do, do you sense that message is from a man or a woman, a relative or boy or girl? Do you have a sense Spirit as to whom this message may belong? What is the message? Is there a name that comes to mind Spirit or a prominent letter in the name or a symbol or sign given you from the relative? Thank you, Spirit. Is there anything else Spirit before we let you go? Thank you, Spirit. Good-bye now Spirit. Is there anyone else of good intent who wishes to make itself known to the medium if the medium would welcome?

Now go on, as you will channeler, for another few moments and allow the Spirit to communicate if it wishes and if you are comfortable. I will be silent now for a few moments.

All right, mediums thank the Spirits and close the channel by thanking them and saying good-bye. As you are ready, take a deep breath, move around a bit, and come back. Thank the Spirit and say good-bye. Thank your doorkeeper for helping you.

Sun Bear

With the Great Spirit of the Universe, the Great Spirit that is beyond the universe, the Great Spirit that is the core of the multi-verse, there is no relationship. At its finest, a being is at one with the Great Spirit. There is no relationship because there are not two to relate. There is one. With the Great Spirit, it is like the spirit of love, the spirit of power, the spirit without limitation. This is infinity.

With your Spirit Guides, it is different. You have relationships with your Spirit Guides. You are not supposed to be one with your Spirit Guides except in the same way you are one with each other. The way that you are one with your Spirit Guides is as if you are one with those whom you love. For example, if you have a parent whom you love or a child, a brother a sister, a lover, a wife, a husband, your love may bring you together in a way that is as though you are a part of each other. However, it is not one because the other one can go away. There is a sense of being together and sometimes of being apart. Sometimes there is a sense of being together with one you love, even when you are apart, but there is still the other.

With the Spirit of the Universe, it is not like that. You are at one. When you are at one, you are not aware of the Spirit of the Universe in the same way you now are aware of the Spirit of the Universe. Right now, in this moment as I speak, you have some awareness of the Great Spirit, right now, but because you are listening to me and learning, your conscious self is present and it has come forward so that you can exist as self and take in what you can. Therefore, when you choose to be aware of, think about or feel the Spirit of the Universe, you may have some ongoing rapport of which you are aware, but it is not the same as being one because you can still think of the Spirit of the Universe. You can be aware of other. When you are one with the Spirit of the Universe, there is no awareness of other.

The reason I am saying all of this is that you are learning how to be mediums. There are those who get into trouble over time with channeling or mediumship. There are certain dangers and if one stays close to doing it the right way, one will not get into trouble with mediumship and with channeling.

One of the most dangerous things that opens the door to trouble with your channeling is thinking you are in fact the Spirit that comes through you. One thinks of oneself as being the Spirit that comes through them in two ways. The first way is the most common way. One does not think it is a Spirit, but thinks they are channeling themselves. That is the most common way. The kind of trouble one gets into with that is one never lets it happen because they think it is they.

Then there is the other kind of trouble. One starts to have a positive outcome when one starts to channel. One enjoys one's own expanded awareness to the point one feels something like more power, more knowing, more ability, and there is nothing wrong with that, and perhaps even that the Spirit that comes through you is really you. Therefore, over time one says I do not need that Spirit to come through. It is really me. I am that which comes through me. I am really Sun Bear. I am really that entity. I am all of the entities that come through me. One tries to take the credit for the Spirit that comes through them because they like either the power they feel or the response they get from other people. They try to transfer the love and adulation that may come toward the Spirit to themselves and move the Spirit out of it.

The kind of trouble one gets into from that is that one's ego becomes inflated and a power trip begins to occur. This kind of power trip is also in many other forms of spiritual work. Some clerics, gurus and teachers may also power trip. What I mean by power trip is that they begin to love the sense of the control and the need for the adulation such that they want more and more and more, stadiums filled, the whole world, things of this kind. Their personality begins to change and eventually they run into trouble along those lines.

The latter is in fact more dangerous. The first one is not as dangerous. What happens in the latter is that when a person begins to power trip and they are something like a channel, you have to remember like attracts like. If you are power tripping and enjoying your control over others, and it is all about what you want to get from others, what you want to take from others, then you are going to, if you are a channeler, run into the kinds of Spirits who want to also control and take from you. You begin to run into problems like conjuring. That means trying to make up a Spirit. By that I mean trying to demand that certain Spirits appear just because you think maybe they would be popular or they would like that or it would get you more attention. Then, rather than having a genuine Spirit entity come, you get a faker to come with other intentions. You get complimentary kinds of entities who love to take from you, as you would like to take from others. Then you run into certain problems.

The way to stay away from these problems is two things. One is you have to have a certain understanding about how we work with you. This is why you have a control Spirit who takes care of the things you cannot think of, a control Spirit or a doorkeeper. That is a Spirit you trust and a Spirit that knows you, gets to learn more and more about you, and takes care of the other Spirits. It makes sure those Spirits that come in can come in as good as possible and also makes sure those Spirits get out, whether those Spirits are good Spirits or they are maladjusted Spirits because there are those as well. Sometimes there is purpose in bringing through maladjusted Spirits, but not for everyone. For some people, it is their work. For example, there may be a very discontented soul who is incomplete when they die and they need to give one final message to somebody before they leave and can move on. This is also the work of some mediums. If that medium has a control Spirit or a doorkeeper, there is no problem whatsoever. That is the first way to be safe, to have a doorkeeper.

The second way is to understand a little more about the construction of Spirit. Essentially, when you die, all that is left of you is consciousness. That consciousness may be more or less well integrated. Your consciousness is formed of many particles like molecules or atoms banded together to form dimensions of self, aspects of self. That is the reason you can have many kinds of thoughts along different lines and sometimes feel divided, all of that kind of thing. Depending upon what is the integration of that consciousness, either more or less, that consciousness can survive the death of the body. However, not all consciousness that survives the death of the body survives forever in any form recognizable to you.

Let us say someone dies and she is fairly well integrated when she died. She will change form when she dies, will have a diminution, a lessening of her particles of consciousness. The particles of consciousness closely associated with the physical world she is leaving behind will go away, immediately or gradually, usually within about three days or so after she dies. That is soul substance you might say, general etheric substance that is released into the ambient nature of the universe, the God nature of the universe and goes off and collects with other particles of consciousness that are also there and becomes a part of what will eventually be other beings.

When the person comes back, she will recognize a familiarity in the other beings into which her soul particles went. She will feel, if she comes back here, an affinity of some kind, a kinship with those souls. Eventually, if those soul particles incarnate when she incarnates again, they will run into her because remember, they are parts of her and she is part of them. They will have certain things in common and their lives will eventually wend their way toward each other for some amount of time, even if it is for a brief meeting, and they will feel a kinship.

Other particles of that person will not remain integrated with her. There are the particles of consciousness that no longer have any use returning to the earth, if she is to return to the earth. They may have completed. The particles that have become complete will go on to a larger collective, perhaps elements of her so-called higher self or other dimensions of God consciousness that have individuated as Spirit Guides. If she incarnates again in the world, when her Spirit Guides come around her in some form, she will feel an affinity, a sense of completeness as if her Guides understand her at some level that makes her feel completed. They are really their own individuated beings, which hold aspects of her completed self as a part of them.

There are also other particles that are simply ambient and not a part of any embodiment or any individuation at all. The integrated person that remains no longer needs them or no longer attracts those particles because those particles that have no place in her and no place in any other integrated being only existed to help bind her in the form she previously was. Since she is no longer to be bound in that form, she no longer has the need for that same binding. That binding goes off let us say.

Let us say that person does not want to come back, but she is attracted to come back because there are other particles of her consciousness remaining in the world that have need for teaching. Remember, any relationship that person may have had when she was here before included aspects of herself that split off, and she needs to learn to integrate with all aspect of herself, no matter in what form. Ultimately, the person must learn to be in a satisfactory harmony with essentially everyone in existence, especially those where she has more affiliated parts. If she could think consciously with all of those split off parts, she may not want actually to return to the earth, but she may be compelled to return to the earth because of the associated karmas with elements of her previous journey left incomplete.

Let us say this person has done this one thousand times as a human. By the time they have split off, mixed, come back with parts here and there, who is that person? She is part of so many beings and so many beings are a part of her that she has become part of a great deal. In fact, this may set up her sense of compassion and connectedness as an older soul here in the world with other being in the world she does not even know. She feels a sense of a part of more and therefore a need to be responsive to that sense of connectedness not only in the world, but also to all of the beings she is a part of who are not in the world.

So that when a Spirit Guide, and this is where we come to you and your channeling, comes to her through a channeler, she says I feel something. I do not care that this does not make perfect sense. I do not care that I am sitting in front of a guy who may be acting and he is doing all of this. He speaks in a funny voice and all of these things. Sometimes he says general things and sometimes he says specific things. She sees past all of that. Why? It is because she is a part of that that is past all of that. Nobody could accept it that is not also a part of something coming through. There are also those people that do not feel the connection.

Once a person comes back here, after a thousand lifetimes, she is connected to a web of people she knows and does not know along with all of those attendant associations those other people may have who have parts in her and their experience over those thousand lifetimes. She also is connected to a web of Spirit she knows and does not know. Over time, she becomes familiar with more than she could ever imagine here on the earth, more life, more beauty, more power and more wisdom than she ever could have imagined or created for herself consciously. She is connected to a web of Spirit that extends so far out into existence and so far deep into existence that that poor little person, who is not really poor, has no comprehension here on earth of how far she goes into existence connected and interrelated.

When that person provides the service of bringing through Spirit for any reason, whether writing, art, music, channeling, healing or whatever it is, she is growing familiar with a comprehension of existence. That existence is so inexplicably vast that while that person is here on earth, she will be amazed with the magnitude and beauty of life, if she will only let it happen, if she will only open up. By the fact of that person opening to Spirit, if she can let go to something greater than the insecurities that at times may bind her, she will find that life has more to offer her than ever she could have created for herself if she controlled it. This goes true for all of you. At times, she will be able to get a vision of what exists for her that is greater than she could have imagined because she is connected to that which is greater than that which she could ever imagine. If she gets that vision, it will help her let go, if she chooses too, if she makes a decision to let go.

What are we? We are expanded beings who reveal the truth, which may or may not at times have something to do with fortune telling, which may or may not at times have something to do with teaching. Our purpose is to expand you to see the truth, to take you out of your frame of consciousness that limits you. Remember, the frame of consciousness that limits you is designed to keep you protected from what you do not want to or cannot relate to, which if you did relate to may tear you down, may take your integrated understanding as you know yourself and rip you apart, tear you down and cause you to decompensate. You may be so identified with a limited perspective, needing it to be something like that, not believing it is limited, that when it is in fact expanded you do not feel expanded at all. You feel broken down.

That is why we warn you about too much closeness with us. We tell you take breaks from us sometimes. When we come through you more and more, more and more begins to take place the more frequently exposed to expanded awareness until you become more and more like us, not us, more and more like us. We understand more and more about what you are here in this world and what others are here in this world. We take that on so others can identify with us.

Why would we do that? What is the purpose of individuation? Why would we individuate as Sun Bear when we exist as part of everything fully? There is a purpose in it that is helpful to others. When we understand your individuation at a more expanded level, we will take on more like you because you are more able to relate to the world and the world is more able to relate to you than the world is able to relate to what we really are, even though you may not always see us like that. We take on more of you so that you can be expanded.

That is why it is even possible to think you are we. This is not a matter of blame. When I say it is ego, I am not saying somebody gets a fat head. What I am saying is there is a reason people become misidentified and get into trouble. However, if you understand, you will not get into trouble.

When you get specific information, the more specific information you get, when it has to do with somebody's life, the more they have the power, if they are conscious, to change it or to make sure it happens. Sometimes it is our duty to point things out in such a way so that that person has a chance to claim the highest available reality, if they are conscious enough, if it is important enough to them. Sometimes people cannot see it and sometimes they do not. That is why some things do not come true.

Other times people see it, but do not want it so that it does not need to happen if they do not want it to happen because some things are a matter of destiny and some things are a matter of choice. Very, very few things are a matter of destiny. This is not a criticism. It is a description. When people from their small mindedness want a specific thing that is not available because it is not a part of their destiny, we cannot give it to them and neither are you be able to give it to them, and then it does not come.

If people from their small mindedness also luckily happen upon something that is a part of destiny, meaning an inalterable outcome, then we can answer it specifically. However, most of the time people do not want to know anything that is a part of destiny. They want to know about something that is a matter of choice or a matter of a series of choices that they must make or not make. We do not know all of the time what choices that person is going to make when they are away from us, when they are not in the expanded moment, when their ego may close them down and they may miss an opportunity. We do not come here to be fortunetellers, but we give fortunes sometimes to direct people where it is important. Sometimes we will pluck out of the air inalterable destiny things to tell people. This is to help guide them with a little bit of hope that they will consider this advice to achieve that. We also want them to believe in us sufficiently to hear our good council beyond the things toward which they are aimed.

I am telling you this because it helps you allow us to come through you with even what formerly may have sounded ridiculous, you will let it come through knowing that sometimes we see expanded things that do not make sense to you in the moment you are channeling. Nevertheless, you will let it happen because you will trust there is something good that we are trying to say.

Usually, if you let yourself go on channeling, we will explain it in a way you can come to understand it. The more we get to know you, the more we will help you to understand the things that come through you that you now do not understand and we will let more come through you. The more practice you have, you will allow more to come through you that is far beyond your comprehension.

You must not close us off to information you have in your own intellect just because you know it already, just because you have learned something already and you see we are about to say something you may have learned from this and that. You must not stop us from using who you are and what you know. Do not remove yourself in that way from the process. That is not what we mean by getting out of the way. We are not interested in producing what you may think in your small mindedness, we should be. We are interested in using everything available to us to express, using everything we can from you and everything we can from us.

Sun Bear

One of the great advantages to having your awareness expanded by Spirit is that your human life in the physical plane can be helped extraordinarily. It is very complimentary to also being able to meditate. However, you cannot use your spirituality to advance or promote yourself in the materialistic world. There is nothing wrong, do not get me wrong, with the materialistic world, but what that does is advances your persona, your ego. Specifically, what I mean is your human animal instinct toward survival creates a persona and that persona is often mistaken as self. The persona is that which forms the specific instincts for security, prestige or social connection with your peers and amongst your peers so that you can have a positioning that would help you better survive, ultimately that is your survival instinct, sex relation, another survival instinct and emotional security. Do not get me wrong, these instincts for survival are necessary for life, but they get way out of proportion in the average person who does not look for something greater than that and is not aware of how that interpenetrates every aspect of their thinking and emotions.

For example, some people think that love is the emotional feeling they have, which when they feel it they have the desire to live with each other, spend their life together, be with each other all the time. Love may be present there also and usually is, at least for a while. However, for the most part, all of that is just ego inflation. Let me explain what I mean by that. That is your survival instinct persona, all the parts that get the validation, your social instincts, sexual instincts, emotional needs for physical security, all of that expands. If there is any love there, of course the love expands your aura and also expands and inflates your persona like a balloon right along with it. So that when people get together, after a while the ego deflates and they are left to see if there is any real love there as they fight to negotiate their survival need conflicts. They may wonder where the love has gone. Love may be present there too, but only dominate if there is self-awareness, self-consciousness, meaning there is awareness of that which is beyond their survival instincts.

I want to make sure this is very clear about the difference between the self and ego and how the ego inflates, the ego being the persona, right along with the expansion of the spirit. So many times the love is lost behind the more dominant struggles of the ego. Why is this important? You must be aware of the price of ego and the danger of ego inflation when you use your spiritual gift to advance your materialistic and worldly motives.

So challenging is this that most teachers of the past would say do not do this at all. I am not saying it should not be done. I am saying in fact it should be done when you are ready and if you have the proper understanding. This is THE proper understanding. You do not have to believe me. You will just find out that this is true.

Your ancestors in the Spirit world love you in every plane and dimension where they exist, in the physical plane, known and unknown to you, but especially in the Spirit world. They want to see you successful as an extension of them. They want to believe that their lives here in this world, while they were here, carry on in some way, the immortality in some way is carried on through you. This is their way of seeing it.

In fact, it is just a lower instinctual level of seeing how they are connected to you and all things, but at a beginning level. They think that they are connected to you by blood and spirit, and they are. However, they actually are connected to you in a greater way. The lesser way of being aware of that is that you are a relative. The higher way of being aware of that is about all of the connectedness through soul aspects or soul parts. They want to help you just as we want to help you.

When you attune through something called channeling, you may also attune to relatives and relations that a part of their spiritual development and work is to help you be successful, help you succeed, help you have the life you want in this world.

You must be aware you cannot get lost in their help and forego that there is a greater spiritual awareness, a greater spiritual perspective you must hold because your relatives will be willing to help you sometimes right into the darkness. I do not mean the material world. I mean right into being lost among things that really do not matter so much on a higher plane, but seem to matter a great deal when you are here.

It is helpful to be aware what is useful for you and useful for them, and what is useful in a higher way to both of you because it teaches you about love. It teaches you about how to be connected to all your relations and not separated by what appears to be life and death, and that you walk in this world right now totally unseparated from all of your available relations. They are not cut off from you. You are not cut off from them. You live in the same world.

The delusion that you are separated is only supported by ignorance, which seems to permeate newer cultures like American society. In the old cultures of the world, particularly amongst our Native people, we always lived amongst our relatives, whether they were born or dead, alive, as you know it, or dead. We called this simply another land, as we called it most often to the west. It was a western world. We had our worldview constructed by a map, the same way you have your globe constructed by a map, but our map included a map of what you would call the Spirit world. Our relatives were just, let us call it, in another city. They were a part of our everyday life and real for us.

Because newer cultures tend not to have that in these days, particularly the descendents of all of the newcomers to this land who seem to be cut off from their roots, from their old people, they seem to lose their way in America. They do not realize they have lost their way, but when you see the American culture at large, what you see is that it lives for consumerism. That is the purpose, to consume as much as you possibly can and then try to give it to your children while teaching them it is good to consume as much as they possibly can consume with very few people being aware that the purpose is to give as much as you can. If everybody gave as much as they could, think how rich everyone would be in a myriad of ways. You could not even comprehend what would happen to your society. That is what happened in the Elohim society. It has created a very wealthy culture full of giving and love. Eventually that will happen here.

Your ancestors who want to help you are also in a world just as interconnected to higher and lower worlds as you are. I am talking about the ancestors who are not incarnated again much as you are currently incarnated, which means your dominant consciousness is in this world, so to speak, even though you have elements of your consciousness in other places.

When you become involved with the awareness of a Spirit world greater than the world you formerly knew, your consciousness, your awareness, your God self expands. That means the self that has a knowing that goes deep inside and hugely expansive apparently outside, becomes super aware to the point that many times there are a great number of people who will find you incomprehensible. Your awareness takes into consideration much that is simply unknown to the vast majority of people and you become like the wise person. You become like the integrated person, the wise and integrated person. Your point of view and your orientation for life take on its higher meaning.

Even though your ancestors will help you more with the expanded understanding of the physical world because they have even more expanded understanding of the physical world than you do, it will not need to lock into a materialistic focus. It will expand you on a spiritual level as well, including the proper use of the physical plane in balance with everything else here in this world.

Why is this discussion important? It is important to understand that to channel, usefully to access the expansive field, makes you the master that you are meant to be. It gives you a knowledge in life, a knowing in life closer not only to what you are meant to have as a spiritual being, but also closer to what, although it is microscopically closer, the Elohim also have. It is a step in the right direction.

Knowing that it is okay for you to permit yourself to receive information with more specificity, you can be more willing to allow us and yourself to bring forth things that, when you are conscious while you are channeling, you may not even know how or why you are saying what you are saying and you may be willing to let it come through you anyway.

Everybody gets into a little trouble now and then, but you will not get into any kind of big trouble if you know what you are doing with your channeling. You have to stay out of the bad neighborhoods. The way to stay out of the bad neighborhoods in psyche work, including channeling, is you have a higher intention. That is, if your intention is to be of service or to be helpful, that intention precludes and shifts all lesser abilities and knowings in alignment with being helpful. So that even your lack of, let us say character development, your lack of awareness, your lack of anything, is then used by Spirit for a better purpose.

Let us say you have a bad habit, for example, of blowing up at people, getting angrier than you want to be and later you say damn, I did it again. I lost it. I have to work on this part of myself. I do not like to be that kind of person. Then one day you are channeling and your Spirit who is coming through you loses it, starts to say, LISTEN! and says something. Then later you think oh, was that me, was that the Spirit Guide or what was that? I should not have done that. My Spirit should not have done that.

That is why you say the prayer. That is why you do the invocation. That is why you think of trying to be of help, to be of service. That sets a greater intention than you could know far into existence. Not that you are trying to justify any sort of lack of development on your own part, but you know we might have chosen you as our channel because now and then you can lose it and we can lose it through you in the instances where it is needed.

Nevertheless, if you are a self-aware, growing person, then you will review you own consciousness and your behavior and say you know Spirit, even though that happened and even though that may have been you, I know that there are higher reasons for this thing. I just want to also say help me in this particular area where I see that I do not always know that this is good. I know that I still need work in this area and please help me with it.

You do not have to be able all of the time clearly to know these things if you are using all of these things within a context as a tool for your own development or a tool for being of service because that is how the universe of help works. The moment you open up to say yes, I want to be a part of a universal good, then whatever level you are at in your development, Spirit greater than you rushes in like angels to protect and guide you and to make you the most wonderful expression of beauty that is available from you at the time. That will unfailingly occur. You never, ever, have to worry about whether it is right or wrong, or getting off track if you are also a person who reviews himself or herself and says I know where my character needs development. I am just going to keep working on it, not because you ever expect to perfect it, but because that is what a higher human being always does.

A higher human being will never be the perfected expression of character they may wish to be because you are not supposed to be that. You are like a diamond that is flawed in the right places at best, and that is what makes you exceptionally unique. Spirit uses the very things that are your flaws, when you are self-reviewing in the highest way.

We want to get you in the habit of being honest with yourself. You will not even have to worry about staying out of the bad neighborhoods because it is not that sort of thing. There are very few bad neighborhoods and you always know them. They are very powerful. That is why you always know them. The bad neighborhoods, they stink. They are not disguised. They are a blight. They smell too high heaven. They are not subtle in any way. I will tell you why.

You can never be fooled at the level where you are, if at all, for too long unless you are really trying to fool yourself, and you will try to fool yourself if you do not understand about instincts. If you do understand about instincts and you are confused about whether you are trying to give yourself what Mataare calls a con job, all you have to do is ask yourself what am I involved in. Does it have anything to do with sex? Does it have anything to do with emotional security? Does it have anything to do with my physical security? Does it have anything to do with prestige or my position in society? If it has anything to do with any of those things, then there is the possibility you are invested in a particular outcome in alignment with those things, which is not wrong, but then you are clear. You are clear right at the outset.

That is what we are talking about, clarity, no garbage, no befuddlement. If it is about sexual and emotional security or position or physical security, then you can say that is part of why I am here too, so let me see if I can bring some higher consciousness to this.

That is not what I am talking about as bad neighborhoods. Every human being must address that, even spiritually awakened human beings. There is no way to get around it as long as you have flesh on your bones and you have bones under your flesh. The bad neighborhoods and the foolers in Spirit come in very poor disguises, which you can see right through because they feel, stink, and smell bad. Why? It is because they do not like masquerading as good. They are proud of their so-called darkness. They are proud of their so-called evil. They think good does not work. They think the good or the bright side, the light, and I am not talking about the void, which is also dark, they think those like you are stupid, idiot fools when you could just be power mongers, power grabbers and users and self-centered. Those kinds of Spirits, you sniff them out in a second once you have had the kinds of teaching we are talking about here. In a minute, you sniff it out.

It does not mean they are bad people. Everyone has a little of that, a little narcissism, but you can tell it right away. They come in very poor disguises. You sniff it out right away. You can never really be lied to too much after you have done some of the work we have done here. What I am trying to say is if they wear one of their poor disguises, they rip it off pretty quick because they do not like it. Soon they will just come right out and say this is what I want. This is what I need to get. They just want to come right out with it.

Another way to get into a bad neighborhood is by trying to conjure, to force what you want out of the Spirit world because when you use psychic force you are going to attract psychically forceful entities. Certain elements of wizardry and magic utilize this. However, you must understand about wizardry and magic, about how to do it properly because a good wizard, a good magician knows how to use that very well. They know how to stay out of trouble with that.

Conjuring can get you into trouble because if you are manipulative and controlling and usury in nature and self-centered and you have no higher intention but that, yes, you can get into trouble. Usually, those kinds of people who go into those kinds of bad neighborhoods start out looking right away for the bad neighborhood. Okay, how can I make this world bend to my will? That is how you get in a bad neighborhood really quickly. It is not necessarily for a good purpose that one does this. Sometimes you want certain things to bend to your intention. What I am speaking of is those who get into trouble, they start right out looking for the most powerful way to absolutely get the world to do their bidding, to get Spirit to do their bidding, to get the universe to do their bidding.

Why is that so wrong? You must understand from the largest perspective, and we will break it down. People who demand the universe serve them miss the point that the universe is already supporting them. They totally miss it. They think they have to demand it, command it to get it to bend to their will.

What, the universe supporting me, you might say. Then why have I wanted this or that for so long and it has not happened if the universe is supporting me? You might miss that the universe is supporting you in certain areas that you feel something is missing.

However, in other ways you might be perfectly able to feel a sense of gratitude and fulfillment from other areas of life, even while in certain areas feeling like you really missed the boat on this and that. That is a normal sort of a way to feel.

Then there are those people who are like the victims of the universe. Victims are very interesting because victims can take the role of the perpetrator too. If one has been a victim for too long, they often turn around and say I will show you, and then they become the perpetrator. Well, I will show the whole world. Then they think I found myself now, and that is so wrong.

What I am saying is that if someone is already in the point of view that he or she has to get the universe to bend to their will, no matter how bright or dark they may appear to be in terms of their higher consciousness, they have missed that the universe is already supporting them. They are absolutely looking to dominate other forces against others, and right away the clashing of the wills of others. Eventually what they will do is seek more and more. It will never be enough. Why will it never be enough? It is because they are already missing the boat. They are already not having any gratitude. They are already miserable. They are already vain. They are already self-centered, negatively. They are already so narcissistic, so closed off to the greater reality that they are being supported and trying to expand that that they have given up on the view that the universe supports them and have taken the position that the universe is against them. That is the bottom line.

If you take the position that the universe is against you, God is against you, we are against you, it is dangerous. Do you know how dangerous that is? That means the more you absolutely believe that, all you can attract is more entities and people who believe and see things the same way. Eventually you will be a perpetrator or a victim of those other powers because you will be in the bad company you yourself have created with your negative thinking. You cannot afford to take that position. You will be in a bad neighborhood.

How do you stay out the bad neighborhood with regard to this, because everybody goes there sometimes? Everybody feels at some time or another like life is against him or her, God is against him or her and he or she is the worst. Everybody goes there. Do not spend too much time there because you will end up desperate. If you are desperate too long, you will be vulnerable, so do not spend too long there.

How do you get out of that? It is so simple. You must force yourself to find what you feel grateful for right now. Force yourself to look around. Even though things may be bad, you say something has to be good. You must be willing to see how the universe must still be supporting you in some way, even if it is one little itsy bitsy way. As long as you have that one little itsy bitsy gratitude, the Great Spirit experiences that as love and pays special attention to you.

Whoever told you that the Great Spirit is impartial must be speaking about the Monad, which is impartial if anything. The Great Spirit, the Spirit of Love, God, the Supreme, whatever name you want to give it, is decidedly partial to the grateful. If you want the help of the Great Spirit, you must find whatever it is that you feel grateful for because the Great Spirit experiences that as love and then gives attention and reward to the grateful.

That is why you can see blind people, for example, who are just happy as a lark. You will find some who are very angry, but why are some happy? They will start telling you life is so good. You will think what is wrong with this person. I would never like to be like that. People with no legs or no arms that are dying, you will see them so grateful for their lives. Why do they feel like that? They are in the middle of being rewarded by the Great Spirit because their gratitude is their acknowledgement of what? It is acknowledgement of the truth that the universe is supporting them rather than an acknowledgement of a great lie that the universe is against them.

How could the universe be against you if you exist? Everything had to be in creation to support your very existence or else you could not be here. A whole universe had to get here before you could exist. That is how much you are supported. That is the very reason why some people hate the universe, because they do exist, which is all backward. That is a condition of being desperate too long and the refusal to find what is good. When you take that rebellious attitude, and I have to warn you about it because it will occur, it is all right to shake your fists at the heavens sometimes. That is actually a good thing at times and I will not go into that now.

Eventually, you have to be willing to see the truth or all you will do is believe a lie. If you believe a lie that is fundamentally against the truth of the universe, at the foundation of what is against the truth of the universe, you are believing in the false path, which will bring you into great karmic troubles.

It is easy to stay out of bad neighborhoods. It stinks and the only time you go in there is when you have business there. Sometimes I go into bad neighborhoods in the Spirit world. Many people there need help. That is for a specific purpose and that is how you stay out of trouble. It stinks to high heaven. The other thing is you stay away from the fundamental lies, which always have to do with poor me. Nothing ever works. I must manipulate everything for it to work. Stay away from that. Instead, see where the universe supports you and expect it.

Ultimately, you are not supposed to believe in us. You are supposed to discover what is true. You are supposed to be able to know what is true for yourself. There is just one caveat. You cannot know absolutely in the same fashion that you may know certain other things absolutely. Once you know a certain amount, you will have to trust eventually. Remember, the greatest knowing that exists is not logical or linear fashions of knowing. You all know how limited knowing can be through linear fashions of knowing because linear fashions of knowing come with a prescription by definition that must be linear. If there are things missing in the linear logic, then how can you know? It defies the very meaning of linear.

You are also beings who can know in a different way than logical. The other way is called intuitive mind, except that outside of situations like this, you have had limited access to anything that helps you develop this intuitive knowing. That is, unless you are totally no good at things that have do with linear learning like school and things like that. Then you probably have a highly developed intuitive knowing because that is the only way you can be successful in life. If you do not have good logical knowing, you are going to cultivate other ways of coming to knowing, streets smarts in the psychic world you might say. If you are very developed in the other learning and successful that way, it is very unlikely, although it happens, that you will very much develop your intuitive knowing because you will be busy with the other way of knowing until such time as you feel limited by that other way of knowing.

Both kinds of ways are important, the linear or logical knowing and intuitive knowing. They compliment each other and they must be together. However, when it comes to the Spirit, the linear at certain points absolutely fails to convince you. It may lead you in the direction of knowing, but it fails to convince you absolutely and it makes very logical sense why. You are dealing with the infinite and you are always finding out something else. Because of that, always something you do not know evades you. Certainty escapes you because you are contending with infinity. When you are dealing with infinity, how do you have certainty?

At some point or another, you have to go over to one side or another. You have to make a choice if you wish to know. You make that choice when you are ready. Our duty is to bring you to that point where you are ready to make the choice, to give you tools, teachings, understanding and help that brings you to a point where you have enough to make a choice. When you make a choice, what is the choice? To believe? No. To trust. Why? Because trust is love and love contains the state of knowing. Intuition occurs in you to that extent there is conscious love in you.

Am I making a connection between love and intuition? Does that mean everybody who is intuitive has love in them? Yes. Does that mean that everybody who has love in them is intuitive? Yes. Why? Because love is God and God is love. When you have God in you, you become knowing the way God knows. If you were completely conscious of love, meaning no fears at all, then you will be completely knowing. It is very difficult to be totally knowing and embodied here in this plane at the same time, but many places exist where it is not difficult.

Every time you take a step in trust, you become more like God, more like love, more intuitive, and awareness pours into you at other levels than linear and logic and you get this knowing that you do not know how you know, but you just do. Of course, as we have said, there are many kinds of knowledge. There is knowledge that you know that you know. There is knowledge that you know that you do not know. You know that you do not know certain things. There is that kind of knowledge. There is the kind of knowledge that you do not know that you do not know.

When you enter into the intuitive, you get that knowledge that you did not know that you do not know, nor do you know how you got that knowledge, but you do, like God. Can that really be true? Absolutely. Why does it not work all of the time for everything you want to know if you are very intuitive? It is very simple. God is very efficient. You are very efficient. If you know that you need to know something, you will know it. If you know that you do not need to know something, you choose not to know it.

Maybe that sounds too convenient. Let me put it another way. You are a human being. You crowd your awareness with useless information. What is the purpose of it? There is useful awareness, useless awareness and harmful awareness. Why would you crowd your consciousness with either that which is harmful to you personally or useless to you personally in your journey? This efficiency opens you up to the good at the right time, in the perfect time, because that would be the perfectly intuitive thing to do, would it not.

What we are saying to you is pay attention to the other knowing, which is simultaneously there also because right there along with your uncertainty in the linear sense, your suspicion in the logical sense is another awareness right there that says, you know what is true. Yes, I know, but I do not know how, so I am going with it. That part is the more knowing self. That is really you.

You eventually come to trust that absolutely. You may not at first, but you eventually come to trust yourself. That is you, absolutely. Think of it. It makes sense. Why would you distrust yourself because of fears when you can trust yourself because of knowing? Eventually you are going to let go of your attachment to your distrusting self, which is really you distrusting some level of your persona. What you are actually distrustful of within yourself is your ego because you suspect that your ego has motive and you can fool yourself. You suspect that because it has happened before. You did not know why. Well, now you know why, because your ego with its motives for security, sex and position, can become invested in directions and can change your point of view, change your perception according to your needs and motives.

What you are suspicious of is what you think is your own mind. It is not your mind. It is your ego. It is your persona, which has always been very egocentric. What you must do is start paying attention to the truth of who you are and see how wise you really are, see how knowing you really are, see how much like the Great Spirit you really are in truth. What begins to happen also when you channel is you begin to become familiar with that whole side of things, and that is what teaches you to trust.

ℳerlin

You will always feel the energy of Spirit when you are channeling, always. You will always have the energy of Spirit when you seek to channel. Some of you will be very comfortable with letting the Spirit take voice. Sometimes you will want to hum or sing or grunt or groan. We had a lot of that with Mataare, although very little of that happens now. You might find your head moving or you body moving. Although it might seem rather camp, you might find your words come out easier when your hands are flowing and your body is moving, but it is not phony. It is what is necessary for the consciousness to claim the body. Eventually, the Spirit and all the entities, if there are many entities, will find their comfort zone with you.

I believe when Mataare saw Lazarus, he did not like what he saw. He loved what he heard in the recordings, but then when he saw Lazarus, he did not like what he was looking at because he saw how strange Lazarus looked when he channeled. Mataare wondered if he looked that strange. Lazarus would speak with his head cocked, eyes closed and mouth contorted, and it looked rather uncomfortable. However, that positioning is what enabled the entity to communicate through him. That is what it found.

Many times persons who channel Spirits do not channel all the Spirits that Mataare channels or they may channel a few or they may channel one that addresses everyone. The Spirit may have no name, but very often will take a name so that that the human being that channels it may create a relationship with that entity. That Spirit may be one that exited inside of time as you define time historically. That Spirit may be one who is an extra-dimensional entity or an extra-planetary entity. It may be your own higher consciousness. Therefore, it is important to understand that all consciousness is connected to the All.

Think of consciousness, the mind, as a great ocean and you swim in a certain part of the ocean. Because it is so familiar to you, you identify with that sector. After a while, it is not a sector anymore to you. It is you. That which is outside of that sector seems as though it is something else, someone else. Those closest to you, you can identify with. Those furthest from you may be more of a challenge to identify with. Those from a place like you, but from somewhere else, you may be in sympathy with those and so on and so forth.

The mind is not yours. The mind is simply that which you identify with as self, your part of the mind or your part of the sea. Therefore, anything that comes from beyond yourself must come through your part of the ocean. Indeed, if you consider for yourself a higher self greater than that which you identify with, that is your aura, your energy system beyond the sea of the mind that you identify with as self, that mirrors you and must sound like you to some degree. Something that is further from you may be shaped by your own sector of mind into something that is comprehensible to you.

We have channels because very often a larger consciousness that exists is unable to be tapped or be literalized or made linear sufficiently that persons can understand it. Therefore, we love our mediums because they translate for us a consciousness that needs to be understood, perhaps by them if they are conscious, or by others. Even if you were not fully conscious, you absorb the energy of it.

We love that over time more and more a person, apart from channeling, begins to sound a little like us. We love that. We are honored. Likewise, we are honored to sound a little like you. We love you. We appreciate you and need you as our channels so that our work here may be understood and that you may have a beautiful experience, a gift from the All That Is of service.

You must let go of the ways you have defined self, consciousness, Spirit, the Divine, God, and let Spirit teach you more, let Spirit reveal to you more by trusting sufficiently that you can get that edification. Over time, you will have that convincement.

Many times a person will say, well, I do not want to be brainwashed by my own beliefs or the beliefs of others. I would say to them that the only danger in life is a closed mind. The only danger in life is a prejudice that is no longer open to anything outside of its own thinking. Therefore, whether it is that you may question, you must be open if you have this calling. That is why you are here, to be edified by the gnosis of your own experience. That is where you grow. The channelies grow from what comes through you, but you grow from being edified by that which comes through you.

Now we are going to do a little channeling. What we are going to do when we go into state to channel is we are going to channel into a tape recorder so that you can hear it for yourself. How we are going to do that is we are going to do an invocation, a prayer of protection and some ohms. As you go into state, you help Spirit come by letting go of the hold on your own body. It is very simple. You let go of the hold on your body when you go to sleep, do you not? You do not even call it letting go of the hold on your body. What lets you let go of your hold upon the body? You shut down the physical senses and you go into consciousness of one sort or another. You let go of your tactile sense. If your tactile sense is too active, you cannot sleep. You have eventually to be separated from body consciousness to go to sleep.

You help yourself let go of the consciousness of the body by relaxing the physical body, relaxing your shoulders, after we do the prayers and the ohms or during it. You relax your eyes. You relax your jaw. You relax your belly. You relax your legs. You relax your feet.

Very often, what will occur immediately or after you are in a rested state is that things will come to mind. Then the mind will settle on something that comes into your awareness. Then you will hear or you will be aware of Spirit actually making a communication, but your mouth is not moving. You may want to allow it to come through you, but Spirit has not claimed your mouth yet. Therefore, you will very often hear or become aware of something and you will actually sometimes close down. Well, I do not really want to say that. How do I know it is Spirit? It is not moving my mouth. Very often the consciousness of Spirit will start before anyone is listening, before your mouth starts moving. This is initially how it works with most people.

It did not work like that for Mataare only because prior to channeling, he was narcoleptic and it was very common for him to fall asleep when he was not channeling. By the same token, he also talked in his sleep, so that made it easier for us, once he trusted us, to come through.

You should not expect that to occur for you. It may, but it may not. In fact, what you ought to expect is just what I said. The consciousness will occur. Your mind will ramble. Then it will become still. Then you will feel a consciousness that is something like I am here or they are here. You will say they are here, hello or some sort of a greeting. If you are that sort of a channel, let it come out of you. If you hear it first, say it. As you start getting loosened up, Spirit will start talking through you.

Do not become involved with the phenomena of oh wow, this is happening. Is it right? Just let it go. That is what it means to get out of the way. Just let your mumbles or words come out and sometimes it helps to say Spirit says thus and so. Spirit says we are doing this. Spirit says this is the light. Spirit says war is not good.

It may be in your own voice. It may be as comfortable as you speak naturally. It may be slow with your head hanging down if that is what is more comfortable. It may be a moving and a dance. I do not want you to worry about any concept of what it should be or worry about anything else. Just allow what happens for you to happen and you will have your recorders into which you will speak.

The time may come when you will not even care what is coming through you, but Spirit will be active, as I said, like water through a sieve. What will happen also, if you are conscious during a channeling, is that you may get tense again. Just relax the body and most of all, relax the breath. Do not go into a meditation because when the energy of Spirit comes in, you may want to be still and experience it, but this is not a meditation. It is a channeling. It is an expression, so we are going to let whatever expression occurs express through you. Do not allow yourself to let it matter if it seems like nonsense to you, if it is grunts and groans. Just remember, we may not be used to you and you may not be used to us. Do not worry about who it is, but if a name pops in, let it pop in for you.

Consider yourself like an instrument. Let us say Mataare is a piano and let us say you are a flute, another is a trumpet and another is a harp. The music may be similar, but the nature of the tambour of the one and the quality of the music it produces is decidedly different. We may try to play your flute. We may try to play your piano. Who knows what kind of an instrument you are. Certainly, you do not know. So let yourself discover the kind of instrument you are.

Some of you may be expert channelers, but you may not channel verbally. Some of you might. Some of you may write. Some of you may paint. Some of you may do art. Some of you may heal. Some of you may teach. Some of you may do different kinds of things and you are used to having the inspirational energy of Spirit around you. However, to allow Spirit to take voice is a precious opportunity for us. We love our mediums because without them we cannot very often communicate exactly in the way that persons need to understand.

Do not be surprised if there are hesitations in your speech because words sometimes need to form. Do not be surprised if you mumble because not all of us speak English. Not all of us are comfortable with your tongue, your pallet and your movements. Even if we have been here before speaking English, we are not used to you. Therefore, you have to lay all of the phenomena aside and the trying to define what all of this means and simply let it be. You are just going to let it be.

This is what we are going to do. I would like you to get your tape recorder. Then we are going to do the invocation. Either you can make it up or you can read or say the invocation that we give to you. Then we will do a prayer of protection and seven ohms. Take as long as you need for the Spirit Guide to come through. As you are ready, allow the Spirit to move you, speak through you or whatever the Spirit needs to do. We would like you to record it for yourself.

Before we begin, I would like you to think of and write down three of your greatest concerns about the world. What are your three greatest concerns about the world, the planet and its people? Just write those down.

Before the invocation, take a big breath, stretch and sigh. Please make sure your shoes are off. The feet are psychic receptors. Now we will do the invocation.

Spirit of light and of truth, inspire our minds and fill our hearts with love. Heal and energize our bodies and receive our thanks for the many gifts we have been given. We ask to be guided on our path that we might please and serve the most high. Amen.

Now we will do the prayer of protection.

Holy art thou, Lord of the Universe. Holy art thou which nature hath not formed. Holy art thou the vast and the mighty one, Lord of both the light and darkness. Oh Adoni, Elohim, Tetragramaton, Ala, Brahma, El, Yahweh, Yohova, Aba, Mutaar, Moot, Quan Yin, be with us. Amen.

Now let us do seven ohms.

I would like you Spirit, if you can, to respond to one of these questions, these concerns that these individuals have about the world. I would like you, if you wish to respond both to the individual that asked and to the world at large. If you do not wish to do this, simply express about anything. Thank you, Spirit. Give yourself roughly fifteen minutes to speak into your tape recorder. When you complete, thank the Spirit and close.

Cassandra

Each of you has your more natural way of channeling and allowing Spirit to come through you. It is organic to allow Spirit on purpose to talk, to converse, to be present. For example, some find that they naturally inspire people. They are not trying to channel, but it comes out in a way that inspires, touches and lifts people. While they are doing it, they do not think about it. It is only after that they may question it, mentally review it and wonder. However, while doing it, they just let go to it at the time.

Some work with healing and persons do not even know except people return. The healer has a comfort with knowing that we are there with them. Yet something in them seeks a more conscious knowing not because they want the recipient of the healing to connect it with them, but rather because the healer knows there is more and does not want that more to be inhibited. I do not mean in some way that they would think was uncomfortable in terms of its appropriateness, but they know that there is so much more as time and time again they have seen the miraculous.

What is that more? They do not know really, but that is where they want to go next. That is opening the door more fully. They may want, for example, to channel information for themselves, for classes, events and so forth.

Some regularly feel us through their creative work and attempt to have that presence initiate and sustain them as they work, initiate the energy and sustain that experience, yet sometimes they do not know it can and then will evolve. For example, if they were to express creatively perhaps through their art more, their natural thinking might cause them to think, do I have a right to spend so much time doing this thing that I love? Is this not indulgent? Yet they have long looked forward to a time when they could indulge without guilt.

One reason one cannot easily indulge oneself is that one develops a culture of thought that involves some self-hatred or another, and I use that word advisedly. That is that if your natural self is not supported, one can develop a world of thinking around why one is not worthy, and then must relentlessly prove their own worthiness to themselves, which gives no time to be yourself because you are busy trying not to fail yourself or others. Having then neglected yourself, oftentimes too much, you are not happy with yourself for what the self-neglect has created.

This is the culture of going round and round in circles with self-hatred, feeling displeased for not taking care of oneself properly. So that when one begins to take care of oneself properly, while it may feel like freedom at times, it also creates the sense at other times that perhaps I should not have done that. As soon as something does not flow right or something goes wrong, perhaps it could have been avoided had I been more efficient with being not myself.

When you open to the greater energy coming through, through more of your sense, including your voice, including your speech, more tends to turn around. This always happens through service. That is to say, over time the going beyond the limitations that restrict a person from giving and being themselves are only overcome because one presents themselves to serve. If you did not have the opportunity to give something, you would stop seeking to connect more deeply with Spirit because you were frustrated. It went nowhere.

When you present yourself and it is drawn through you and has a place to go, you will then put aside those limitations, at least temporarily and let yourself become more at one with who you are. When this takes place frequently, your thinking will change. When you allow Spirit to pass through you in the name of giving service, everything changes. You in fact enter a different world. You enter a greater reality.

You must remember that you do not live in everyone else's reality and they do not live in your reality. You share, if you want to, their reality with them and your reality with them, but they do not live there. You are the inhabitant of this greater reality. Therefore, you cannot be fully normal because your references have changed. What is important to you is more intense than it is for other persons. Your spiritual expression becomes more a part of your ordinary life, almost every waking minute integrated with it. It would only occur that way because you make yourself available.

If you did not serve, I promise you would forget all about this and be reabsorbed into the same world as where others live. It is the nature of the human function. So you instead become at one with the Spirit and we become at one with you.

You do not know fully what we are doing with you. There are doorways into the realms of Spirit and it is all very simple. It is very natural. It is not as complicated as we describe it. In fact, if not for the energy, you would think nothing of it. When we work with you, you open to let us move you and be with you, and you are aware and an impulse comes. Impulses are different for different persons and different even within one person. An impulse comes and your hand moves, or an impulse comes and it says move your hand. However, you do not sit there and say, is that the impulse? You move the hand. The impulse may translate into words, but most times, it does not.

Most of the times there are inhibiting persona-based impulses that say I do not know. However, if you lay those aside, you will also become aware of comforting, supportive presences that do not judge, but that gently say let me move. Let me speak. Let me respond. Let me. You will be aware of that. Then you may choose, if you are still there and not one with it as sometimes happens, you might choose to say or think, all right, I will. This is why many start giggling and laughing because you are in a conversation with us. That tickles you and some part of you begins to think, it is happening. It is happening, and you become excited.

If that sort of thing occurs, it is all right. When you are being creative artistically, writing, painting, drawing, making music, performance arts, dancing, speaking, whatever it is, when you are letting go to this, be aware, not while you are doing, but when you are setting an intention, remember, be aware this has some place it wants to go. Even if nobody is there, we have some place we want this to go. You may not know where it is. Very likely, you will have no idea, particularly if you are being creative by yourself sitting in front of a canvas or writing. It will occur at some points, why am I doing this. The answer is it has somewhere to go. You just do not know yet.

Sometimes you have the gift of seeing little things here or there, but most of it you will never see where it goes. However, regularly you will feel so wonderful. I knew it happened. I knew it was not useless. Many times something will happen and then you will read something, watch television, see a movie or a performance or talk to a friend or relative and you will say, ah, that already happened. I already was told that. This is a part of it all, a part of my teaching and a part of that teaching. You will see how you are integrated into everything and you will be amazed. Things so ordinary you cannot help but think at times, I am confabulating. I am putting all these meaningless things together in my own mind. This is how the world is supposed to be for you. When you are not in that world of seeing the connection, at that point you are miserable.

It is true some who do not have their consciousness raised in the right way will enter into harmful, psychopathic and schizophrenic awareness. If they do not understand what is happening or if they have been trained in the ways of fear or their heart or mind has been seriously disrupted in their lives, they may see connections that hurt them. However, you will not. You must remember that you do not live in the same world as those who have separated themselves out from the rest of their experience of self because they are just that special to be able to be disconnected. We call it terminal uniqueness, that somehow, whether they are spiritual persons or scientific persons, they are somehow pushing away meaning and connectedness until they must become at one with uniqueness because the need of their persona, their ego disconnected from truth is to make itself significant through separation. That uniqueness becomes terminal. We are not speaking of that, nor are we speaking of becoming fearful that your connectedness is self-created, but rather that it is observed. How could you be separate from anything when in fact you are at one with everything?

This knowing is natural. You do not even need to think about it. It is organic. However, at times, because you have presented yourselves in such ways as you do, there are gifts given to you that are wondrous beyond wondrous.

Sun Bear

The ancestors tend to come around when you are open. Understand that when you do things like this, contacting the Spirit world, Spirits who are available, they are happy and will all come. Sometimes you may get annoyed that they say, hey, hey, I need to tell someone something. You know, some of them want you to pass messages on to others. You can choose whether you wish to do that or not, but they must come check with your gatekeeper if that is okay. If it is annoying you, tell your gatekeeper, get rid of that guy. I will call you. You do not call me. Your gatekeeper will usually handle that.

However, you will become aware sometimes of ancestors. They are proud of you. They love you. They are glad you are here and they lend you their support, whether you are aware of it or not. So any chance they get, they like to tell you they are proud of you. They tell each other and us all about you.

There are worlds here that they and we inhabit, just as we come and inhabit your world. It is easier for us to contact the world where your ancestors are because we do not need mediums. Nothing is strange in those worlds to them. I pop out. They do not know me. They just know my heart, and out of nowhere, I say, hey, this one or that one, she remembers you. They say, oh really, thanks.

Now if one of us you know or not one you know, maybe some lizard man, pops into your bedroom and says, hey, grandma Nana says she remembers you and that you are never alone. She visits you and she is waiting to meet you when you come over. That might be a little off putting. However, to us over here, particularly with us, some strange one shows up and says something, no problem. They are used to it. They are not in the time patterns that you are.

You know, there are some mean people in the Spirit world who harass people, but not you because you are protected. You are not the type of persons they would harass. No matter what you think of yourself negatively or positively for that matter, you are just not appealing to them. You are not their type. Sorry. The bad guys, you are not their type. Therefore, even if something weird comes around you, I promise you it is not a bad guy. It is just like if a lizard showed up and the personality can be very different. If we show up in a personality from some other type of incarnation, not of this world, whether human or not human, it can throw you for a loop. You can think it is some kind of strange person.

You will often have one of those show up in your dreams, and it may scare you. The scare is, more often than not, a pattern interrupt to make you conscious that you are in another state. Then if you were interrupted sufficiently to say, oh, oh, this is that dream again or this is that, the whole character would change. The being would change because you had been interrupted and then the teaching would begin. Oftentimes we will come and do whatever we need to do to interrupt your normal dream, and then the dream becomes a teaching.

Bad guys cannot get you. They just cannot. If there is anything that is like terror, it is an unresolved emotional state in you from sometime in the past that is regurgitating, that is coming up for clearing, and usually an entity there, whether you recognize that entity or not, that is causing it and healing it, like a teacher. Usually that is what it is. I would have to talk about specific things that have happened to you to show you how and what those things meant.

When you meditate, have you seen the appearance of faces? Sometimes they are right in your face with the eyes or the mouth. Most of the time people see eyes and eyebrows starring at them from very close. Sometimes people do not get scared because they think it is a reflection of their eyes, but there is no reflection on the eyelids. There is not even any light there. That is your consciousness. There is not light behind your eyes. That is in your consciousness. You close your eyes and you see light that some people say are nerve endings. No, they are not. A nerve ending cannot spark, and if they could, your eye could not see it because your eyes need outer light to reflect. Really you only see reflections of things. Therefore, nothing you see is real. It does not mean there is nothing there, but what you are seeing, it is not real.

What we tell people is sometimes those you seek who may be on the other side, may not be available. Those ones who are not available, they cannot or do not come. What we mean by available is, they cannot come or it would be hard for them to come. Oftentimes, when you call someone in, he or she called you first and you are hearing it. You are receiving it. You may have grandpa say, hello, and then you might say, you know, I am going to call grandpa in. Do you see? Oftentimes they initiate it, and then you think of it after.

That is very much how we communicate with you where we will say, I am here, and you will say, oh, I just suddenly thought of Sun Bear. It is not that you necessarily know we are speaking to you, but almost all the time we contact you first and then you say you are contacting us. One of the reasons why, it is a little convoluted, but follow me, we say you must ask questions, must be inquisitive is that oftentimes when you say I wonder if it means that or this when this occurs, it is because you already got the message that this means something. You heard it in the way you hear, and then you start thinking, I wonder if... It is because you have gotten part of an insight, part of an answer. When you say, I wonder if... that means you acknowledged you got a part and you want to know the rest. So oftentimes your question is a sign you have already begun to receive the answer.

Any time you have a question that seems that you cannot answer it, if you have asked it, that means you have already begun to get it. So you ought to ask yourself, well, what do I feel then? What do I think that means? Then you will realize you already got it or part of it. That is why you are asking the question.

If you do not ask a question, if you reject questions thinking its doubt, you will shut yourself off. If you start thinking about something that you are not sure about, and you are thinking you are hallucinating stuff, then you will never know what the truth might be about that if you do not ask. That thing will just have passed you by.

A common occurrence is there will be many in Spirit wishing to speak. The problem is that it feels like there is so much to communicate, so much to express, so much to say that it could not all come. You just have to ask your doorkeeper to pick one, pick what is most important. We have that issue because communication comes energetically. Words are such a slow process and the nature of true communication is instantaneous. That is why you will get a picture, a scene, a bunch of things all at once. Then it has to be turned into this linear thing so it can be understood. Normally a scene, imagery, whatever it is, would take someone months to process. It impacts and downloads, and then it comes up later in events. You start to see things in events and you never know it was connected to that particular revelation that came previously in energetic form.

These kinds of things are always going on in the presence of someone who is aware and who is in service. You can be getting things all the time, but your processor has not translated it yet. The same is true in your channeling for another or even if you are trying to channel music, art or anything. There is always something left. That is why there are so many books a writer writes, so many paintings and so much music.

Mataare was trained in music and he was so frustrated because most of the time he wrote music mathematically, based on the chord structures and the difference between the various tones and the scales and it did not flow like a song into him for him to write. It was an avante garde sort of music and classical style and then in jazz, which was very free form. He was frustrated because that is how he had to write because he would hear music all the time, but when he tried to write it, it would go away or he could not figure out on what note to start. There was not a way he could get it out in the linear threads in the scores. He was so frustrated not being able to get all that out into music. All he could do was mathematical equations. He stopped trying to write music based on what flowed through him.

That was not music. It was us, and he could grasp it in a musical expression, but could not express it in a musical expression. He can certainly express us in this sort of expression. He is wide open here, but not for the form of music, which was his love. Certainly, this was not Mataare's love. He would love to be as far away from this sort of thing as possible. He could not stand New Agers and people who go around asking the question like what is the meaning of life. These things would drive him crazy. He would say, oh, those people are crazy, but now he is one of those people.

Philos and Enoch

The nature of eternity is your spirit and not the mind, for there is a distinction between the two, the mind being nearly infinite, the self being eternal, usually. The mind is a tool of the infinite, a tool to establish an expression, otherwise, the All exists as an All, which for all intent and purpose is nothing, no thing. Mind allows it to express.

So why do we say these things to you? It is important to understand that as teachers this mind seeks always to be a tool of your eternal self. You have come far enough to recognize this, and further still to make a decision, a firm choice to be consciously an expression of that. You are willing and allowing mind to take form whether it be higher self, alternate self, Guides of self, expressions of God, angelic and otherwise, and to allow the translation of that as a function through mind and allow it to express according to its desire and the capacity that you allow this mind to enable.

The very nature of this expression is simplicity itself. However, the need of persons oftentimes is to complicate this simplicity. It may not appear complicated in terms of what you would naturally expect others in their seeking to understand, but it is in fact made complicated.

The nature of Spirit is to express simply. The nature of the recipient, not you as a channel, but a recipient outside of the channel, is to have that understanding made clear for those who seek to understand coming from very different, complicated and tangled sets of life experiences. Therefore, the more others seek to understand through you, the more you and Spirit must present through the tangles that represent their understanding. Without you as the translator, then what would those out there have to identify with?

You, as a vehicle for Spirit recognize time and time again the power and simplicity of this internal consciousness that rules the heart and brings peace and light. You have also that which surprises you from time to time in the form of the miraculous for no reason whatsoever, which serves sometimes to remind you of where and who you are and that you are loved, that you are love itself. Spirit expands you in this way. Likewise, others are expanded through you.

The more frequently this Spirit is drawn through you, the more complex ways this Spirit begins to express, but understand, the nature of Spirit is simple. When you channel for yourselves, you often will not get anything but the most expansive things of awareness and teachings in general. Spirit, knowing you understand already through your own experience of Spirit, knows you grasp the meaning even when expressed simplistically, being that the very nature of Spirit is simple, and once reminded of this whole simplicity, no further complicated message is required.

It is for this reason one's persona, one's personality, one's unique individualized flavor of mind that each of you may possess, sets upon the judgment of the Spirit that passes through you, wondering if indeed this has meaning, wondering if it is genuine, save for the experience of the energy that you feel. It makes you question it, and in the presence of others, you may judge whether or not that which seems to come through you is of value. Nonetheless, you should let this express and allow the recipient to draw through you through time that which is less real and more complex to be expressed that the mind, individualized mind, has the tendency to judge as better, when in fact it is further from the truth. Therefore, we allow and accept the things that in fact are further from the simplicity of truth because we trust you. We know you. We love you as vehicles. Otherwise, we would not empower you and you would not seek us.

When we speak to you even now, it may seem like the complex explanation of things to which you might say, ah, I see. Really, it is only because you draw from us that way in which you need to understand, and so it comes out this way. It is not because Mataare or we invent this or that the channel is so fluid. It is that you draw your need and sense it and we are drawn in this manner.

If Mataare were more conscious, he would not let this out. He would hear so much that is untested while perhaps inspiring and makes sense that he would ask, Mataare do you know this. How can we know this? How can you say things that are so far outside of normal perception that there is no way to test it? That which comes through me may have an influence on persons when I myself do not even know its value and cannot vouch for its value. Therefore, it serves us to have Mataare a little more distant from this so we can be more fluid.

Being less distant from this, you will have the tendency to judge yourselves, but you will still let it through because of your decision to be vehicles. You are the ones. You are the ones because you are the ones. Who else would it be? Would you decide it is that one, but not you? Nevertheless, you are here. You are the ones. Did you make a mistake? What made you the ones? You are available. You have sought further calling. The Spirit called and you said, all right. Who are you? Whom would you be to judge that Spirit somehow in your case made a mistake and you are somehow right again?

Think of it this way. Your desire, being so sincere, so consistent, so insistent throughout your life, has done nothing except seek the answer and await the call. You have been alert. Now, some would ask and they keep themselves away for one reason or another, lack of faith or interest or it may not be right, but why do you keep asking? Why do you keep seeking? Why do you keep finding? Why have you heard it while others, in their waiting, may have grown impatient and turned away. You see, you are the ones. You are it. I will just leave it there.

Merlin

One of the most challenging things about trying to get messages across to people, especially if they are spiritually open and aware, conscious and connected is that they think they have heard it all before. That is exactly the reason why one would gloss right over it. It is something one assumes they have already integrated. However, what if there comes a time when you particularly need that message and it just cannot get through because it is something that is already integrated into your awareness. In other words, it is not anything new, and while you may be looking for something new, what is coming is what is old and is applicable in that situation and not in anything new.

Let us say that something came up in a particular day and you already had the knowing, had the answer. What might occur is the event was new, the circumstance, the details, the particulars and logistics of that circumstance were new, but the karma, the karmic positioning is the same as what might have occurred before. The tenor and the tambour of the moment are similar to other things you may have experienced in the past even though in a new set of circumstances. What if for you, some old message or insight applies to the new circumstance?

Most people tend to think I have been here before. Why am I here again? I am speaking now as if that particular event is a sort of unhappy challenge let us say. You might be looking for an insight or a path relative to that circumstance that has some connection with that particular circumstance. In fact, the message you have already gotten, you have already learned, the knowing you have already come to applies there, that this is not a new thing.

Everyone has those old knowings applying to new circumstances. Sometimes one can easily see that. What of those times when you cannot easily see that and the same thing applies? You are not easily able to see your way out of this particular challenge and some old awareness, some awareness that has predated that event is in fact applicable, but you just do not see it. You call upon some guidance. You open your awareness, you try to find some insight and what seems to come is something like what you read in a book, your consciousness giving you one of those old things. Your response might be, come on. That is not what I need right now. What I need is something else. Your response might be how did I get myself here in this situation again? I am so stupid. Why does this keep happening to me?

What if the reason persons miss their message is the blind spot at that particular time, when in fact they are getting the message, but it is in their blind spot? Let us say, for example, it is someone else for whom you find yourself in the position of being the carrier of that message. Spirit has imbued you with the insight and there you are in the presence of another who needs, and there you are holding the message. You therefore, become the channel. What do you do with that message?

If that person is seeking counsel, you will let it through. However, if that person is not seeking counsel, then what do you do with that message? Especially if you sense the message will not be received or cannot be received, what will you do? There you are with the knowing.

This is the position we find ourselves in all of the time with those who call upon their higher guidance. Many call upon our guidance, and you are their vehicles for that guidance. You will find yourselves in the same position as we do. However, here is the rub. They are with you, like it or not, because at that time you are the agent.

You must find a way, if you want to, to shape that message in a way that it can be received. That is your value as a medium. That is your value as a channel because you are uniquely equipped to make the vibration of that message receivable to the recipient, to the querent. This is required. Do you not see that we need you as channels because we cannot get the message through for those who need or who are in fact asking without you who are translators of that message? That is why we love our channels. That is why we need our channels. That is the function of the Spirit of the Universe, to express itself through its many forms.

When we come to you, whether we are identifiable as Merlin, Sun Bear or any one of the others of us or whether we come collectively to you in forms of energy we do not want you to shape into a particular character, you are the ones who make that accessible to others. That is what we are in fact asking of you when you make yourselves available for it.

You define those terms, not us. You define the ways that you would like us to work with you when it comes to channeling. You ask us to come to you in the ways that are useful to you so that you can help others. It is a rather altruistic pathway on your part. By that, I mean it is a simple expression of your desire to serve.

We are telling you outright, tell us how you want us to come to work through you. Tell us. Say, I would like you to help me in this way to help others. Not necessarily, how can I serve, but I want it to come in this way for myself because of my particular needs. I see a need to be met in this way and that way. You also can ask us in that way for yourselves. We will not necessarily respond to that because most of the time if we received your request to come to you in the ways that you want for your particular needs, you would have done that for yourself already.

If you cannot create it for yourself in that particular way, then perhaps we are not supporting you in creating it that way. Therefore, we are not going necessarily to support you in that way because you are asking. In a way, you have your answer already that we cannot come in that particular way. We will not come to you in that particular way and that is why you are stuck in that particular way. There is no help there. Perhaps it is up to you to keep going, but more often than not, perhaps it is up to you to change.

When it comes to being altruistic, you will still have selfish concerns. Believe me when I say you must be selfish to a certain degree. You must have certain selfishness in your life. You just have to have it. It is necessary. You must be self-concerned in many ways in your life. I do not want to tell you that it is important to be completely selfless. In fact, it is dangerous to become completely selfless. You come here as a self because you have something to do as self. You are a unique expression of the Divine as self, so we do not want to eradicate that. You do not want that to be snuffed out. You came here to be that.

However, when it comes to that matter of service and you humbly present yourselves as agents, and I do say humbly because it is in fact a humble thing to do, why should you want to serve others? Compassion. You have so much love in you that your love nature, your compassion heart, has commanded you, has forced you to assume responsibility, to take responsibility. I must help. I feel this in my heart. I love. What can I do with it? Where can I go? I feel it. It is bursting inside of me. It is going to tear me apart if I cannot give it away.

We are looking for you, so tell us what you want when it comes to this. Tell us, I would like you to come in this way if you can. Tell us what you need. In order for me to do this, I think I will need this.

With Mataare, we came to him. He wanted to do it. He wanted to be of help and we came to him this way, but when we came to him, he did not know what to do. We did not know how to work with him. We just answered his prayer and we knew that it would shape itself. Then he began to define it. First, can you come in at a certain time so that it does not frighten me? Second, he wanted to do it free of charge. Then we told him no, no, no. You have to receive something for it. Then he never received enough. We told him at that time what to ask. No, no, no. He did not want to do it. What he tried to do was other work to support doing this for donations or for a very small fee. Of course, it was too small. Later it came round like this. He said, listen, I can do this under this circumstance. Is that all right? I need to be able to make my living from this. That is what I need. Can you do that? Yes.

Tell us what you need. Then be prepared to embrace it. Think about it. You do not have to tell us all at once. You do not have to figure it all out now and then say these are the terms because they will evolve. You say, for now, this is what I need so that I can be of help in this way.

We are trying to develop you further as channels. How will you be received as channels? How will that be created? You and we will create that in a way that suits not only your desire to serve, but also fulfills your heart's nature, reconstructs your life along the lines of greater beauty and pulls you from those places where you have felt stuck.

One thing about being stuck, a person does not just get stuck by accident. Usually a person puts themselves in those situations where they wind up stuck either because they cannot see anything else to do any better or because they are faithless. They do not have sufficient faith to go forward beyond that place. When you ask Spirit, especially when you are presenting yourselves as agents, when you have that compassionate altruistic nature to want to be of help in this sea of light, then it is impossible not to get that help. When that help comes, it changes those places that you may have held onto calling yourself stuck. It changes those things. You will have a hard time holding those things in place that you may have held onto, not realizing those things have made you stuck or realizing they have made you stuck, but still holding onto them for dear life. You will not be able to do that. It will unstick you.

If you look at your history, it has already occurred in some places. Your desire to give has changed your life, has it not? Have you not built your life around that already? Perhaps some of you not as much as you may have liked. There is no more powerful way to do it than to ask us to express ourselves through you. Ask Spirit to express ourselves through you. Ask your Spirit Teachers and not simply Spirit, which is beautiful in its expansive nature, because you are spirit too as a part of that, but we are sent to you as Guides, some of us as teachers. If you ask your teachers to come under your roof, into your home, into your lives, we certainly will. We will not rule. We will not command. We will not cajole. However, you will be in the presence of your teachers and you will be with us all of the time, whether you realize it or not. You do not have to follow us. We will not badger you, not intentionally, but our very presence near you may be cause for concern at times. You will know we are there and it will be like looking into a mirror. You will not be able to avoid that mirror when you need to look into it.

If you are in need of having your lives accelerate toward your greater fulfillment, toward your greater completion, there is no better way than to bring your teachers near. When the time comes for us to draw back, we will draw back. When the time comes for us to come near, we will come near.

Do you know that in all the many years we have been coming through Mataare, we cannot get him to listen to one single full recording of himself in trance, not one in decades. He will not do it. I wonder if you have similar reservations. The biggest reason he will not do it is it is too confronting. I do not mean our message. If he would listen, he would find it supportive and not confronting. The confronting part of it is hearing us coming through him. He still cannot accept that it is all right. He accepts that it happens. He accepts that it is good and useful. He is glad that it happens, but when he is presented with listening to himself, listening to that which comes through him, he is still frightened. There is still too much fear there.

I would suggest to you to listen to the recordings of you channeling and you will become more comfortable with the phenomena of it. Let go of the phenomena. The only thing that makes persons who are channels uncomfortable is the phenomena of the personification of Spirit demonstrating itself through you. That is a phenomenon because it is usually your consciousness that expresses through you. Now it is your consciousness plus. That is a phenomenon. It has certain things involved. This is how it works. You said, Spirit, God, help me. I need to give. This is who I am. This is my heart. Then the Supreme Divine says, yes, I choose you. You have been chosen. You accept the mantel. Listen to yourselves. Read what is written through you. Accept the mantel. Accept it.

Books channeled by Mataare
Compiled and edited by Carolyn Hawkins

The Old Soul's Guide
A compendium of quotes on various subjects to introduce and reframe one's construct of spiritual awakening.

Masters' Guide to Love, Relationship and Soul Mates
An investigation of the concept of love beyond a need based emotion, including how the experience of divine or spiritual love infuses and plays out through partnership. Also provides information about what a soul mate is and how most effectively to work with soul mate relationships.

Masters' Guide to Prayer and Meditation
Why prayer and meditation are vital to the spiritual path and for right alignment when one is offering oneself in service, including examples for how to pray and meditate most effectively.

Masters' Guide to Self-Review, a Workbook
Through lectures and worksheets, the progression of this workbook allows one to identify where their innate survival instinct is running the show. Once identified, one is walked through the process of disarming their reactiveness to the survival instinct through awareness and prayer, including asking for Divine help and guidance, which deepens one's relationship with the Spirit of the Universe.

Masters' Guide to Extraterrestrials
To understand oneself, one must have a clearer picture of the structure in which they experience life. Included here is an introduction to other expressions of life within this universe that help the growth and development of life on this planet

Masters' Guide to Wealth

Wealth, in its truest form, including financial, is a vital part of spiritual growth, especially for those committed to service and struggling with the collective paradigm of service as sacrifice. Outlined here is a realignment with the higher principles of wealth that allows one the experience of connectedness to all of life, consciousness, the world and the universe, which is a safe and supportive cradle designed to advance and prosper life as one engages in the exploration of life.

Masters' Guide to Psychic Development

The natural byproduct of spiritual development (consciousness development) is the opening of one's innate psychic gifts. Offered here is instruction for the harnessing and empowered use of those gifts.

Masters' Guide to Magic and Numerology

A continued exploration of and instruction in harnessing and empowered use of one's innate human gifts.

Made in United States
North Haven, CT
28 June 2024

54191120R00128